No God but Man

ON RACE, KNOWLEDGE,
AND TERRORISM

Atiya Husain

Duke University Press   *Durham and London*   2025

© 2025 DUKE UNIVERSITY PRESS. All rights reserved
Printed in the United States of America on acid-free paper ∞
Project Editor: Ihsan Taylor
Cover design by Dave Rainey
Typeset in Garamond Premier Pro and Retail
by Copperline Book Services

Library of Congress Cataloging-in-Publication Data
Names: Husain, Atiya, author.
Title: No god but man : on race, knowledge, and terrorism /
Atiya Husain.
Other titles: Global insecurities.
Description: Durham : Duke University Press, 2025. | Series:
Global insecurities | Includes bibliographical references and index.
Identifiers: LCCN 2024017842 (print)
LCCN 2024017843 (ebook)
ISBN 9781478031369 (paperback)
ISBN 9781478028116 (hardcover)
ISBN 9781478060345 (ebook)
Subjects: LCSH: Shakur, Assata. | United States. Federal Bureau of
Investigation. | Terrorism—Government policy—United States. | War
on Terrorism, 2001–2009—Social aspects—United States. | Fugitives
from justice—United States. | Crime and race—United States. | African
American Muslims—Political activity. | Muslims—Political activity—
United States. | BISAC: SOCIAL SCIENCE / Ethnic Studies / American /
African American & Black Studies | RELIGION / Islam / General
Classification: LCC HV6432 .H87 2025 (print) | LCC HV6432 (ebook) |
DDC 363.3250973—dc23/eng/20241031
LC record available at https://lccn.loc.gov/2024017842
LC ebook record available at https://lccn.loc.gov/2024017843

Cover art: Middlesex County Workhouse correspondence form, 1973.
Derived from a letter in the Black Panther Party Archives of Frankye
Adams-Johnson, Margaret Walker Center, Jackson State University,
Jackson, Mississippi.

No God but Man

GLOBAL INSECURITIES
A series edited by Catherine Besteman and Darryl Li

To Issra

Contents

Acknowledgments ix

INTRODUCTION 1

1. *L'HOMME MOYEN* AND
AMERICAN ANTHROPOMETRY 23

2. ASSATA, THE MUSLIM 51

3. THE RULE OF RACELESSNESS 83

4. ASSATA, BLACK MADONNA 107

CONCLUSION. Race: Theirs and Ours 131

Notes 139
Bibliography 169
Index 185

Acknowledgments

The idea for this book has been in my mind since 2013, when the FBI added Assata Shakur to its Most Wanted Terrorist list. The decade between her addition and the completion of this book has been enough time for me to start down one line of inquiry but see that better answers are to be found elsewhere. I started this project with one set of assumptions about race, and over the course of the next decade, deeper engagement with these archival materials—the FBI Most Wanted program's posters and Assata Shakur's published and unpublished writings—forced the realization that my assumptions were getting in my way. This sort of journey significantly broadens the scope of who must be acknowledged: I am grateful to everyone who has contributed to my thinking over these years. I am indebted to those whose scholarship helped inform my earlier exploration, as well as those who offered critiques and disagreements in good faith as I have sought to do in this book as well.

I would like to thank everyone at Duke University Press who has had a hand in publishing this project. Ever since Jonathan Horowitz kindly mentioned my project to Gisela Fosado on a delayed flight, her support has been unwavering. I appreciate the careful attention of Alejandra Mejía and Ihsan Taylor on the production process and Paula Durbin-Westby's indexing. The reviewers' comments have improved the manuscript significantly.

The analysis in the book relies on the work of archivists including Angela D. Stewart at the Margaret Walker Alexander National Research Center at Jackson State University, Sojourna Cunningham at Boatwright Library at the University of Richmond, Maureen Moran at the William Taylor Muse Law Library of the University of Richmond School of Law, and Jennifer Fauxsmith at the Radcliffe Institute at Harvard University, as well as the archivists at the Schomburg Center and New York University's Tamiment Library and Robert F. Wagner

Labor Archives. Their dedication made some of the archival work of this project possible during the height of the COVID-19 pandemic.

Although this book is not based on my doctoral research, the generous mentorship and sharp thinking of the faculty I worked with while at the University of North Carolina at Chapel Hill must be honored. Thank you to Karolyn Tyson, Charles Kurzman, Eduardo Bonilla-Silva, Linda Burton, and Andrew Perrin.

The students at the University of Richmond who pushed for an Africana Studies department inspired me during my years there. I thank the dean's office as well as colleagues with whom I exchanged preliminary work in formal and informal working groups at UR: Julietta Singh, Nathan Snaza, and Rania Sweis; the writing circle for junior faculty organized by Eva Hageman and Lauren Tilton; and the Humanities Connect program. The research for this book began with funding from the University of Richmond, where I was lucky to work with a great group of undergraduate research assistants: Unitha Cherry, Sarai Duran, Shira Greer, Maha Hassan, Jaide Hinds-Clarke, Jennifer Munnings, and Ali Munro. The research was completed thanks to the Social Science and Humanities Research Council of Canada, which funded my wonderful graduate research assistants, Catalina Hernandez, Mohammed Jahirul Islam, Leila Mahmoudi, and Nadeea Rahim. Thanks also to Michael Agnew for dedicated application support.

Support for the project has also come through invitations, collaborations, and conversations that provided space to think and explore. Thanks for speaking invitations from Hana Brown, Daniel Chard, Huma Dar, Verena Erlenbusch-Anderson, Nabila Islam, Azeezah Kanji, Neda Maghbouleh, Shabana Mir, Alaina Morgan, Saher Selod, and Stanley Thangaraj. Invitations to write came from Sami Al-Arian, Adam McGee, and Meara Sharma, as well as the University of Chicago Divinity School Race and Religion Essay Contest Committee. Collaboration with Anver Emon has helped give space to this work, and Michael Fischbach, Mike German, and Teishan Latner answered niche questions about the research. Sohail Daulatzai and Junaid Rana's generous engagement with the book has improved it. Darryl Li's support and feedback on the manuscript was invaluable. Laura Lopez-Sanders offered helpful comments at a critical time. And the opportunity to stay in conversation with Jihad Abdul-Mumit was one of the greatest gifts of my time in Richmond.

Colleagues at the Carleton University Department of Law and Legal Studies offered an encouraging institutional home to do my work. Many thanks to colleagues and collaborators in Ottawa: Melanie Adrian, Gulzar Charania, Michael Christensen, Ryan Conrad, Stacy Douglas, Nana'aba Duncan, Malini

Guha, Rehana Hashmi, Adrian Harewood, William Hébert, Vincent Kazmierski, Azar Masoumi, Jeffrey Monaghan, Hollis Moore, Umut Özsu, Carolyn Ramzy, Dale Spencer, Rania Tfaily, Christiane Wilke, and Liam Cole Young. And special thanks to Students for Justice in Palestine.

From quick exchanges to reading chapters and debating ideas, my brilliant friends and family have made their mark on this project. I benefited from periodic catch-ups with Fatema Ahmed, Neel Ahuja, Felicia Arriaga, Neda Atanasoski, Trenita Childers, Samah Choudhury, B. Brian Foster, Naseeha Hussain, Danielle Purifoy, Antonia Randolph, Victor Ray, Aiza Siddiqi, Louise Seamster, and Nafisah Ula. Thanks are also due to new friends and collaborators Fahad Ahmad, Aseel Qazzaz, and Susana Vargas, who arrived on the scene just as the book was being finished and made an impact in a short time. I am deeply indebted to Corey D. B. Walker, whose refrain "Black studies is not race studies" made all the difference; together with Carthene Bazemore-Walker, you are role models in mentorship. Hafsa Kanjwal and Azad Essa's principled engagement inspires, and I could always rely on the intellectual curiosity and sincerity of Saadia Yacoob and Zaid Adhami. The all-around support of Eram Alam remains unmatched.

My North Carolina family kept me company and made critical interventions as I finished a key draft of the book: Anusha Hariharan; Kumi Silva, David Monje, and Ruby; Rhon and James Manigault-Bryant, along with Cy and Vale; and Rakhee Devasthali, Sijal Nasralla, and Tasneem. I appreciate Juliane Hammer and Cemil Aydin for their encouragement and feedback as generous thinking partners since my graduate school years.

I appreciate the Husain, Islam, and Towns families for every act of care, support, and cheerleading—with special thanks to Armond. Thank you for your companionship, your unrelenting faith in me, and your brilliance. You and Issra have all my love and gratitude.

INTRODUCTION

What the Federal Bureau of Investigation keeps under lock and key has been of greatest interest to scholars, lawyers, and social movements.[1] What the FBI seeks to actively advertise, however, is just as important as what it tries to keep to itself. The bureau has regularly produced wanted posters as an archive that exists to be seen. This heavily stylized, heavily reproduced public document can tell us much about the very same issues of social movements, repression, and even bureaucracy that draw scholars, journalists, and activists to secret files to begin with. Wanted lists and posters stand out compared to other sorts of FBI paper.[2] If redacted FBI files and never-to-be-released secret files are one end of the spectrum of FBI documents, then wanted posters are on the opposite end. Wanted posters are what the FBI proudly displays and distributes for public consumption. The wanted poster format is standardized and familiar: a heading, a name, photographs, and then a stack of categories. The categories in use are date(s) of birth used, place of birth, height, weight, occupation, hair, build, eyes, sex, nationality, languages, citizenship, complexion, scars and marks, tattoos, and, of course, race. There is often a line at the bottom of the poster offering a cash reward for information leading to capture, or an additional note that the individual is armed and dangerous, with some written narrative on their crimes, affiliations, where they were last seen, and memorable details. These sorts of FBI posters have been in circulation since the early twentieth century.

Their production and distribution were formalized in the 1950 creation of the FBI Most Wanted program.

Wanted posters are fertile grounds for classification and categorization. There are at least two clear sites of category formation in the Most Wanted program: first, the columns of physical attributes and other identifying information under each individual's photograph on a poster (e.g., nationality, citizenship, race, scars and marks, etc.); and second, the several wanted lists that constitute the program. The Most Wanted program began with just one wanted list of ten people, but since the 1990s it has developed several more lists and expanded in size. By the 2010s, there were about three hundred to four hundred posters of individual wanted people in the program at any given time.[3] The lone Ten Most Wanted in 1950 would be joined by lists including Parental Kidnapping, in 1998; Seeking Information—Crimes against Children, in 2004; Cyber's Most Wanted, in 2013; and Human Trafficking, in 2014. By 2021 the largest list was Fugitives, consisting of more than one hundred posters, while smaller lists like Cyber's Most Wanted could include as few as six or seven posters. Individuals are sometimes moved from one list to another, suggesting that the difference between the lists is meaningful for FBI categorization practices. The importance of these categories exceeds the confines of the FBI since posters are made for public distribution and thus with some sense of their intended viewership's understanding of particular categories in mind. Posters are ideological, as they both establish categories and reflect existing categories enough to make sense to their viewers.

Perhaps the most important list, for both the bureau and the purposes of this book, is the Most Wanted Terrorist (MWT) list. The list began with twenty-two men when then president George W. Bush announced it to reporters in October 2001. It was the first terrorism list of the program, later accompanied by Seeking Information—Terrorism in 2002 and Domestic Terrorism in 2006.[4] It is indeed possible to say that this list and its roughly two dozen posters are even more important to the FBI than its Ten Most Wanted: the MWT has rewards for information leading to capture in the millions, far surpassing the rewards offered for the Ten Most Wanted and other lists, which have reward amounts in the thousands or none at all. Though seemingly singular or small, since it comprises just a couple dozen people, the MWT list is inherently significant beyond its relevance for the FBI. Massive structural shifts have taken place in the name of capturing these few people and whatever they are presumably tied to. More specifically, the federal government restructured, creating the Department of Homeland Security. These names were offered as justification for the invasion of Afghanistan and Iraq, all part of launching a global war on terror that hammered Bosnia, Sudan, Yemen, and many more.[5] Hundreds of thousands have perished, and entire geographies have been restructured via drone warfare.[6] The climate impacts of the war on terror are considerable. Generally, wanted posters are designed to identify and criminalize one individual at a time, but this atomizing has repercussions far beyond the represented individual. Bombing campaigns are conducted in the name of killing just one person on a wanted poster. How many thousands of people did the United States and its allies kill in their global war on terror when the single individual named Osama bin Laden was their most wanted enemy? The claim to having targeted or successfully killed one or two *terrorists* allows for the killing of masses, facilitated by certain kinds of thinking sedimented in the form of the wanted poster, as this book and its many sources show. Given the constellation of issues to which the MWT list is connected, this list drives the questions of this book.

Scanning the posters of the Muslim men on the first version of the MWT list in 2001, observers of the early years of the war on terror would initially be unsurprised by the images: dark hair and eyes. Beards. Flashes of the word Al-Qaeda. Osama bin Laden is a familiar face. Muslims with birthplaces listed in Comoros, Indonesia, Kenya, Kuwait, Palestine, Saudi Arabia, and Somalia, as well as Alabama and Wisconsin, have been added to this high-priority terrorism list in the two decades since its creation. Looking at their photographs, one would notice faces that would easily be classified all over the US color line and its current official categories of white, Black, and Asian, even while most individuals have markers like names, places of birth, and affiliations likely indicating Muslim status. Several others have been added to the MWT list since 2001 that do not match the familiar profile of the Muslim terrorist, like Daniel Andreas San Diego, associated with environmental terrorism, and Assata Shakur (Joanne Deborah Chesimard on her wanted poster), formerly of the Black Panther Party and Black Liberation Army.

The list is home to a puzzle and a history that are perhaps counterintuitive. For this reason, they are useful to explore for pushing prevailing thought on race theory and category formation in the humanities and social sciences toward my argument that race is largely incoherent as an analytical category. The puzzle stems from the categories of use on the MWT list that distinguish it from others throughout the Most Wanted program. The MWT list differs from other posters across the Most Wanted program in at least one striking way: most of its Muslims are lacking an official race category. For those who match that image of the Muslim terrorist, the category of race is missing in the columns of attributes on each poster. Like most posters, there are entries for categories like eyes, height, sex, scars and marks, and so on. Nearly every possible category is used on their posters except race. Race has sometimes been missing on posters in the past, but as one of many missing categories on a poster. On the MWT list, however, race is rather systematically missing, and that absence is limited to the archetypal Muslim terrorist. Those who do not match this image but who are still on the MWT list, like Shakur and San Diego, still have a race category. However, this difference should not be taken to mean that racelessness can be easily attributed to simple identifiability as Muslims. The hundreds of posters in the rest of the program include fellow Muslims who are easily identified as such because of their names and descriptors like *imam* in the occupation category, for example. They are accused of nonterrorism crimes, and their posters do have race categories. It is absolutely critical to note that race labels are not simply different for Muslims, and those associated with them, on nonterrorist as compared to terrorist lists. Rather, race labels disappear altogether.[7] This basic comparison between Muslims accused of terrorism (raceless) and Muslims accused of other crimes (racially categorized) suggests that simply being visibly or identifiably Muslim is not the factor leading to racelessness. There are many questions to ask about this.

One of the main questions of this book is: What can this singular official racelessness tell us about race?[8] The racelessness signaled on the Most Wanted Terrorist list is the substantial puzzle from which this book's broader agenda expands. This racelessness is not accidental nor a careless omission, as chapter 3 demonstrates in detail, but rather a puzzle illustrative of a broader racial epistemology in which the FBI is but one powerful node.[9] Each chapter moves chronologically, looking at four very different cases: the poster form as based on the concept of the average man in late nineteenth-century statistics and race science, Assata Shakur's brief years as a Muslim, the official racelessness described earlier, and Shakur's post-9/11 trajectory in which the FBI represents her as a non-Muslim alongside Muslims on the MWT list. These cases offer a look at race from different angles and all come down to the MWT list, but with regard to very different moments and peoples, supporting an argument about taking seriously the defects in race as a mode of organization and thus as an analytical category. Although many have argued against race as a mode of organization before, this argument departs from much scholarly work on Muslims and the war on terror, largely sociological, that tends to find race useful as an analytical category, which is an opening for this book's interest in making room for more generative thought in this area of study.

After 9/11, there was an eruption of knowledge that sought to understand what the experiences of violence and discrimination against Muslims in the war on terror meant and how best to theorize them. Was it a problem of religious discrimination? Racial discrimination? Was it religio-racial? Was it orientalism? Was it Islamophobia? Was it a problem of capitalism? Of imperialism? All these options in various combinations and with different approaches were offered up in the important work of scholars like Hisham D. Aidi, Evelyn Alsultany, Talal Asad, Sahar Aziz, Moustafa Bayoumi, Hatem Bazian, Khaled Beydoun, Louise Cainkar, Edward E. Curtis, Sohail Daulatzai, John Esposito, Neil Gotanda, Zareena Grewal, Yvonne Haddad, Juliane Hammer, Sherman A. Jackson, Deepa Kumar, Arun Kundnani, Erik Love, Sunaina Maira, Nasar Meer, Tariq Modood, Nadine Naber, Jasbir Puar, Junaid Rana, Sherene H. Razack, Omid Safi, Salman Sayyid, Saher Selod, Kumarini Silva, Leti Volpp, and more. To the question of how to understand what the war on terror meant, race rose as a winner, moving up from being a marginal arena of explanation to a central concept in the debate. Knowledge producers in the halls of universities, at marches, in nonprofit organizations, and increasingly in policy circles advanced the argument that Muslims' experiences, in the United States and around the world, bore some relationship to race. Some argued that Muslims who previously experienced the comforts of whiteness in the United States fell from that status. Some argued that 9/11 might have had an intensification effect but that the Muslim has long been a racial or racialized category for the West more broadly. In contrast, others argued that Muslims' status as a religious group or an immigrant group in Western countries is far more important than race for understanding their post-9/11 predicament; but for my purposes, this counterargument suggests above all that the appeal to race was gaining enough traction to merit a direct rebuttal.[10]

A theoretical shorthand—"the racialization of Muslims"—permeated debates and analysis that had little to do with criminalization. It also traveled to scholarship not centrally about Muslims. For example, Ruth Wilson Gilmore and Angela Davis use this phrase to refer to post-9/11 violence against Muslims in their work on prisons addressing a popular audience. The dizzying array of definitions of racialization notwithstanding, this concept was adopted as especially useful for theorizing the relationship between race and Muslims, again, both inside and outside academe. A few core questions guided the knowledge produced on race and Muslims: How are Muslims racialized? Where does the figure of the Muslim fit in the racial taxonomy? What is the relationship between race and religion? These questions, and the assumptions folded up inside each of them, continue to define much of the literature on Muslims and race in the twenty-first century.

The crown jewel of the evidence marshaled to support the argument that Muslims are racialized is the stereotypical image of the Muslim terrorist. One might then reasonably expect the MWT list to serve as evidence of this argument. What might such a reading look like? Analysis of the racelessness of Muslims on the terrorist list based on the Muslim racialization argument briefly described so far may proceed by reading racelessness as itself a racial category. This reading has its merits. It rightly recognizes the lumping together of people who are otherwise connected to very different religions (Sikh, Hindu, and Coptic, for example) and geographies (Italian, Syrian, Bosnian, and so on). Similarly, the word *brown* appears in literature on post-9/11 surveillance in connection with some hazy sense of *Muslim-looking*. Such works seek to capture the commonsense quality of the brown/Muslim image, a common sense that is unimpeded by its imprecision and awkwardness.[11] Such a reading may appear to account for what is obviously a case of group formation. However, interpreting the MWT list as a case of the racialization of Muslims, or locating a definition of race that allows for defining Muslims as one, would leave too much unaccounted for. The great flaw of these sorts of readings is that they defer the question of why race is the factor used to single out Muslims on the MWT list when it could be anything else. What is *race* to the FBI such that Muslims on the Most Wanted Terrorist list do not have it? And what can this tell us about race more broadly in the twenty-first century, coming off the complex contestations around race in the previous few decades? Rather than making a transhistorical argument about Islam, race, or terrorism, assuming that these have a single meaning or uniform expression across time and space, this book instead draws its conclusions from the specific historical, empirical case of the MWT list and connected issues that, owing to their particularities, have much to reveal about policing, race, social science, religion, blackness, and Islam in the United States.

The Average Man
One of this book's arguments is that the MWT list demands an analysis outside of those racial terms of engagement on which the sociology of race and much of the social sciences and humanities have relied. These terms bear a genetic relation to the identification practices in policing that produced the raceless Muslim terrorist pattern to begin with. If these terms are then applied to analyze this pattern, we risk suffering from what Barbara J. Fields so aptly calls a problem of trying to "lift something up while you are standing on it."[12] The book therefore begins with attention to those racial terms of engagement in chapter 1. After all, answers to the question of what race means to the FBI on their wanted posters is not just a question of what fills in a blank on wanted posters; it is a question of

the very presence of that blank, which takes us to the form of the wanted poster and the bureau's categories of choice.[13]

The history of the form of the wanted poster grounds this analysis. The wanted poster form descends from the work of nineteenth-century Belgian astronomer–turned–social scientist Adolphe Quetelet. Sometimes cited as a founder of sociology, he is credited with establishing the quantitative paradigm in the social sciences. Part of that probabilistic revolution, his influence is diffused across the social sciences. His innovation in statistical methods continues to wield influence today. Most importantly for this book, he came up with the concept of the average man.

Quetelet's statistical invention of the average man, *l'homme moyen*, was an ideal figure of what he called "beauty" and "goodness" whose perfection was represented as the very middle of the normal curve, or bell curve, that Quetelet imported from astronomy into the study of human difference. Quetelet modeled physical features of the body and moral propensities on the bell curve. The average man was the fictional, normative figure in the middle of the curve against which all others were measured as *deviant* to a greater or lesser degree; he even referred to measurements on either extreme of the bell curve as monstrous. For Quetelet, the *average* of the average man suggested not mediocrity but a particular kind of perfection. It was an overvaluing of a certain way of being human that he deemed best based on the curve. It was an immediately controversial concept in statistics. It was rejected by many statisticians. Scholars have debated the extent to which the average man concept is important at all for the statistical knowledge that would follow.

Although the average man was indeed rejected by many prominent statisticians of the day, it was put to use by police decades later. French police clerk Alphonse Bertillon adopted Quetelet's average man to organize police records of arrestees as part of his foundational work on introducing scientific rationality into policing. Bertillon created small index cards featuring standardized photographs we call mug shots—also his invention—and a standardized list of body parts with measurements and descriptive details resembling wanted poster categories. Each arrested person would have a card. The collected measurements on each card would be reduced to a single measurement. Based on that one measurement, the tens of thousands of cards would be filed in a particular place in massive cabinets. That particular place was determined by the measurement's distance from the average man. The appeal of this method was that an arrestee could be identified, so it was claimed, by measuring them and seeing if those measurements already belonged to a card, thus suggesting a repeat offender. This method, *bertillonage*, would expand from France, across Europe and its colonies, and, of course, to the United States and Canada. The FBI would adopt this method as well. As Simon A. Cole has shown, the American uptake of these methods was sloppy, departing from Bertillon's fastidious and exacting vision.[14] J. Edgar Hoover, for example, complained that inconsistencies in measurement made it an unwieldy system for the bureau; he lauded fingerprinting as a much more efficient alternative to *bertillonage*.[15] In fact, Hoover's own genealogy of criminal identification asserts that *bertillonage* was replaced by fingerprinting.[16] However, traces of the form of *bertillonage* remain. The categories used on Bertillon cards match many of those still used on wanted posters, such as hair color, eye color, tattoos, and scars and marks, for example. The FBI's uptake of Bertillon's methods and episteme of scientific rationality for identification led to the creation of the identification order, a precursor to the FBI wanted poster with all the same information as a wanted poster, plus fingerprints. Identification orders are distributed by federal and local police internally between cities and offices. Wanted posters, in contrast, are distributed to the public. These earlier forms would find their full expression in the Most Wanted program years later. The retention of the same form of the FBI wanted poster is one piece of evidence that the epistemology of the average man lives on.

When it comes to wanted posters, the average man as an organizing feature of the poster categories is where race can be found. The point here is not centrally to argue that the average man is a racial concept, which others like Ian Hacking have already done well, as chapter 1 discusses, but to highlight how the average man conforms to a definition of race that considers its universalism and its purpose as a way to organize knowledge long before the obviously racial categories of black and white become definitive. Theoretical work, much of it from Black studies, that analyzes the figure of man as a centerpiece of race is especially useful here. R. A. Judy's definition of white supremacy offers several important features extending to a useful definition of *race*. He defines white supremacy as the "hyper-valuing of the noble man ... the noble man of heroic virtue, *arête*, or the noble man of *virtus*, in the Roman tradition ... or the Kantian *anthropos*"; "It's about that particular anthropocentrism ... that can only think about civilization in terms of the hero," he explains. This understanding of white supremacy, which is "not about white people in Europe or anything as simple as that," he emphasizes, highlights instead a particular understanding of the human that constitutes a definition of race.[17] That view of the human is a major anchor of race for this book.[18] In this understanding of race, I wish to highlight two aspects: (1) its materiality, and (2) its relation to a theocentric turned biocentric understanding of nature.

First, the average man, a statistical version of the noble man Judy critiques, is not merely a colorful metaphor or a cultural figure. Rather, given legs through *bertillonage*, it is made concrete as a statistically derived way of organizing humans with direct consequences for their freedom or captivity. Man is an abstraction but is made materially concrete, as its statistical iteration of the average man demonstrates. As Baidik Bhattacharya observes, nineteenth-century human sciences gave "their object—*man* himself—its empirical solidity" by borrowing "epistemological models and conceptual tools from the sciences of life, labor, and language."[19] And still, "the materiality of man remained elusive." Bhattacharya's approach to this need to locate the materiality of man is that resolution is not found in European history or the study of epistemology alone, but in the "governmental practices of the empire, which combined knowledge and techniques of managing the material body ... and thus provided legitimacy to such disciplinary inquiries into the human body."[20] The average man, and its path to the MWT list, is a site of all these: scientific knowledge production, the later-baptized-as-neutral basic methodology of the social sciences, and the exercise of imperial power. The average man therefore helps us see how race is material via its epistemological dimension. In other words, the epistemology of race cannot be dismissed as distanced from material conditions and social structure.

Second, this understanding of race rooted in the concept of man also highlights the place of religion, not only as an identity of some on the MWT list but as an epistemology based on some understanding of nature. Most analysis applying the conceptual frameworks common to post-9/11 studies on Muslims in the war on terror would locate questions of religion in the (majority Muslim) religious identity of the list. Attention to the medium and history of the wanted poster, however, requires a reorientation and a different framework. As historian Theodore Porter and sociologist Frank Hankins mention, Quetelet's work came out of religious thought as a counter to it, though not antagonistically, while also retaining similar forms. Statistics were once used in tandem with theological explanations for social phenomena. Quetelet secularized statistical explanations for regularly occurring phenomena, once understood as an outcome of divine planning and then explained by Quetelet, and others, as an outcome of an autonomous system of nature. But in both the theocentric and biocentric, there is an arbiter of knowledge, and that goes from being God to being man. Quetelet's thought and his figure of the average man are examples of what Sylvia Wynter calls *Man2*, a secular version of the earlier religio-secular understanding of man that emerges toward the end of the eighteenth century and into the nineteenth.[21] For Wynter, *man* refers to one way of being human structured on western European ways of being that are then overrepresented. The West represents man as the only, universal way of being fully human, and it distributes this understanding across the globe. This monopoly on humanity begins with a figure she calls *Man1*, or *homo politicus*, which is an earlier variant of man in explicitly religious and political terms. *Man2*, in contrast, is a purely secular variant emerging in bourgeois capitalist terms. The supreme source of legitimacy moves from a religio-secular understanding of man built on a Christian idea of God to instead a purely secular or, as Wynter says, de-godded source of legitimacy that continues to be structured on the theological model. God is replaced with a secular understanding of nature as the knower and arbiter of truth. Along similar lines, nature, Quetelet argues, determines man's fate, but there is a critical caveat—nature can be shaped by the average man.[22] In a move that most indicates Quetelet's secular turn but using the form of religion, he indicates a conditionally omnipotent and omniscient element of the average man. He believes that everything could be known and categorized in relation to the average man, or the ultimate human, pending enough observations.

The cut-and-dried categories on wanted posters come out of this epistemological rupture of the secular, which, I argue, cannot be neatly severed from its religious roots. What, then, is the place of religion for wanted posters? This epistemological rupture suggests that race and religion are not intersecting or intersectional (which implies separation sometimes and combination at other times), nor are they simply entangled or laid on top of one another—metaphors that perhaps obstruct understanding. Instead, I emphasize the shift from the theocentric to the biocentric alongside the maintenance of a similar knowledge structure across both.[23] This emphasis helps us apprehend subsequent happenings in the Most Wanted program and its categories, such as the FBI's inclusion of Assata Shakur, who was added to the MWT list in 2013. Her representation in the program, as well as her legal cases, require an understanding of the epistemological dimension of race, specifically its grounding in the epistemological rupture of the secular. Frameworks like intersectionality that are commonly employed to interpret Assata Shakur's thought and experiences have little room for such an understanding. Such frameworks may not only serve as a placeholder for mapping out relationships between what are understood as the identity categories of race and others like gender; as chapter 4 on Assata Shakur shows, they may enable the very same powers that seek her extradition from Cuba. To instead understand the trials of Assata Shakur with an emphasis on the secularization of knowledge is to illuminate the nature of the challenge that she and others in the Black liberation movement posed to this epistemology of man since, as Enrique Dussel argues, "the quintessence, the backbone" of Eurocentrism is the theology of Latino-German Christendom.[24] The theological challenge that she and the rest of the Black liberation movement made requires an understanding of the theological nature of what they fought, which, as *No God but Man* emphasizes, hinges on the Negro category.

Islam and "the Negro"

On its wanted poster for Assata Shakur in 1983, the FBI used the word *Muslim*. Convicted in 1977 of killing a police officer, she escaped prison in 1979 and was granted asylum in Cuba. The poster followed her prison escape. It described her as wearing "Muslim or men's clothing." By 2013, when the bureau added her to the MWT list, the word *Muslim* was long gone from her poster even as she was surrounded by Muslims. Further, a race category has always appeared on her posters; she does not bear the mark of the Muslim on the MWT list. Featured on wanted posters on and off since the 1970s, she has also been wanted longer than anyone who has ever been on the MWT list, including Osama bin Laden. The FBI announcement of her addition to the MWT list notes that she is the first woman; however, she is also the first and only representative of the mid-twentieth-century Black liberation movement. She is a lightning rod of a figure for her enemies and her supporters: police unions, the state of New Jersey, and the federal government have sought her extradition from Cuba, and protestors in the recent Black Lives Matter movement could be heard chanting her words at protests and wearing T-shirts that read "Assata Taught Me." Her autobiography has been on university course syllabi since its publication in the late 1980s, which further distinguishes her from most others on the MWT list. In representations of Assata Shakur by both her enemies and her supporters in the twenty-first century, she is not a Muslim.

And yet, there are records from different types of sources that make clear that she called herself a Muslim at some point. According to court records, her correspondence from prison, and her attorneys' biographical accounts of her criminal trials, the use of the word *Muslim* to describe Assata Shakur on her wanted poster is not a complete FBI fabrication put forth to malign her. In fact, she had some connection to Islam from the mid- to late 1970s that materialized in a religious freedom case. She asserted her Muslim status in the courtroom, demanding court proceedings stop on Fridays to respect her religious freedom.

Islam appeared in the opening statement Assata Shakur intended to read at her murder trial in 1977. The court did not permit her or her attorney to read it. In the statement, later published in several sources, including bulletins put out by the Assata Shakur Defense Committee and the Attica News in February

1977,[25] she sought to address the jury: "During the jury selection process you were asked whether or not you had heard of the Black Panther Party, the Black Liberation Army and of the Muslim religion. You were asked those questions for a reason. Although my religious and political beliefs are theoretically not on trial here, so much misinformation and plain nonsense was put out in the media about my political affiliations, that I feel compelled to set the record straight."[26] As chapter 2 demonstrates in detail, her Islam was sometimes respected by the court and sometimes not. But of interest is the way in which Islam arose—she brought it up as a move that asserted her power. The ways that Islam appears do not suggest that it is a subordinated religion or identity on the basis of which remedy is required, as per contemporary racialization arguments. Instead, Muslim status appears in moments in which she is pushing against courtroom efforts to punish and control her. This is a show of power (the little power she had in that situation), which is otherwise a major theme of her autobiography, to the point that it has been subject to critique for this. Through this show of power, she sent the message to the courts that she was not going to simply submit to their will.

Her Muslim status comes up in the courts and the media, and is discussed by Assata Shakur herself, as though it differs in some way from what she ordinarily is or would be. It is posed as a counter to her racial status, as part of an "alternative modality of blackness," to use Sherman A. Jackson's words.[27] In the rest of her opening statement, she gestures to this: "Unlike Alex Haley, the author of *Roots*, I am unable to trace my family back to Africa. And so, in an effort to return to my roots and to rediscover my culture and identity, I chose an African name, Assata Shakur, and adopted the Islamic (Muslim) religion."[28] Her point here is part of what Sylvester Johnson argues was "the most consequential epistemic shift effected by Black ethnic religions" such as Islam: they claimed "that Christianization and slavery were essentially processes of cultural destruction," which included the destruction of connections to Islam.[29]

In her opening statement, she situates Islam explicitly as part of a project of recovery of what was denied her as someone positioned inside the racial Negro construct as lacking history, culture, and civilization. For Cedric Robinson, this erasure is central to race. I would add that race is less a construction per the ubiquitous sociological "social construction of race" and more borne of obliterations—the obliteration from historical memory of actual encounters between (those who would go on to be called) Europeans and Black Africans, and, of course, the obliteration of peoples to form something new, like the Negro and other races. "This 'Negro' was a wholly distinct ideological construct from those images of Africans that had preceded it," differing "in function and ultimately in kind."[30] Robinson notes the centrality of Islam to that process. "Where previously the Blacks were a fearful phenomenon to Europeans because of their historical association with civilizations superior, dominant, and/or antagonistic to Western societies (the most recent being that of Islam)," he argues, "now the ideograph of Blacks came to signify a difference of species, an exploitable source of energy (labor power) both mindless to the organizational requirements of production and insensitive to the subhuman conditions of work." This is part of a planetary shift. "In the more than 3,000 years between the beginnings of the first conception of the 'Ethiopian' and the appearance of the 'Negro,' the relationship between the African and European had been reversed."[31] The reversal involved Europe's rise to world influence and unprecedented levels of control over the fate of much of the planet and its living beings.

In Robinson's account of race, Islam is part of what was erased from Africans to make the Negro. This is important to understanding not only the place of Muslims vis-à-vis race but, as he argues, European racialism more broadly. For this, he explains, four moments must be understood, and "Islamic domination" is one of them:

1. The racial ordering of European society from its formative period, which extends into the medieval and feudal ages as "blood" and racial beliefs and legends.
2. The Islamic (i.e., Arab, Persian, Turkish, and African) domination of Mediterranean civilization and the consequent retarding of European social and cultural life: the Dark Ages.
3. The incorporation of African, Asian, and peoples of the New World into the world system emerging from late feudalism and merchant capitalism.
4. The dialectic of colonialism, plantocratic slavery, and resistance from the sixteenth century forward, and the formations of industrial labor and labor reserves.[32]

Most analyses of racism, Robinson summarizes, begin with the third moment, partially consider the fourth, and ignore the first two.[33] The debate on whether or not race is modern continues, and this book is not engaged in it, but rather notes relevant continuities from before and through modernity.

The analysis of enslaved African Muslims' writings in the work of Sylviane Diouf, Michael Gomez, and R. A. Judy shows how the Negro was configured in part through a specific sort of obliteration that extracted Africans from Islam in the Euro-American worldview related to the construct of the Arab.[34] This is an important aspect of the Negro and, by necessary relation, what it meant to be

Muslim, for that worldview: Muslims—specifically, those Europe recognized as Muslim—represent rivalry and power, in contrast to the Negro, figured as already defeated. By such relations, the Negro could not be Muslim in Euro-American categories. In a reprisal of this earlier formation, the nature of the Muslim threat for the war on terror is as a powerful rival force requiring extreme measures to defeat, and not as a weak sort of enemy, per the concepts of the Negro as well as the Indian who have been figured as already defeated.[35] These categories of Negro, Indian, and so on were never purely descriptive of natural phenomena, as their makers claim; these categories continue to suffer incoherence, as the case of raceless Muslim terrorists initially suggests, and these categories are also subject to being bent toward very different goals, as Assata Shakur shows.

Assata Shakur's brief period as a Muslim is important for this book's argument on race. The knowledge of Shakur's years as a Muslim has receded from public—and indeed the FBI's—memory, too. Further, in popular culture, and in the recent Black Lives Matter movement, she is heavily represented, but not as a Muslim, whether in past or present tense. Islam is absent from popular and scholarly biographical treatments of her story, with few exceptions. Likely, cues are taken from her autobiography, in which she writes that she always had respect for Islam but had "never practiced it." Although disappeared, her brief Muslim status is important for what it enables and for what it can clarify about race and the big themes of this book. Based on analysis of how Islam came up in her battles with the state, in both courtroom and prison, I argue that her Muslim status pushes against race and gestures toward other ways of conceiving of relations beyond the terms of race. The nature of that push lies not in her simple self-identification with Islam for the sake of it, which is to say not as a matter of her simple use of her own will in ways that were disliked by those she leveraged it against. Rather, her identification with Islam has a particular significance in the racial context of the United States as just described. Her Muslim status militates against the particular obliteration resulting in the Negro, which is to say a particular racial arrangement. She considers and also does not use those rules to make her moves. That rejection destabilizes the very basis of race (the average man, noble man, *Man2*, and so on) in posing a challenge outside its logics. This rejection of man, specifically its white divinity, and Black people being drawn to Islam as an alternative to that racial experience, is not unique to her but was rather a basic feature of Islam in Black America in the mid-twentieth century. A major feature of Black Islam is rejecting that white divinity (the theological character of man), and her seemingly uneven engagement with Islam proceeds in that tradition.

It was common enough for Panthers to be Muslim or consider Islam, which held a political meaning entangled with Black Power. Huey P. Newton's perspective on religion is instructive, as it articulates the alternative humanism of the Panthers and their relation to God, which differs in key ways from the average man, *Man2*, the noble man, and so on. In *Revolutionary Suicide*, he explains what was meant by the phrase "All Power to the People." It was based on "the idea of man as God." Further:

> I have no other God but man, and I firmly believe that man is the highest or chief good. If you are obligated to be true and honest to anyone, it is to your God, and if each man is God, then you must be true to him. If you believe that man is the ultimate being, then you will act according to your belief. Your attitude and behavior toward man is a kind of religion in itself, with high standards of responsibility.[36]

Unlike the version of man critiqued by Judy and Wynter, and that proposed by Quetelet, Newton's version is not a peak version of the human, but rather each human stands in for the divine, owed whatever God is owed. Black Power continues to have its critics: for its cultural nationalism, masculinity, misogyny, strategy, alliances, and more. But an aspect of it that I seek to emphasize, these critiques notwithstanding, is the theological challenge it poses: that the problem of race is not just its essentialism, or its erasure of history from people, or that it classifies poorly, but also that it has a false divine figure that persists into the most powerful articulation of the secular and shapes our sense of reality and possibility.[37] Newton is clear that his own notion of man was once religious, then turned secular: "It was especially important to me that I explore the Judaeo-Christian concept of God" because it led Black people to believe, he writes, that they will live better in the next life and experience justice then.[38] "All Power to the People" was intended to ground Black people in the present. At the same time: "The Black Panthers have never intended to turn Black people away from religion. We want to encourage them to change their consciousness of themselves and to be less accepting of the white man's version of God—the God of the downtrodden, the weak, and the undeserving. We want them to see themselves as the called, the chosen, and the salt of the earth."[39]

Along these lines, Assata Shakur's Islam, like that of other Black people in the mid-twentieth century, was a show of power, not weakness. It was as much a restoration project of seeking one's history and practices that were violently erased by chattel slavery as it was a project of creating the cultural intricacies that make Islam a Black religion in the United States.[40] If Islam is a restoration of that which was obliterated in the making of race for those pushed into the

Negro category, then to be Muslim, in this context, is to move against the US racial order and its logics.

On Race Theory

It is widely acknowledged in scholarship on race that the meanings of race are contested. They are stretched and played with toward various ends, and defined and redefined a thousand times, as Stuart Hall emphasized. And my point is not only that there are clear limits to that stretching but also, perhaps, that there is promise in the limits of that stretching. In other words, the liberatory potential of some reclaimed understanding of race has proven itself to be illusory, and another option has always been possible. This option is useful not only as an end goal imagined to be part of some distant future, but it is analytically important right now; it is necessary for simply understanding the MWT list and its version of race.

Theories of race coming from thinkers as different from one another as Sylvia Wynter and R. A. Judy in Black studies discussed earlier, as well as Stuart Hall and Paul Gilroy in cultural studies, and the social scientific approaches of Adolph Reed, Barbara Fields, and Karen Fields, all tend to emphasize the limits and boundaries of race. This case of the raceless Muslim terrorist provides fresh evidence of these scholars' conclusions. It is one entry in a larger sort of archive that exceeds this book, an archive of phenomena that do not quite fit the terms of race, an archive that these thinkers have also engaged to come to their conclusions in various disciplines and with various, sometimes contrasting, commitments. It should be noted that none of them study those who are considered racially ambiguous, or those in the intermediate category between Black and white on the racial hierarchy, to argue that race is limited. This would be an easy conclusion to reach when empirically studying those who are not readily identifiable as either Black or white in the black-white binary that has defined race in the United States in many ways. Rather, many of these thinkers examine exactly that which (supposedly unambiguously) defines race: race as fabricated by law, plantation economy, eugenicists, statisticians, and so on.

While studying the experiences of Black people and blackness, that great metonym for *race*, they find that, still, race is not a concept worth holding onto as analytically useful for understanding those to whom it has been applied as a presumably obviously useful means for understanding. For one, as Fields and Fields emphasize, race clouds any solid understanding of racism. As they explain, the social practice of racism produces the conception of race, and not the other way around. They emphasize the difference between these terms and problematize their conflation. "The shorthand" that allows "race" to mean many different things all conflated together makes the nefarious move of transforming "*racism*, as something an aggressor *does*, into *race*, something the target *is*, in a sleight of hand that is easy to miss."[41] There are other ways scholars have distinguished between race and racism. Some will define race as what comes first and racism as activity based on the reality of race rather than the assumption of race along similar lines; there are presumably antiracist attempts to maintain a distinction in order to end racism but preserve race. For me, Fields and Fields's reason for distinguishing between the two is useful, and not these latter reasons (which may be what Anibal Quijano critiques in a footnote poking at Americans for their obsession with differentiating between the two).[42] Following decolonial thought that emphasizes the racialization of knowledge structures, I position race as a problem as well, and not only racism, as Judy's intellectual project would suggest. Judy considers how race is one system of knowledge that stands in contrast to that of Frantz Fanon, whose project Judy seeks to build on to think toward alternatives. At the very least, this suggests that race is not always already part of every system of knowledge. What these otherwise very different thinkers share is a notion that race is not a sprawling social construct common to all that is social but is bounded by time and space as historic fabrication that should be treated analytically as a fabrication that, as David Theo Goldberg puts it, is to be *mentioned* but not *used* as an analytical category.[43]

Philosopher Tommie Shelby makes a useful distinction between an external attribution, what we may call race, a blackness of white creation, or racial blackness, on the one hand; and a blackness of Black creation that, for me, is not a case of race.[44] Both sorts of blackness appear in the idiom of *Negro, Black, African American*, and so on, so the important differentiating feature here is not the word *blackness* itself but the contextual question of the goals and activities around which it is oriented. There is thus a critical difference between the epistemological and material creations of that plantation economy, for example, and the epistemological and material practice and creations of affinity among those otherwise different peoples pushed together by such an arrangement. The blackness of Black creation runs counter to European *race* and the presumed promise of being recognized as such in European categories, and this, too, may use racial language but does not align with man in its interests, desired outcomes, or methods of knowing and living. Their separation is a valuable heuristic. This heuristic does not require adhering to some notion of ontological differences between Black and white, nor does it establish a clean line between the two that ignores Black actors acting in white interests and the reverse. It also does not rely on reducing or romanticizing the blackness of Black creation.[45] The value of limiting the definition of race by making a distinction between the goals of that blackness of white creation and Black creation becomes apparent when considering the relation between Muslims and race.

Research on Muslims and race in the United States tends to collapse this distinction. There is indeed some notion of a Muslim of American creation that clashes with Muslims' own ideas of what it means to be Muslim. Junaid Rana rightly points out a related problem in the contemporary task of producing knowledge about Muslims inside of "race": "the danger is a complicity with liberal modes of thinking that would render the figure of the Muslim as simply a racialized subject without addressing issues of sociality, theology, and even alternative modes of political thought and liberation."[46] Junaid Rana and Gilberto Rosas note that there are two understandings of *Muslim* in conflict, a collapse of two very different meanings of *Muslim*. It refers to "a religious community to be policed and disciplined into the American polity," on the one hand, and then a related but different enough definition that is part of racial epistemology "as a general category that situates Muslims as an ambiguous racial community that encompasses the 'Arab–Middle Eastern–Muslim' ... South Asians (including Christians, Hindus, Muslims, and Sikhs), and possibly Latinas/os, and African Americans."[47] And yet, theoretical frameworks used in the study of the racialization of Muslims cannot get out of this problem of unintentionally doing the work of subsuming Muslims into race. Race, while fueling this problem, remains an attractive framework for understanding the experiences and positioning of Muslims in the war on terror and for resisting it. It is clear, and I agree, that race has something to do with what Muslims have faced after 9/11, and my overall point in this book is that precision about that something is critical. For me, that something is in the world of epistemology, and less so in what is called racial identity. Those who have argued that Muslims are racialized have fought against the incorrect (often right wing or liberal) idea that race has nothing to do with violence against Muslims in the war on terror because Islam is a religion, which is connected to the charge that Muslims are exaggerating about the violence and discrimination they face. The arguments against this charge fail, however, because they are using the same general categories. This book's interest is in clearing some of the barriers to exploring the promise of rejecting expressions of racial epistemologies in the study of Muslims and race.

A sprawling definition of race is adopted in literature on Muslim racialization. Race is used to "bear the weight, metaphorically, of other kinds of difference" and a wide range of activity.[48] Michael Omi and Howard Winant are among the most frequently engaged scholars of race in this area of study. Their approach to race is then instructive: "While race is a template for the subordination and oppression of different social groups," they "emphasize that it is also a template for resistance to many forms of marginalization and domination."[49] The first part of Omi and Winant's definition of race describes race in a way that would account for the average man as a template for the human to whom others are subordinate. Scientific race is certainly in the business of producing templates. The second part of their definition of race, however, while true in some cases, is more debatable for movements like civil rights and Black Power that are nevertheless read as squarely racial. Then, either the second part of their definition reflects a misreading of movements that have adopted race language to push for something very different from a racial order, or the second part itself does the work of race, which is to endlessly organize and categorize persons, places, and things as subordinate or subordinated, however sympathetically, to a godlike figure whose position at the top of this hierarchy is natural/ized. Here, critical versions of race theory run into a problem: Omi and Winant begin by arguing that race is a particular sort of violent construct coming out of Europe, then conclude that it becomes a liberatory project as well. All is read back into race. These two parts of a race definition for Omi and Winant are simply one example of a broader consensus in much scholarship on race and Muslims discussed in chapters 3 and 4. When Muslims are put into this very broad theoretical understanding of race, in which race is a template for violence and all that is against that violence, the observation that the war on terror treats Muslims as the enemy (race) comes to serve as the basis for stretching the definition of race to remedy this situation (antiracism), in an anxious appeal to a liberal antiracism that requires self-definition in man's image, as chapter 4 argues.[50]

The bigger question raised is whether scholarship engages the logic of race to understand it or whether some other kind of logic is engaged, a question I ask not from ungrounded theorizing but from the empirical realities of the MWT list.

Overview of Chapters

The chapters are organized chronologically, all approaching issues related to the Most Wanted Terrorist list. I begin with the history and epistemology of the MWT list in chapter 1 and then move on to case studies more directly connected to individuals on the list in the remaining three chapters, with the fourth chapter and conclusion considering contemporary expressions and challenges to the racial epistemology organizing the MWT list.

Chapter 1 has three goals: to offer a genealogy of the wanted poster as organized by the average man; to trace the religious roots of the secular, racial knowledge formation that continues to nourish it; and to provide an overview of the Most Wanted program. I argue that the statistical invention of the average man is defined by race as the overvaluing of one way of being human. After an introduction to the average man, I show how late nineteenth-century French police clerk Alphonse Bertillon adopted Quetelet's average man decades later to organize French police records at home, in the colonies, and in major cities across the world. Lastly, I trace the FBI's uptake of the methods and episteme of scientific rationality for identification, leading to the creation of the identification order, a precursor to the FBI wanted poster, and ultimately an entire FBI program dedicated to the distribution of wanted posters. Rather than accepting the narrative that modern science is secular (defined as free of religion), chapter 1 excavates the theological aspects of the history of the wanted poster.

Chapter 2 considers archival materials related to Islam surrounding Assata Shakur in the 1970s and 1980s, including her wanted posters from those years. This chapter advances the argument that, rather than another case of racial particularism in a critical frame, the blackness of Black Power—again, that blackness of Black people's creation—is an argument against race. In other words, I argue that her invocation of Islam functioned as a move against racial logics. The chapter moves chronologically, beginning with a discussion of how Islam appeared in courtroom matters during her various trials. It then analyzes how the New Jersey state police and FBI have used Islam to describe her on her wanted poster and identification order. She is ungendered, per Hortense Spillers, in posters, the courts, and the media in relation to the Muslim label. She is gendered in whatever contradictory ways serve the purposes of those doing the gendering. Lastly, the chapter covers the period after her escape to Cuba, from where she writes in her autobiography that she "never practiced" Islam. The contradiction between her claim never to have practiced Islam, alongside archival material in which she called herself Muslim, is then interpreted through a discussion of an essay by Safiya Bukhari, another former Panther who was a devoted Muslim. Bukhari's discussion of fearlessness draws attention to the social role of the theological dimension of Black Islam that resonates with the less overtly theological approach of Shakur, in which Bukhari sought to kill her potential to be owned by anything but God.

The goal of chapter 3 is to offer the wealth of examples of wanted posters of raceless Muslims on the MWT list. The chapter highlights the distinctiveness of the MWT posters by making key comparisons between their posters and those of Muslims on nonterrorism lists, as well as non-Muslims on terrorism lists. I argue that the fact of their racelessness is something to think with rather than to consider as a case of the racialization of Muslims. The racelessness of Muslims on the MWT list marks paradox: they are at once off the charts in their (social scientific) deviance (from the average man), while also marked as rivals, which is to say as formidable rather than weak enemies. The chapter concludes with a discussion of the crashing together of frameworks of difference that make this paradox, modeled on Nasser Hussain's argument regarding Guantánamo as a place not where law is absent, but where different legal systems converge to create hyperlegality. The FBI's posters are in a scientific paradigm, and the Muslim enemy is in a theological one. These converge to produce the paradox expressed as racelessness.

Chapter 4 approaches debates on Assata Shakur's 2013 designation as a terrorist as a moment illuminating some of the problems of how race, blackness, and Islam are theorized by those critical of the war on terror. Some of Shakur's supporters' attempts to save her from the terror designation turn her into a Black Madonna, to use Dhoruba Bin Wahad's phrase—an abstract, innocent, heroine figure. The racial logic of innocence that challenges her addition to the MWT list in 2013 but not the list itself, I argue, renders her a kind of average man. This logic of the average man is also reflected in research on the war on terror for those signified by acronyms like SWANA (Southwest Asian and North African) and AMSA (Arab, Muslim, South Asian) based on its use of concepts like racialization and intersectionality. The chapter locates traces of the average man in these concepts through their treatment of racial blackness. It raises the question as to whether these concepts, even when put forth as merely descriptive, are analytically relying on racial blackness and thus doing the epistemological work of race. A review of Shakur's posters from the 1980s onward, and state and political organizations' pursuit of her, then lead to a discussion of how her baptism as innocent by her supporters resonates with the atomizing function of wanted posters and the FBI's view of a "Black messiah"—an atomizing to make guilty, rather than innocent. Critiquing racial blackness as a model, the chapter points to the original conception of Black studies, as it is already connected to Islam, as holding useful ways of thinking and pursuing the change that we, who are concerned with the position of Muslims in the war on terror, seek. The conclusion chapter revisits Eqbal Ahmad's famous speech, "Terrorism: Theirs and Ours," and discusses the promise of his notions of *theirs* and *ours* but put toward this book's analysis of race.

1

L'HOMME MOYEN AND AMERICAN ANTHROPOMETRY

Questions of knowledge are not a distant concern for those involved in the practical, everyday exercise of police identification. Glen King, executive director of the International Association of Chiefs of Police (IACP), argued in the 1970s that the "development of our national criminal identification system is not primarily a story of expanding police technology."[1] Rather, "its place is better described among the history of ideas."[2] Former FBI director J. Edgar Hoover was also concerned with ideas, as his 1929 article in the *Annals of the American Academy of Political and Social Science* suggests. The article provides a genealogy of criminal identification, per its title. In this genealogy, Hoover attributes revolutionary developments in criminal identification to "men of science" Adolphe Quetelet, Francis Galton, and Alphonse Bertillon. Their world of ideas, particularly Quetelet's concept of the average man, or *l'homme moyen*, transformed modern policing. The average man is also central to the genealogy of the wanted poster, as this chapter traces from its origins in statistics, to the Paris Prefecture of Police, to the FBI and its Most Wanted program.[3] The wanted poster retains traces of the average man that make it a scientific racial artifact.

Adolphe Quetelet (1796–1874) was an astronomer and statistician born in Ghent. Allan Sekula views Quetelet as the most important "early architect of sociology" other than Auguste Comte, while George Sarton insists that Quetelet is much more deserving of the title than Comte; either way, Quetelet does not live on in sociological memory as competitive with Comte for the title, despite having an important influence on foundational theorists in the discipline like Marx and Émile Durkheim.[4] Still, Quetelet is typically credited for laying the foundation for the quantitative paradigm in the social sciences, or at least, for Paul Lazarsfeld, for marking "the beginning of what one should consider modern efforts at sociological quantification."[5] Quetelet was in the business of what John H. Goldthorpe describes as "sociological science," or the study of probabilistic regularities in social life that are understood as properties of populations themselves.[6] Quetelet's version of social science was about measuring not just the physical but also the moral, since "moral phenomena," he claimed, "when observed on a great scale, are found to resemble physical phenomena."[7] Employing the same techniques to study abstract human attributes, physical qualities, and moral propensities, Quetelet rendered regularities as a matter of the traits of the individuals and groups, abstracted from history.

Quetelet made wide-ranging contributions, and he is "almost unique," Theodore Porter observes, for how he made a connection between the study of humans and of celestial bodies in the nineteenth century.[8] His contributions were as wide-ranging as his interests. From his formative years, Quetelet maintained a connection to the arts. He published poetry, performed in a local theater, and wanted initially to become a painter and sculptor. At the age of eighteen, however, he became a mathematics teacher, and from there completed his doctorate with a thesis on abstract geometry. He was heavily involved in starting an astronomical observatory in Brussels. While doing the work of setting up the observatory, he was sent to Paris to learn about the tools and technology required. In Paris, he met the mathematicians Fourier and Laplace. Quetelet was impressed by their work on probability.[9] By combining the statistical social data they worked on with his own work on abstract mathematics, Quetelet was able to essentially combine his interests in natural sciences like astronomy as well as the humanistic side of his interests; Lazarsfeld holds that Quetelet's later work cannot be understood without an understanding of his humanism, including his background in literature and his humanist friends.[10] Similarly, Kevin Donnelly emphasizes the relationship between Quetelet's intellectual work and his institution building, arguing that the various parts of his life cannot be fragmented in order to be understood.[11] Indeed, he was involved in creating many Belgian institutions of science and recordkeeping, establishing some of the first actuarial tables used in Belgium and helping to found an international society for the promotion of statistical methods in 1853.[12]

The major, if loose, argument Quetelet made was that all phenomena have statistical stability, and a figure he called *l'homme moyen*, or the average man, is the basis of stability.[13] The average man, which will be explained in detail, is what he called an ideal of "beauty" and "goodness." It is fictional, he asserts, but still the average man is of utmost importance for Quetelet because it is the departure point for his entire scientific project. Locating and determining the average man "ought necessarily to precede every other inquiry into social physics, since it is, as it were, the basis," he wrote.[14] The average man was a controversial concept, critiqued for implying that mediocrity was an ideal, and for involving too many assumptions.[15] Although also critical of the concept, this chapter is most interested in its secularity, its resonance with other versions of man, its proliferation through policing, and the means by which it treats description as neutral even as it is openly normative. This chapter argues that the average man is a racial concept, and specifically as a matter of "the hyper-valuing of the noble man," of R. A. Judy's understanding of white supremacy. Quetelet's average man is an easy example of what Judy describes as "that particular anthropocentrism... that can only think about civilization in terms of the hero."[16] This figure of man is foundational to the understanding of race that informs the FBI Most Wanted program.[17] Further, as Sylvester A. Johnson and Steven Weitzman remind us in their research on the FBI, religion is critical to understanding the bureau.[18] This argument rings true not only in the FBI's explicit attention to religious groups but also because of the religious structure of the secularized epistemology of criminal identification that the FBI adopts, which takes us to the early years of statistics.[19]

Secularizing Statistics

Rates of birth and death—the most human experiences, as Carlo Ginzburg notes—animated the earliest statisticians.[20] They calculated probabilities that served the needs of states and militaries for information. Statistics emerged with the informational requirements of the state as its motivational impulse. Indeed, the word *statistics* has a root word meaning *state*.[21] The modern state and statisticians were interdependent; statistics were useful for the state to represent social relations and maintain legitimacy, while the data provided by the state was necessary for the basic work of statistical analysis. Official statistics bureaus developed in the nineteenth century, along with new political uses of statistics, in a time when the probabilistic style of statistical reasoning was forming.[22] Large-scale social statistics became available in the early nineteenth century due to expanded census taking. The idea that social phenomena could be subjected to quantitative analysis became prominent in the early seventeenth century, and statisticians up until the nineteenth century saw statistical regularity as evidence of divine planning. They explained regularity in birth and death rates as a matter of divine wisdom, an explanation based on theological naturalism. Theological naturalism faced a theodicean struggle when it had to contend with what it understood as deviance, as the unnatural. Some sorts of statistical regularity did not seem easily attributed to divine wisdom and planning without raising that thorny question of theodicy and the nature of God. For example, was the stability of rates of theft, murder, and suicide also from God? These domains of deviance were also part of the earliest statistical inquiry—suicide, crime, vagrancy, madness, prostitution, disease—rooted in the notion that control through enumeration and classification can improve deviants.[23]

The collapse of theological naturalism was an epistemic upheaval, constituting new conditions of modernity that complicated the question of what it means to be human.[24] The meaning of reason and rationality shifted along with this epistemological change from an understanding that the way to know the human was through God to instead a knowledge that was in and through humans.[25] This new understanding not only shifted the locus of understanding from God to man but also was valued as the best means of knowing. With belief in God relegated to the private and personal, God was put at a distance from the order of knowledge.[26] However, religious epistemology lived on after the epistemological shift of Enlightenment rationality, as Charles Long explains, through the very categories of Enlightenment reason that must create "empirical others" to dominate.[27] Quetelet is one example of many who facilitated this epistemological shift while maintaining a private concern with the divine that could come in rhetorically to defend his work but was distanced from the structure of his thought. For example, he says it would be "injurious to divinity" to think that humans are the only life forms to whom natural law does not apply.[28] He further reflects that such an understanding would be more injurious to divinity than the research he proposed to carry out, which suggests an acknowledgement that his work might be injurious.

In what some call *premodern protorace*, with its theological naturalism, the natural is inseparable from the theological: the divine makes the natural, and the unnatural is a deviation from Christ. Jews and Moors enter here. The etymology of the term *race*, as *raza*, is instructive to this end, where *raza* referred to stock, the breeding of horses, and also to Jews and Moors.[29] Lewis Gordon points out a specific feature of horses and dogs that *raza* referred to—they are made through human involvement. "Thus, their 'natural' form was heavily mediated or, under another interpretation"—like Quetelet's, for my purposes—

"deviated."[30] "It would be odd to consider dogs and horses 'unnatural' however," Gordon explains. "That they are domesticated animals signals a relationship between them and the human beings they serve.... They are, nevertheless, deviations through supposedly human hubris. Comparing them with domesticated animals, then, signaled also the social role they were expected ultimately to play."[31] A similar understanding of the natural and unnatural is expressed quite explicitly for Quetelet through metaphors from astronomy about deviation: instead of a deviation from Christ, the unnatural is a deviation from the norm, or the average man. The paradoxical understanding of the unnatural as deviating from the natural, while also being available and domesticated/controlled in service of the natural, is also in Quetelet's thought, as he believed that the average man could shape nature for his own benefit.[32]

Quetelet helped resolve the theodicean question of the unnatural through a cosmology that was both physicalist and theological, and almost lawlike, where all phenomena are defined by mass regularity.[33] Where theologically oriented statisticians like Süssmilch explained observed regularity as evidence of a divine order, Quetelet removed God from the explanation and in a way made the regularity its own explanation: it was social law.[34] This secularizing resolution was part of key principles of statistics he helped usher in. In his 1908 dissertation situating Quetelet in the history of statistics, Frank Hankins argues that three principles were important for the development of the statistical method: that social phenomena have causes; regularities in statistical results reveal the rules of the existing social order; and large amounts of data yield constancy in results. These principles run through Quetelet's work. He explored them in the binomial curve, the center of which was the average man.

Deriving the Average Man

How did Quetelet derive the concept of the average man statistically in a process that, I would argue, cannot be reduced to being purely methodological but that speaks to the theological and theoretical as well? Quetelet mapped cases, those deemed natural and not, onto the model of the bell curve he imported from astronomy. The Gaussian error curve of astronomy was used to estimate the location of stars. As Goldthorpe summarizes, Quetelet extended the logic of the curve in astronomy that made "differing observations of features of the same object" (like different individuals' observations of the location of one particular star) to "observations of the features of different individuals" (like many individuals' propensity to commit a crime).[35] That it was an error curve is important here. It was as though nature or society aimed to form a specific sort of individual, and some degree of error would occur each time, thus creating variation around that type (the average man), which was in the middle of the curve. When Quetelet plotted heights and weights on a graph, he noticed that they resembled the distribution of errors on a normal curve.[36] From this, he came to believe that the distribution of any physical characteristics could be analyzed as if they were a normal distribution on a binomial curve. The formulas he came up with based on the study of birth and death rates, among other rates, were "based partly on curve-fitting, partly on analogy, and were not interpreted concretely or grounded in physical models," Porter summarizes.[37] It thus took on the flavor, though not the substance, of empirically derived truth.

The average man, *l'homme moyen*, is the basis of Quetelet's work, as he says, and yet it is also notoriously unclear, read differently by philosophers and sociologists like Durkheim and facing many critiques like that of determinism.[38] It was plainly normative, and, by Quetelet's own admission, "fictitious."[39] As Hacking reasons, there were and are no such actual, individual men whose bodily measurements, by any measure, altogether, simultaneously, meet the determined average on every bodily measure—which is to say nothing of how average morals are figured into the composite of the average man.[40] The average man was therefore a fictional type of statistical derivation, derived as a mean between limits and hypervalued by definition, thus fitting Judy's analysis of the overvaluing of the noble man. Quetelet models his average man as the norm based on measurements of the natural organism that, per Sylvia Wynter, cannot be cleansed of its religious epistemological roots despite scientists' best efforts. It is this epistemology, a methodological hypervaluing of the average man, that is essential to that "rational absurdity" called race.[41]

The statistical character of the average man differentiated it as a norm from notions of ideals or venerated attributes that have an important place in other contexts.[42] The difference between norm and ideal is significant, as Lennard J. Davis points out. Societies with an ideal do not expect humans to live up to that ideal, as Davis explains; it is reserved for mythic figures like gods. Norms, on the other hand, are presented as though they reflect natural variance and a neutrally determined peak in actual populations of people. Humans are thus supposed to naturally, already, be like the average man, an ideal made real, or an ideal for humans and not (only) the divine. Again, then, the average man is prescriptive but in the language of the descriptive. As Davis argues, one consequence of the idea of the norm is that it divides the total population into standard and nonstandard subpopulations, which means that the next step is to try to norm the substandard—the aim of eugenics. Drawing our attention once again to the theological, the average man is also a case of what Wynter calls *Man2*, or *homo economicus*, a secular figure that occupies the epistemological position once held by God for western European Christians. Reading the trajectory of average man in criminology as a case of *Man2* highlights the religious dimension of the episteme, rather than leaving the assumption of the secular uninterrogated. This is a specific type of secular, but it is not the only secular. It is not like what Sherman A. Jackson calls "the Islamic secular," for example, which refers to a limitation that Islamic law or *sharī'ah* places on itself, in which certain areas fall outside of its legal gaze but are nevertheless recognized as falling under God's gaze, like all things. Further, the development of law on those areas outside the purview of *sharī'ah* does not proceed as though man has replaced God, like the secular epistemology of Quetelet.[43]

"It is this being," that is, average man, "whom we must consider in establishing the basis of social physics," Quetelet proposes, which means "throwing out of view peculiar or anomalous cases."[44] As Quetelet explained, "*One of the principal facts of civilisation is, that it more and more contracts the limits within which the different elements relating to man oscillate.* The more knowledge is diffused, so much the more do the deviations from the average disappear; and the more, consequently, do we tend to approach that which is beautiful, that which is good."[45] Part of Quetelet's method, then, is that deviations from average man dissolve by design when many cases are considered; put differently, in terms that draw attention to the racial character of his statistical imaginary, deviations are necessarily obliterated.[46] He calls deviations from average man "beyond the natural," as "preternatural, or monstrosities."[47] "When the deviations become greater, they constitute the extraordinary class" of limits, which are "beyond the natural."[48] He uses the astronomy-related concept of oscillation to describe the disappearance of deviations as a natural process, since observations in astronomy can be mapped onto human traits and behaviors quite neatly, as though neutrally describing rather than what Quetelet was doing through description: establishing a norm and a seemingly systematic means of identifying it.[49]

The relation between the average man (the natural) and deviations (the unnatural) is modeled on the astronomy-related concepts of gravity, equilibrium, movement, and perturbation. As Porter remarks, Quetelet certainly "developed an extravagant system of metaphors and similes."[50] For example, Quetelet wrote, "The average man ... is in a nation what the centre of gravity is in a body; it is by having that central point in view that we arrive at the apprehension of all the phenomena of equilibrium and motion."[51] He frequently returned to the notions of equilibrium and movement. Not only did he claim that we can understand equilibrium and motion in a system through maintaining the centrality of the average man in our analysis, but further, the average man is himself the center of the social. The center of gravity is a kind of "equilibrium," and everything else "belongs to... the movement of the system."[52] That which is in motion—which is to say that which is not average man—perturbs average man.[53] The metaphor of perturbations is used to explain away not only individual cases that do not fit the binomial distribution but also large-scale social phenomena like revolutions, a metaphor introduced in the first paper he wrote after the September revolution.

Quetelet's importation of concepts and models from astronomy, and putting them to use in the study of humans to define, organize, and order human difference, to explain away what he deemed to be deviations or perturbations, thus made his knowledge apparatus just as racial as those of the more familiar names of Immanuel Kant and Galton. This discussion on deviations suggests one way in which the average man is racial, but not just in the sense that the average man could be said to map onto the white and deviations map onto the nonwhite. Quetelet's work cannot totally be reduced in this way without missing a significant aspect of his work and influence on that racial order. Again, Judy's definition of white supremacy is useful. In "Kant and the Negro," Judy describes Kant's human as colorless.[54] The Negro as a lesser human is understood on the same model as Kant's colorless human but with color added. The word *white* is not what is important here in his definition of white supremacy, but that others are seen as being on the model of this particular human, just as lesser. That is the universalizing of man or, more specifically here, the average man. Similar to this understanding of a raceless or colorless template of the human on which color is added is David Lloyd and Paul Thomas's argument that Raymond Williams's concept of "the whole man" in his earlier work is prepolitical. Much like Quetelet's man, it rests on an undivided concept of humanity.[55] It is prepolitical because, resonant with Judy's description of Kant's "colorless human" with color added, "the political stands in for the division of the human into partialities. The same... applies to every other conceivable division."[56] The implication is that man—the whole man, or noble man, or average man—is "above economics and above class" or, as Lloyd and Thomas phrase it, "cultivatedly disinterested."[57]

For Quetelet, different races/nations each have a different average man, which suggests further that a white-nonwhite binary is insufficient as a way to capture what is racial about the concept of the average man. Quetelet explains, "Every race has its peculiar constitution, which differs from [the average man] more or less, and which is determined by the influence of climate, and the habits which characterise the average man of that peculiar country."[58] There are a few different ways we may identify this aspect of the average man concept as racial. For Ian Hacking, Quetelet is putting forth something racial because he is creating a biological type that is specific to each nation. Peoplehood was no longer to be defined as a matter of culture, geography, language, or religion, Hacking summarizes, but through "a new objective measurable conception of a people. A race would be characterized by its measurements of physical and moral qualities, summed up in the average man of that race."[59]

While Hacking's latter contention about an objective-measurement-based conception rightly pinpoints the heart of scientific/biologistic race, I locate the racial in the universalizing, overvalued character of Quetelet's average man and not only in the notion that each race/nation has its own average man. Specifically, for Quetelet, there is a penultimate average man who is not yet determined but can and must be. Pending sufficient data, with enough observations, Quetelet often repeats, anything can be known, and more specifically, it will be possible to find an average man of the entire human race: "I think it is not only not absurd, but even *possible*, to determine the average man of a nation, or of the human race; the apparent absurdity of such a research only proceeds from the want of a sufficient number of accurate observations, so that the conclusions may present the greatest possible probability of truth."[60] Consistent with his thinking on deviations from the average man generally, he elaborates that this model holds true when the comparison is not between individual men plotted on the bell curve but between nations: "individual peculiarities tend to disappear more and more, and... nations assume a greater resemblance to each other."[61] Any conclusions must be based on observations of many individuals; the more individuals observed, and the more precise the measurements, the more that the conclusions reflect laws of what he calls the social body. The necessity of a vast number of observations to draw conclusions is a foundational assumption of statistics and the quantitative social sciences to which Quetelet made many contributions. Quetelet is relentlessly hopeful about the promise of more definitive scientific conclusions simply with more observations. His interest— the "science of Man"—had been rather limited, in his view. The key piece missing was the measurements of man: "The void resulting from this neglect must be filled up by the sciences of observation."[62] For Quetelet, "Experience alone can with certainty solve a problem which no *à priori* reasoning could determine."[63] For example, he notes the work of other thinkers who seek to determine the standard of beauty for humans as proportionate to intelligence.[64] He reports that studies of comparative anatomy find that facial angles nearly approaching a right angle are associated with the maximum level of intelligence, "which would give the pre-eminence to the Caucasian. I do not know if any observations have been made on a somewhat larger scale, having in view the measurement of the degrees of size of the facial angle at different ages, in order to determine if these are at all proportionate to the degrees of the development of intelligence."[65] Quetelet is method-forward: observations and the statistical procedures for interpreting them remain neutral for him. They are a view from nowhere—a God's-eye view, a phrasing that draws attention to the theological element of Quetelet's average man that also makes it a racial concept.

Race is the obliterative, biocentric paradigm that Quetelet, among others, would help to inaugurate, with its new theology/science in which man replaces God as the arbiter of knowledge. "It is not at all my intention to propose a Theory of Man," Quetelet wrote, but he nevertheless understood man as having "in himself a moral force securing to him the empire over all living beings on this globe.... By means of them, also, he possesses the power of modifying, at least to appearance, the laws of nature affecting him, and perhaps by causing a progressive movement, [he] tends to approach a happier physical condition."[66] The average man was in control of other planetary life, including human others, as guaranteed by nature (different from God). This a basic outline of the philosophy of Western colonialism. His specific average man very much lined up with the theory of man of his time. The fact that eugenicists Francis Galton and Karl Pearson would find his work so inspiring is instructive. Still, Quetelet's average man had a mixed reception. French and English statisticians rejected the average man.[67] Others have argued that the average man is not essential to Quetelet's work or is not the most interesting and important thing about it.[68] These critiques notwithstanding, the average man does have an important role in the case of interest in this book because it becomes the figure around which FBI records are organized.

To America: *Bertillonage*, Fingerprints, and the FBI

The average man, via anthropometry, found a rich life in American policing, informing categorization and cataloging procedures. Alphonse M. Bertillon (1853–1914) adopted Quetelet's average man to build the first modern criminal identification system in the late nineteenth and early twentieth century that continues to inform FBI identification practices well into the twenty-first century. Bertillon became a police clerk for the Paris Prefecture of Police in his early twenties, coming from a family with connections to science, medicine, and anthropology.[69] It was his grandfather, Achille Guillard, who coined the term *demography* for a new discipline he would help establish that was interested in locating underlying laws and causes, oriented toward improving administrative statistics. His elder brother Jacques became the director of statistics for the city of Paris, and his father cofounded the École d'anthropologie. Quetelet was an important influence for the Bertillons.[70] His father incorporated some elements of Quetelet's social physics in his own work, such as using the same bell curve mapping method as Quetelet to show how it can be used to distinguish races.[71] He would gift thirteen-year-old Alphonse a copy of Quetelet's *Physique Sociale*, and the boy reportedly took a great interest in it at the time.[72] With a father and brother who were physicians, Alphonse, too, began medical school, but he left after passing the first exam.[73] Despite the young Bertillon skipping around between several jobs, medical school, and the army, his father used his connections to get him a job as a junior clerk at a bank, in which he lasted three months, and then a position as a police clerk in which his job was to copy out forms.[74] This gave him his start as one of the key "men of science" to introduce scientific rationality into policing.

He began the position at the police prefecture in March 1879. Within months, he decided to pursue a method for the identification of recidivists.[75] Within years, he would revolutionize police identification, a revolution that would be legal, social, and moral, and that would make him an architect of the contemporary conception of criminal justice.[76] Recidivism was a prime concern when he joined the prefecture. An 1885 French bill banished "recidivist" criminals to penal colonies.[77] It was one of a series of legislative efforts, and first offenders and recidivists were the two categories at play in this and similar laws adopted at this time. Enforcing this law hinged on the ability of the police to identify individuals they had encountered multiple times. Identity had to become fixed and verifiable for this goal, given what was already available as means of identification. Identity had already become textualized under Napoleon, as passports were issued to all French citizens and foreigners in both metropole and colony.[78] These identity papers, however, were easily forged, which made the goal of identification on their basis difficult in the context of recidivism. Earlier methods, such as branding by hot iron and cropping the ears of recidivists, had been illegal since 1832.[79] Additional pressure came from the aftermath of the Paris Commune. The 1871 Commune burned all city records prior to 1859, so Paris residents over a certain age were able to invent any sort of identity.[80] Changes in the perception of crime accompanied the birth of an international association of workers and the repression of workers after the Paris Commune, signaling the place of class struggle.[81] It was in this context that Bertillon made the case for his method: "There was need of a method...analogous to that in use in botany and zoölogy," Bertillon wrote; it must be a system "based on the characteristic elements of individuality, and not on the station and occupation of the accused, which may be erroneously given."[82] For Bertillon, anthropometry provided a way. For the problem of identification and verification, it was a solution that Baidik Bhattacharya calls somapolitics, or an imperial paradigm "distinguished by its remarkable attention to the material surface, or the *soma* of the criminal body (as opposed to its more elusive *psyche*), formulated in close collaboration with imperial 'race-thinking.'"[83]

The Bertillon system, or *bertillonage*, was its namesake's anthropometric method and system of organizing police records. Its main tools were small cards, calipers, cabinets, and the camera. *Bertillonage* involved a process of measurement-based description of an arrestee listed on a small card, followed by an elaborate process of classifying the individual cards based on those measurements. These measurements of certain body parts were understood as a method of elimination: they could be used to prove who an individual brought into the police station was not. The negative nature of this method was its "principal defect," Ginzburg observes.[84] It did not, however, stand alone. To make a positive identification, Bertillon used the *portait parlé*, a "spoken portrait," or detailed physical description of the individual, and some cite this as among the more lasting parts of Bertillon's legacy.[85] Descriptors in the *portait parlé* included weight, hair color, eyes, complexion, location, size and shape of scars and marks, moles, and tattoos—that is, much the same categories appearing on today's FBI wanted posters.[86] Bertillon cards also included a photograph of the front and profile of the face, a method of photography that was also a Bertillon innovation. The photography department of the Paris Prefecture of Police had been taking photographs of "distinguished criminals" to create an archive of photographic records since the department's creation in 1874. However, the photographs were difficult to retrieve and to use for identification since they were so irregular. In response, Bertillon rationalized crime photography: the camera type, the distance between camera and object, pose, and brightness were all standardized, in effect becoming the mug shot as we know it.[87] Although police photography predates Bertillon, it was a valuable part of his method for law enforcement. The photograph was a "feature of the Bertillon system" that Hoover called "an invaluable aid to all agencies and organizations that deal with offenders."[88] Photography was essential to Bertillon's method and intertwined with the history of modern policing in general. "It was not until the advent of photography that law enforcement agencies began the development of modern methods of criminal identification," Hoover wrote.[89]

The Bertillon system was elaborate and thus challenging for operators and institutions, but solved some problems, like the problems of photography. While calling photography invaluable, Hoover and many others believed it had its limits for policing. The problem with photography for the purposes of the police was that the use of aliases made the cataloging of photographs by name difficult.⁹⁰ But Bertillon helped channel the powers of photography into identification by not relying on individuals using the same name in every encounter with law enforcement and instead relying on bodily measurements. The question of the meaning and significance of photography is debated. It may appear at face value that the photograph is the most important aspect of the Bertillon card for identification purposes because it is the product of a chemical and mechanical process compared to other sorts of visual representation and verbal description.⁹¹ A sense of objectivity surrounds photographs as the "purest of archival documents," as Nancy Armstrong writes in her critique of this presumed purity.⁹² Photographs do not speak for themselves or exist outside interpretation. The optical, or the photographic, image is made legible through categories.

Categorization and cataloging processes gave photographs meaning they would not otherwise necessarily have had. Bertillon described the procedure for organizing the thousands of cards that would come out of his anthropometric method and the theoretical concepts that structured his procedure as follows. Cards were first divided by gender, then by age. They were then divided by the length of the head, followed by the width of the head, the length of the middle finger, the length of the foot, the length of the forearm, height, the length of the little finger, then by eye color, then the length of the ear. For the Paris Prefecture of Police, this process turned 120,000 photographs into 10,000 groups with a dozen pictures in each, Bertillon reports.⁹³ The measurements would be calculated into a particular proportion, and the cards would be filed in massive cabinets according to those proportions.⁹⁴ Each measurement and proportion was not defined by its absolute value, for Bertillon, but was based on its distance from the mean on a bell curve. This is where Quetelet's average man came in. This bell curve and the average man directly informed record keeping and which Bertillon cards went in which "Bertillon cabinets," leading Sekula to observe that "Bertillon can be said to have realized the binomial curve as office furniture" to the point that the "central artifact" of the "bureaucratic-clerical system of 'intelligence'" that would emerge in the late nineteenth and early twentieth century "is not the camera but the filing cabinet."⁹⁵ On this borrowing of the average man from Quetelet, Bertillon said in 1893, "The ideal card of the average man, more exactly the *français banal*, that is to say an individual in whom all the measurements correspond exactly to the average dimensions, quite simply does not exist. It is never found even in the most central section of my cabinets. There are, of course, cards which approach this ideal configuration, but the related measurements never approach each other so closely that they can be confused."⁹⁶ Bertillon's main concern is defending the effectiveness of his system in allowing law enforcement to retrieve the desired card out of tens of thousands of cards. His statement nevertheless confirms that the average man is both a fiction and an organizing concept in the practical matter of how to classify arrestees' information in a cabinet to facilitate expedient identification.[97] His work is crucial to inscribing Quetelet's thought into practical processes that, from social science to the FBI Most Wanted program, established description relative to the average man as neutral.

The practice of *bertillonage* was not to match photograph to photograph, but to match photographs to an idealized image.[98] The saturation of images in the policing context, and outside of it as well, for Armstrong, like the accumulation of sets of photographs of composites like families, criminals, and natives, for example, corresponded to categories.[99] Bertillon card photographs acquired meaning based on their difference from other images in the cabinets, from the generic average man standard.[100] The saturation of standardized images narrowed the sorts of categories used to identify almost every person, place, or thing, Armstrong writes. These standardized, obliterative categories, and the generic in comparison to which they are meaningful, are my interest here. As Bhattacharya points out, the comparative framework is key, "where individual identity is always already a deviation from the standard, just as 'savage' bodies are deviations from white European bodies. 'Savagery' is not seen as an autonomous phenomenon but as a deviation that can be mapped, compared, and arranged by neat tables.... In other words... the statistical ordering of these peculiarities is the means through which the meaning of the body can be produced."[101] Traces of this relationship between photograph, description, and this statistical history remain in the wanted poster form.

Race is a defining feature of this revolutionary technique of anthropometry but, as with Quetelet, perhaps not obviously so for those who deem the language of color as the sine qua non of race. Bertillon was influenced by the criminological theories of his day but also differed from them in some ways, particularly when it came to racial categorization. For example, Italian anthropologist Cesare Lombroso famously argued that criminals were "born" as such, marked by the large size of their bodies, asymmetrical faces, and oblong skull shape.[102] Bertillon did not advance this sort of perspective. For example, Bertillon rejected "the old physiognomists" who "pretended to compare the different forms of the human face to those of animals" because, as Bertillon wrote, "there is not among the men of the white race an individual physiognomic characteristic that cannot be compared very simply with some similar but exaggerated form that is normal among one of the colored races—the red, the black, or the yellow."[103] Although different from Lombroso, he had written on race elsewhere in ways that indicate his relation to European colonial endeavors. While at the School of Anthropology in 1878, he considered writing a book that would go on to be published in 1882. *Ethnographie moderne: Les races sauvages* is a patchwork of previous ethnographies' observations and conclusions organized into chapters based on each savage race. He writes that *le nègre* is not suited to freedom, and so will allow themselves to be enslaved rather than die, whereas *l'indigène du nord de l'Amérique* would rather die than be enslaved; this is the reason, he continues, that Africa has been a center of the slave trade.[104] *Les races sauvages* was completed as Bertillon was attempting to introduce his method to the Paris Prefecture of Police but was not finding much success.[105] But soon, success came, and *bertillonage* spread. In 1882, the Police Prefect Jean-Louis Camescasse created an Identity Bureau in the Paris Prefecture of Police, and over the next five years *bertillonage* would be institutionalized both throughout and far beyond France in concert with colonialism and racial science. Anthropometric laboratories were established in the United States and Canada in 1887, and then later in Argentina in 1891, colonial Bengal in 1893, and Great Britain in 1894.[106] Bureaus also appeared in French colonies in Africa as well as Indochina. *Bertillonage* was part of colonial identification practices for French colonial subjects in both metropole and colony, and Bertillon personally played a role in establishing the judicial identification service in Algiers.[107]

The development and growth of several identificatory practices in the colonies suggest that identification is a feature of colonial policing as well as race. Anthropometry had a special place in the policing of radicalism in the metropole as well, specifically anarchists. Though this method was well established by 1892 when the anarchist Ravachol was arrested, Bertillon's successful identification of Ravachol using anthropometry famously validated the method. Further, the International Anti-anarchist Conference of 1898 endorsed *bertillonage* in order to create a standardized system for finding terrorists and radicals across borders.[108] Not only was Quetelet's average man put to use to find a new means by which to control populations, but it was relatedly about developing a new way to know them.[109] This situated the average man as not a neutral concept that could be assessed only through its explicitly oppressive application to the colonies and the Western proletariat, but rather as political in its very constitution. Anthropometry presents itself as based on the neutral, painless collection of measurements of body parts. But its "innermost dreams," as Hacking says, are about the control of populations; after all, this new method emerged in the context of the late nineteenth-century French state as it experienced industrial growth, urbanization, and colonial expansion.[110]

Policing the proletariat and colonies is an obvious warrant for the development and demand for efficient identification procedures, but the deepening of technologies to better execute colonial violence does not itself capture the full extent of the significance of scientific rationality in policing and its revolutionary quality. This suggests that analysis of the problems of Quetelet and Bertillon is not over when France leaves Algeria and Vietnam, or when the police doing the work of identification invite people of color onto the force; rather, as Wynter says, the end of this particular epistemology itself is what would end the problem of race, necessitating other means of knowing.

BERTILLON'S VISION WAS FOR a standardized and universal system like the metric system, but this did not transpire.[111] The adoption of *bertillonage* in the United States was not comprehensive, despite Bertillon's pleas. Identification bureaus would use some of his method and not other parts of it. Modifications would leave warped, uneven processes at identification bureaus. This was certainly the case in the United States. Simon A. Cole offers a helpful account of the reality of *bertillonage* in the United States, in which most operators learned the method from Bertillon's training manuals translated into English rather than from the man himself. It is more accurate, Cole argues, to describe what ensued as "anthropometric identification systems inspired by the French system."[112] For example, the New York State Bureau of Prisons adopted anthropometric identification in 1896, after which New York's Sing Sing Prison's registers included spaces for prison clerks to fill in descriptions of the prisoner's complexion, eye color, hair color, stature, weight, ears, nose, lips, forehead, eyebrows, mouth, teeth, and general features. In *bertillonage*, these descriptions are standardized morphological terms and can be found in his instruction manuals. But on the Sing Sing registers, clerks entered an array of descriptors like "good size good shape," "good bald head," "fair small face," and, most commonly, "regular."[113] Inconsistency in how measurements were taken was also a limitation of the adoption of *bertillonage* in the United States. Hoover, too, complained of inaccuracies in practice. He lamented, "one operator would take [measurements] 'loose' while another would take them 'close.'"[114] For a means of identification that relied on minor differences in measurements, this deficiency compromised its utility in the eyes of identification bureaus.

The adoption of a patchy version of *bertillonage* in the United States through sloppy application of the presumably precise and detailed system is important for the argument of this chapter. I am arguing that the form of the wanted poster has traces of the statistical average man, and that *bertillonage* connects these. The uneven US employment of the method did not compromise the American appreciation and adoption of the thought behind the method. The looseness of the adoption of *bertillonage* continued into the wanted poster, and its logic remained even after the bureau dropped *bertillonage* formally. Fingerprinting seemed to solve the FBI's problems with the unwieldy Bertillon system.[115] Galton, who coined the term *eugenics*, was looking for an external marker of internal character—piety, beauty, idiocy, criminality—and thought that fingerprints held the secret. If discovered, these external markers could be used to determine who should and should not procreate. After failing to discover a fingerprint pattern unique to each race or to people with particular traits, which he attributed to extensive race mixing having taken place already, he concluded that each fingerprint was both unique and permanent, which made fingerprints useful for individual identification. By the early twentieth century, Galton's fingerprint method, combined with Scotland Yard commissioner E. R. Henry's system for filing and classifying fingerprints based on two types of patterns, was adopted by all identification bureaus in the United States.[116] This new system made it possible to file fingerprints by patterns and not by name, crime, or description/measurements of individuals, per Bertillon. Bertillon sold his method by claiming that it was possible to identify potential recidivists in just a few minutes; his method was replaced for the same reasons when fingerprinting seemed to be faster.[117] Also more efficient than Bertillon's system at retrieving records, the Henry system reportedly allowed an identification in less than five minutes.[118] Efficiency was among the greatest values in this emergent bureaucracy, and as historian John F. Fox Jr. argues, the FBI's recordkeeping system was guided by the drive for efficiency that characterized the progressive era.[119] Hoover's filing system suggests this.[120] He cultivated a passion for bureaucracy and defined the bureau as a "white-collar sanctuary" in which agents were "more like lawyers than bona fide policemen, at least as far as their official duties were concerned," in the progressive era.[121] Social statistics, already oriented toward the state and with a long relationship to criminology, were easily employed toward this capitalist drive for efficiency; the nexus of policing and social science matured. However, this drive was not independent of race making, as some historians imagine it. As historian Khalil Gibran Muhammad finds, the progressive era was "the founding moment for the emergence of an enduring statistical discourse of Black dysfunctionality."[122]

The institutionalizing of statistically supported identification practices took place in the 1920s through congressional bills, police lobbying, and the creation of new national units. The International Association of Chiefs of Police, which encouraged the adoption of *bertillonage* in the United States and

Canada, pushed the establishment of a national identification bureau in Washington, DC.[123] The establishment of the National Bureau of Criminal Identification changed federal recordkeeping. Fingerprints were previously stored at one of two national identification centers that existed before 1924: one in the Leavenworth, Kansas, penitentiary, and the other in a disorganized and understaffed location maintained by the IACP.[124] The collection at Leavenworth, which included fingerprints, photographs, and Bertillon records, was managed by prisoners.[125] The fingerprint records of the IACP's Identification Bureau and the Bureau of Criminal Identification at Leavenworth were merged and consolidated following the passage of a bill funding the merger by Congress.[126] "The Division of Identification is your child," Hoover said to the IACP.[127] The division began and was absorbed into the FBI in July 1924, during Hoover's tenure as director of the FBI. In the 1920s, the National Bureau of Criminal Identification used *bertillonage* as well as fingerprinting, which led to a massive number of records: this fingerprint collection grew from 810,000 records to over 10 million between 1923 and 1945.[128]

Reception of fingerprinting and the expansion of identification practices among the American public was initially mixed. Efforts to convince the public, to gain public support, attest to this contestation.[129] The St. Louis World's Fair of 1904 was a site of enthusiasm for fingerprinting: the National Bureau of Criminal Identification was moved to the fair for a few months to promote their work with the Bertillon method; the annual IACP convention was even held at the fair; and commercial firms that sold Bertillon's identification system and fingerprint equipment hosted exhibits.[130] The involvement of the public in national identification is notable here, an earlier moment of the essential role of public appeal in the FBI wanted posters to come. Not everyone was enthusiastic, however. Standardization of fingerprinting procedures in policing was still an ongoing project in the first two decades of the twentieth century, and, perhaps in part because of this, it was not yet convincing to the public, who saw it as a violation of defendants' right not to incriminate themselves.[131] This had resonance in the courtroom, particularly in criminal trials that depended on fingerprint evidence. Juries did not take fingerprints as a given. They required convincing by identification personnel called upon by the court, since much of the American public viewed fingerprinting as "vaguely mystical" and not scientific.[132] Labor unions were also opposed to the creation of state identification bureaus, viewing them as an advancement of police agencies' ability to break strikes. Unions and communists rejected the idea of universal fingerprinting for its other repressive possibilities as well.[133] The IACP attempted to define unionism in a way that supported their own arguments, while of course separating out and condemning communists:

Other groups were afraid they might lose some of their constitutional liberties. The communists, of course, oppose anything which would tend to unify society, as they make their greatest gains among disorganized people. Union Labor, through some false prophets, has consistently opposed it. This is strange indeed because one thing for which unionism has always fought is social security or similar legislation, and when you think of the hundreds of thousands of workers affected by such legislation who have identical names and descriptions, it is at once apparent that such laws would not work without fingerprints. The union men who make the most furor against fingerprinting have as their sole reason the potential "blacklist" made possible by fingerprints, but this is a lame reason when examined by any thinking union man.[134]

The mid-1930s brought an effort for the IACP to launch a campaign to complete its national network of state bureaus.[135] The anxieties of World War II also made room for arguments expanding policing through keeping track of "aliens."[136] The FBI expanded during this time to keep up with the paperwork that this sort of policing required: the FBI had 4,370 employees in January 1941 and then 7,910 by the following January.[137] An article in the *Detective*, a monthly magazine largely recognized as the IACP's official publication from 1898 until the association developed a newsletter, reported that resistance to fingerprinting of aliens in the context of World War II had been defeated: "These obstacles consisted chiefly of opposition by communists, nazis [*sic*], parlor pinks and fellow-travelers together with an inborn prejudice of the public against the use of fingerprints except in dealing with criminals. Viewed as a measure of national defense, this widespread prejudice was removed. And it is most significant that the only remaining opposition came from the organized ranks of the radicals against whom the measure is now aimed."[138]

As other important moments in the rest of this book show, this will not be the last time that the question of public support is important for the FBI, nor the last time that FBI powers expand and fight for public acceptance in the context of war. War is an important part of the history of the Most Wanted program and its wanted poster form. Lynching souvenirs of the Jim Crow era and the Pentagon's deck of Iraq's Most Wanted playing cards are also comparable as souvenirs of war for Rachel Hall, who further argues that the playing cards are the military's version of the FBI Most Wanted program.[139] The first FBI posters distributed in 1917 by the Department of Justice for draft dodger Grover C. Bergdoll brought together the two print genres of war propaganda and tabloid journalism.[140] Devastating, all-consuming, sensational events like war, and the drumming up of public support for it, do not negate the continual role of racial theories and methods in establishing identification and policing infrastructure, but often become moments in which warmakers find reason for urgently doubling down on these methods despite public opposition.

Identification Orders for the Police, Wanted Posters for the Public

The methods of both Bertillon and Galton, who Sekula says "mapped out general parameters for the bureaucratic handling of visual documents," come together in the emergence of the identification order.[141] It is an important precursor to the wanted poster as we know it today.[142] The FBI (then the Bureau of Investigation) issued its first identification order on December 15, 1919, for William N. Bishop.[143] Identification orders consisted of photographs, description, and fingerprints, and they were intended for communication between the FBI (headquarters and field offices) and local police.[144] Identification orders also "carried the crisp, compact appeal of index cards," Hall points out, combining the features of Bertillon's format and Galton's fingerprinting.[145] Bertillon's format not only included cards with descriptions in list form, but also the photograph: he created stamp-sized mug shots, photo albums of criminals, and descriptive notices, thus making him "the architect of a new brand of *police memory*."[146] The medium of the wanted poster owes some of its features to Bertillon's design, which are also shared by the identification order. Identification orders are bureaucratic forms, or "pieces of administrative paper" that are part of the repeated and regulating social practices through which the state creates itself as a "coherent entity"; David Theo Goldberg calls this administrology.[147] In an example of administrology, Hoover suggests that identification orders expanded, and their production was centralized, due to the success of the fingerprint identification system developed further by Galton: "It is based upon the admittedly marked success which has attended the centralization of fingerprint data in the Identification Division of the United States Bureau of Investigation. It is based upon the theory that similar success will follow the establishment of a centralized division to which may be directed wanted notices by law enforcement officials everywhere in connection with fugitives whose apprehension is desired for the commission of major crimes."[148]

While identification orders were made for police and other law enforcement officials, wanted flyers and placards were made for the American public. Of course, wanted posters have a longer history than the scientific rationality of Bertillon and others, as Valentin Groebner shows.[149] Cities in central and western Europe have exchanged lists of wanted criminals and outlaws since the early thirteenth century. By the fourteenth century, and well into the fifteenth and sixteenth centuries, these lists of names would be accompanied by a description of the appearance of the wanted individual. This description was based primarily on clothing. There was little by way of a description of the face or body. The description of Jos Fritz, leader of a peasant uprising in the upper Rhine in 1517, for example, was mostly about the color of his coat and stockings but also noted that he had a black mole on his left hand. Noting a visible mole on the left hand may appear to be a neutral observation of a simple fact of the body, but in the *Secretum Secretorum*, a mole on the left hand is the mark of a traitor. Description is not a neutral practice even when it may appear to be. Other sorts of wanted posters operate similarly. Wanted notices for escaped enslaved people included a physical description of the body in narrative form along with names and a sketch of a figure running. Notices for outlaws who were "wanted: dead or alive" might include a photograph with a description of the outlaw. The operative categories and physical descriptors on all such media or memorabilia "seem to reveal less about a person's identity as such than about the conditions and practices through which it is constituted, about the flexible 'arts' by means of which unambiguous certainty is produced," Groebner concludes.[150] Bertillon's contribution to this long history of criminal identification is scientific rationality. His contribution is not limited to the selection of body parts as physical identifying signs, since earlier identification practices also saw the body as a site for identification; rather, he made his mark in the extent to which he rationalized identity and body. Scientific rationality gave way to the format of the FBI wanted poster, presented in the form of a neat list of descriptors of the face and body, circulated in internal FBI publications as early as 1923 and officially distributed to the American public in 1950.

In 1950, the FBI created its Most Wanted program. Dedicated to producing and circulating wanted posters, the program sent posters across the country and eventually across the globe. These notices could be found plastered on the walls of post offices, police stations, on billboards, lampposts in targeted areas, and other public areas with increased foot traffic. The program is regularly commemorated on the anniversary of its birth. Its captures are rehearsed as successes. The FBI publicizes descriptive statistics on how many fugitives it has captured through the program, and in what time frame. The FBI's histories of the program include cartoonish quotes from its captured fugitives who invariably recognized the effectiveness of the program, admitting they did not stand a chance once a poster with photographs of their face began circulating. These captures are career making for the bureau's agents involved.[151]

Precursors and one-off wanted posters notwithstanding, it was not until the mid-twentieth century that the FBI formalized the creation and distribution of wanted posters in a new program, whose founding, form, and functions are outlined next. The FBI's official story of the Most Wanted program takes the public's interest in 1950 as its starting point. The official tale of the history of the Most Wanted program begins with a newspaper story published on February 7, 1949, in the *Washington Daily News*. The story was about ten of the FBI's most sought-after fugitives. The story generated increased public interest in "crime solving," as the FBI tells it. This interest prompted the bureau to formalize this into a program.[152] Hoover established the program on March 14, 1950.[153] Told this way, the FBI appears to be a democratically responsive institution, with the demands of the people in mind; the FBI's story of the program has a hegemonic foundation in the enthusiastic consent of citizens. The Most Wanted program is a classic post–World War II development in this and other ways that further divorced racial science from its context of emergence. The Jewish Holocaust made plain for the West the horrors of scientific racism in a way it could understand, though it was not qualitatively different from the horrors of colonial rule elsewhere, as Aimé Césaire and others have pointed out. The new racial order after World War II delegitimized scientific racism in part through the 1950 UNESCO declarations on race, which argued that differences of appearance are not differences of intellect, that race is not revealing of biological realities. The general scientific racial method of Quetelet, Bertillon, and Galton that gave scientific racism teeth, however, was maintained through all this change and further institutionalized that very same year in the founding of the Most Wanted program. Scientific racism was condemned with one hand and fortified with the other.

Wanted posters are a site of communication—unilateral missives—from state agencies to people who are then deployed to assist the state in its work of apprehending criminals.[154] After all, as Guy Debord argues, "The spectacle is not a collection of images; it is a social relation between people that is mediated by images."[155] Wanted posters were circulated widely, signs of state-citizen relations posted everywhere. The FBI distributed its posters to police stations for further dissemination, after which posters appeared in public places, on television, in some newspapers and magazines, and abroad.[156] They were even found as an advertisement in the pages of a dermatology journal, much to the distress of a physician for whom the "major question" was "whether medicine should be encouraged, or even allowed, to be an extension of the police functions of the society."[157] They could be found rather consistently on the walls of post offices until June 30, 1995, when the FBI created a website.[158] Now, the internet is the primary home of the bureau's wanted posters, although they are still selectively posted at US embassies in other countries, in neighborhoods, at border-crossing waiting rooms, and on billboards on US highways.

The Most Wanted program now comprises several lists, but its first and most famous list is the Ten Most Wanted. Since 1950, the official criteria for placing individuals on this list have not changed: to be added to the Ten Most Wanted list, a person must be wanted on federal charges, or commit a state crime and then commit unlawful flight to avoid prosecution.[159] Considerations include the frequency and type of crime, but there are no hard-and-fast rules. The official FBI criteria are rather subjective: the fugitive must be considered particularly dangerous, and the bureau must believe that nationwide publicity will likely help capture them.[160] Thousands of cases fit these criteria every year, but few make it to the Ten Most Wanted list. A combination of limited oversight and accountability of the FBI and its own recordkeeping issues limit what is known about the FBI's process for creating Most Wanted posters and lists.[161] The bureau reports the following process for getting a suspect on the Ten Most Wanted list, specifically.[162] When a spot opens up on the Ten Most Wanted, agents submit candidates to the FBI Criminal Investigative Division, which reviews and narrows the list down to be approved by the assistant director of the division and the deputy director of the FBI. As for crime-specific lists, any FBI agent can request for an individual to be added.[163]

The FBI Most Wanted program has long served as a place for announcing and reminding the public of law enforcement priorities. On the occasion of former Black Panther and Black Liberation Army member Assata Shakur's addition to the Most Wanted Terrorist list, a bureau representative said to a reporter that "the list is not necessarily a reflection of the people who pose the most imminent threat to the US, but instead is a tool to draw attention to those whom it believes it can capture with increased public awareness."[164] Although the FBI notes the importance of public awareness and links it to the increased chances of capture, research has shown a decrease in captures alongside expansion of the program.[165] This would suggest that these posters serve another purpose. Apprehension is not so much the purpose as announcement and advertisement. In other words, the very naming of the wanted person, the very existence and distribution of the poster, is itself the point. As Sara Ahmed writes on documents in another context, "If passing the document [around] is the point of the document, then the point can simply be *to create a trail*."[166] It is not only a trail through which the wanted poster itself passes, but also a trail that the wanted poster suggests by virtue of its existence. Wanted posters name an ongoing material pursuit. The production of a chased enemy legitimizes the pursuer through publicizing the criminalization of the pursued; it serves as an announcement to all those who could imagine solidarity or even sympathy. The wanted poster as a document, therefore, announces the existence of danger and deviance true to its roots in Bertillon's uptake of Quetelet's average man, compared to whom everybody else—from fugitives to terrorists—deviates to some degree. It names who and what is dangerous, and it puts forth who has the right and responsibility to protect us from that danger—and as such is productive of what constitutes *us*. It also creates a narrative of apprehension even though rates of apprehension have slowed in recent years. The viewer of the poster is to contact the FBI with a tip to receive the reward, but it is notable that tips through the circulation of posters are not the main means, or even a significant means, of capture. If it is increasingly easier, technologically speaking, to catch fugitives, why have rates of apprehension not increased as surveillance technology has advanced? To partially answer this question, the FBI Most Wanted program's design further suggests that apprehension is not the only purpose. The circulation of documents and consequent production of the idea of a chase—and not only apprehension—are part of the purpose that the posters serve.

Despite consistency of official criteria for selection, the demographics of those on the Ten Most Wanted list and the types of crimes that the bureau focuses on have changed since 1950. These changes do not mirror increases or decreases in crime rates. Specifically, the years after the 1950 creation of the Most Wanted program saw an increase in murders over a decade, followed by a decrease in murders over a decade, but fugitives wanted for murder by the FBI grew steadily over this time.[167] Indeed, criminologists continue to struggle to construct an agreed-upon measure of crime rates. They struggle to explain increases and decreases in crime rates in their assessments of the effectiveness of various policies. As such, trends in the FBI Most Wanted program cannot be explained by the argument that it has simply responded to crime rates or other sorts of trends. If the composition of FBI lists mirrored any larger trends, it was the law enforcement priorities of specific presidential administrations and the passage of legislation giving specific powers and priorities to law enforcement.[168] In the 1950s, the Most Wanted program, which was limited to the Ten Most Wanted only, focused on prison escapees, bank robbers, burglars, and car thieves. Most were white. In the 1960s, 181 people were added to the Ten Most Wanted list.[169] The first women were added in the 1960s for aiding a kidnapping. More women were added in connection with anti–Vietnam War protesting. In the 1970s, the Ten Most Wanted list grew to sixteen—exceeding the size of the list as it is named. This was the largest it had ever been until that point, with revolutionaries such as the Puerto Rican separatist organization Fuerzas Armadas de Liberación Nacional (FALN) being of the greatest interest, along with the pursuit of neo-Nazis like the Order. The program has grown in size since: it expanded from ten fugitives in 1950 to a bit over 100 over the next decade or two as fugitives were swapped in and out of the Ten Most Wanted list, and then ballooning in the early 2000s when the program began to have over 300 wanted people at any given time.

Popular opinion of the FBI tanked in the 1970s, presenting a problem for a bureau whose wanted program relied on winning or at least competing for hegemony.[170] The low public opinion of the FBI in the 1970s occurs contemporaneously with a reduction in tip-based arrests and the revelation of COINTELPRO. In contrast, in the 1950s, over 40 percent of fugitives were arrested as a result of a tip or surrender. This rate faced a sharp decline to 20 percent in the 1970s, which was also when the FBI reports that its attention turned to what it calls "organized crime and terrorism."[171] Revolutionaries of anticolonial and anticapitalist movements had decent levels of popular support in these years. Most of the people added to the Ten Most Wanted in the 1950s were made famous, or notorious, by their addition to the list, but not in the next two decades. In the 1960s and '70s, revolutionaries added to the list were already well known before their addition.[172]

The Travels of L'homme moyen

New media forms have opened up the distribution and organization of wanted posters. The digitization of wanted posters plays a role in the significance of their distribution, particularly in the appearance of an organized, bureaucratized archive and a categorization system that reflects the modes of knowledge at play, accumulated from that racial, scientific rationality of Quetelet, Bertillon, and Galton. The repository of current posters is maintained on the FBI's website. The format of its website, available as far back as 1996 with the Internet Archive, has changed every few years. This format change is relevant because it is what structures the organization of the wanted posters and has involved various listing practices.[173] The website would sometimes organize its wanted posters in the form of a recent archive by featuring lists of posters from the previous months. For example, the FBI's website in 2000 had lists called January 2000 Fugitive Archives and February 2000 Fugitive Archives. This archival style, characterized by the display of careful attention, storing, and organizing of data, appears objective and neutral. The FBI's website has a page with frequently asked questions about its Ten Most Wanted, and on the sixtieth anniversary of the program's founding, posted a page with a list of all individuals who have been on the Ten Most Wanted list. This archive design fell out of practice on the FBI Most Wanted program's website in favor of the type of crime as the organizing feature of the Most Wanted program after 2001. By 2016, when the FBI website design was again overhauled, the Most Wanted program lists and sublists were organized on the bureau website as follows:

- Ten Most Wanted Fugitives
- Fugitives: Crimes against Children, Murder, Additional Violent Crime, Cybercrime, White-Collar Crime, Counterintelligence, Criminal Enterprise Investigations, Seeking Information, and Human Trafficking
- Terrorism: Most Wanted Terrorist, Seeking Information—Terrorism, and Domestic Terrorism
- Parental Kidnapping
- Bank Robbers
- Endangered Child Alert Program

The format of Most Wanted posters bears an important resemblance to Bertillon cards and identification orders, as previously mentioned. Many of the same categories on posters are still in use, such as scars and marks; the general form of the wanted poster has remained stable in the face of changes like the creation of new lists and the use of different categories or entries.

A spectacularly public archive, the Most Wanted program is a source for plenty of popular culture. Perhaps an accomplishment of its public efforts, references to "the FBI Most Wanted list" are familiar enough in American popular culture. The television program *America's Most Wanted*, for example, was one of the longest running on Fox at the time of its cancellation in 2012 after about two dozen seasons, only to be revived in 2021. The few scholarly and journalistic works on the FBI Most Wanted program also take a largely celebratory approach, repeating the FBI's narrative of success or seeking to assess the program's effectiveness.[174] Mention of FBI wanted posters is scattered elsewhere. Most of the research on the FBI tells the story of the program as part of a larger analysis of FBI bureaucracy.[175] Research most relevant here mentions the Most Wanted program as a brief but important part of the story of a famous individual wanted by the FBI, or as part of a larger story of state repression of mid-twentieth-century radical movements.[176] The limited works on the Most Wanted program historicize the program, approach the form of the wanted poster from a media studies perspective, and assess the success of the program in meeting its stated objectives.[177] This chapter, in contrast, traces the scientific genealogy of wanted posters and excavates their relation with the secular, with statistical description, and with policing the proletariat and colonies. The ubiquity and visual intensity of the wanted poster and some of its most famous subjects may make it appear as though name recognition and photographs are the posters' most important feature. However, this book shifts our attention to the power of textual categories on and around the posters.

As this chapter has shown, the FBI and social science are genetically linked in their shared ancestor Quetelet, and his average man continues to organize identification in policing via the form of the wanted poster, and to wield influence in social science in its very methodological approach.[178] Through work like Quetelet's and others, Ginzburg summarizes, "The body, language, and human history for the first time were exposed to objective examination, which on principle excluded divine intervention. We are still today the heirs of this decisive turning-point in the culture of the *polis*."[179] Even though Quetelet rejected the charge that his work was godless, this chapter highlights the move to a secular episteme that built on the religious and lays the groundwork for the rest of the book's arguments on the ongoing significance of the average man. The FBI's wanted posters and its attendant program are a case of how the repressive capacities of anthropometry, as well as its spirit and principles, live on in the procedures and scientific objects it would give way to. In this way, the average man extended past the presumed end of scientific racism. Influenced by Quetelet and his thought, FBI posters are an important medium that keeps his thought and its problems alive. Race ran all through the very method of anthropometry, or *bertillonage*, that Quetelet's work would be adopted to facilitate, from the obviously bloody effects of *bertillonage* in the colonies to the veins of contemporary policing and social science based on continued use of this framework and methods. These methods directly inform the format of the wanted poster. The poster form is thus imbued with the racial episteme of the method: Quetelet's imperial, obliterative average man; Bertillon's organization of criminal records according to this average man; and the FBI's adoption of all of this.

Men of science helped establish and institutionalize procedures for knowing and managing populations that would become neutral ways of knowing, abstracted from the colonial and capitalist policing contexts in which they were developed and tested. Quetelet and Bertillon are intellectual ancestors for much race thinking after their time, both in the FBI and outside of it.[180] The specific French, European racial categories they constructed are not what traveled; rather, what traveled to US policing were the categorization practices, a version of the formal techniques, and their epistemology.[181] The FBI's adoption of these methods informed twentieth-century policing, but also twenty-first, even after the bureau officially abandoned *bertillonage*, and even after it adopted surveillance and identification measures more technologically advanced than fingerprinting.

Read as a post–World War II institution in the tradition of official antiracism, the Most Wanted program developed in this political moment in the thick of the decolonization era and civil rights, which weakened the plainly biological race perspective and shifted it to a seemingly antiracist version of the same in which biological definitions of race have continued to permeate racial common sense.[182] The FBI has been on the slower side to come around to official antiracism compared to other state agencies and corporations in the 1980s and 1990s as such entities began to move toward using affirmative action, quotas, and diversity policies.[183] For example, diversity rhetoric increased under FBI directors Robert Mueller and James Comey, while the number of FBI agents of color fell: by 2016, 4.5 percent of special agents were African American, which makes the number even less than it was in 1992.[184] The FBI was also late to the use of the word *Black* rather than *Negro*, as wanted posters show. It was not until 1980 that the FBI began to use the word *Black* instead on its wanted posters. Official antiracism enables the continuation of material racism under cover of representation; for example, the material pursuit of "deviants" does not change and only ramps up for the FBI, all while using the newly more respectful self-identifier *Black* instead of *Negro*.

"At the end of the sixties or at the beginning of the seventies," Assata Shakur recalled in her autobiography, "it seemed like people were going underground left and right. Every other week i was hearing about somebody disappearing. Police repression had come down so hard on the Black movement that it seemed as if the entire Black community was on the FBI's Most Wanted list."[185] Wanted posters played an important role in the mid-twentieth-century Black liberation movement, to the point that DIY wanted posters featuring police officers who had killed Black people could be found in Harlem and Detroit, as Stuart Schrader shows. "On all of these DIY wanted posters, the killers were white, the victims Black. By reversing the expected race/class polarity... these posters became instruments of critique, revealing not only the pervasive political whiteness of police, but policing as a machine of racial stigmatization."[186] Assata Shakur's wanted poster from the 1980s would become iconic, and in her journey through the legal system, we see the power of moves that begin as reversals, or appear to be reversals, but mean much more in their ability to undermine what Quetelet calls the average man's "empire over all living beings on this globe."[187]

2

ASSATA, THE MUSLIM

Mid-twentieth-century Islam in Black America has its major figures and official representatives, and Assata Shakur is not one of them. If asked to locate such figures, it is Malcolm X, Muhammad Ali, and Elijah Muhammad who appear more forcefully. Men typically dominate that imaginary, despite the major contributions of women, but that is not the main or the only reason Assata Shakur does not have an easy place in the history of Black Islam.[1] Archival materials, including her own writings, show that for a few years in the mid-1970s, she called herself a Muslim, but in her 1987 autobiography she writes that she "never practiced" Islam. What lies in the gap between these archival materials and her autobiography?

On the heels of the Nation of Islam's initial growth and Malcolm X's assassination, it was not unusual for Black Panthers and Black Liberation Army members to be Muslim, inspired by many of these earlier figures. Many had converted in the late 1960s and early 1970s, not as a separate endeavor from their revolutionary activities, as some Muslim Panthers would emphasize, but as central to them.[2] Salahdeen Shakur was the patriarch of the Shakur clan, a family united by a shared last name but not by blood, for the most part. As a disciple of Malcolm X and having completed his hajj in the 1960s, he would play a role in welcoming many young Panthers into the fold of Islam in those years when Assata Shakur was active. He taught Islam to young Black men and women from his home in Jamaica, Queens, where they also studied Marxism-Leninism and pan-Africanist thought. "As advisor, elder, and spiritual mentor, Salahdeen provided a bridge between Garvey and Malcolm X; between the UNIA movement of the older generation and the nascent interest in Islam among younger blacks."[3] As Bilal Sunni-Ali reflected, "A lot of young people that were in the liberation struggle, many who later joined the Panther Party, as it developed, related to Salahdeen Shakur as somebody that we could talk to about Islam, learn Islam from."[4] And still, Assata, coming out of this family of the Shakurs for whom Islam was important, would not be considered among the important figures of Islam in Black America, even as her story speaks to this story, as this chapter discusses. Nevertheless, Assata Shakur's travels through state institutions, from courts to prisons to hospitals, shed light on the role of Islam relative to race during this time, beyond the well-known biographies of Malcolm X, Elijah Muhammad, Muhammad Ali, and similar figures. Further, former Panthers and collaborators have described Shakur as a rather ordinary member of the movement, not an overwhelmingly influential leader or movement strategist, which also gives her experiences a particular kind of importance for understanding how Islam has functioned as a counter to Western race in the context of Black radicalism that exceeded the choices of the most dedicated and devout converts and leaders.[5]

A short biographical overview is necessary at this point. Just three years after the Oakland Black Panther Party (BPP) began under the leadership of Huey P. Newton and Bobby Seale, Assata Shakur joined a chapter of the party on the other side of the country. It was 1969, and she was a student who still went by the name Joanne Chesimard at City College of New York.[6] The Harlem chapter's leadership were incarcerated in the Panther 21 case the year that she joined the party. Lumumba Shakur was incarcerated, and Sekou Odinga was in exile in Algeria; those who were out on bail—like Afeni Shakur, Joan Bird, Jamal Joseph, Michael "Cetewayo" Tabor, and Dhoruba Bin Wahad—worked with her.[7] By the end of 1969, state and federal counterinsurgency campaigns across the country resulted in about thirty Panthers facing capital punishment. Forty faced life in prison, fifty-five faced prison terms of up to thirty years, and 155 were in jail or wanted.[8] This repression relied on informants, agents provocateurs, lengthy trials, and other techniques that ultimately propelled a split in the party. Even as ideological differences already existed within the party, as some Panthers and their historians have argued, state exploitation of these differences through infiltration and surveillance made them irreconcilable and led some former Panthers to create an armed underground East Coast formation called the Black Liberation Army (BLA).[9] In this cauldron of intense state repression of Black revolutionaries feeding extensive distrust within movement ranks, Assata Shakur joined the BLA in 1971. In many ways, she faced the fate common to many Panthers and BLA members, as she would be among the growing numbers of incarcerated Black revolutionaries in the 1970s. The FBI and local police were already looking for her in 1973 when a state trooper pulled her over on the New Jersey Turnpike. Her 1972 FBI identification order notes that she was wanted in connection with a bank robbery.[10] Because she was one of the few women associated with the BLA, local bank robberies and police deaths in the New Jersey and New York areas involving a Black woman were quickly attributed to her, she would later write.[11]

When Assata Shakur, Sundiata Acoli, and Zayd Shakur were pulled over by a New Jersey state trooper on May 2, 1973, all were in the Black Panther Party and were suspected to be members of the Black Liberation Army. There were two deaths that day. Zayd Shakur was killed, along with Werner Foerster, an officer who arrived at the scene later. Sundiata Acoli was able to escape into the nearby woods, where he remained until his capture a few days later. Assata Shakur was shot in the back; the trajectory of the bullet, which broke her clavicle, suggests she was shot with her hands in the air, according to medical testimony at her trial.[12] Shot and injured, Shakur was captured by police that day on the turnpike. In the wake of the turnpike event, Assata Shakur and Sundiata Acoli faced multiple charges and were ultimately convicted of kidnapping and murdering a police officer. Over several years, she would be tried for multiple robberies and other crimes while incarcerated in various prisons and jails, including some for men only, between 1973 and 1977. She saw acquittals and dismissals in every case except the charges related to the death of Werner Foerster. For these charges, she was convicted and sentenced to life in prison. She escaped prison in 1979 and gained asylum in Cuba, where she has remained since. In the early 2000s, there was a resurgence in the federal government's interest in advertising their pursuit of her. In 2005, the bureau added her to their Most Wanted program as a featured fugitive. Then, in 2006, they moved her to their Domestic Terrorism list, where she remained until 2013, when she was moved to the Most Wanted Terrorist list (see chapter 4).

During at least 1976–77, the later years of her court trials, she called herself a Muslim. Evidence of this appears in her own writings and correspondence from that time, her supporters' published materials both then and years later, mainstream media, and court records. The courtroom was an especially important site for competing claims about Islam and what it meant. She invoked Islam in the courtroom as part of defining who she was and what her politics were. At one point, the *Black Panther* reported that she had won the right to have Fridays off from court for what was called the "Muslim Sabbath," "since she is an orthodox Sunni Muslim."[13] Islam was also commonly mentioned in mainstream newspaper reporting on her trials. For example, "Because she is Muslim, Assata can not [sic] eat pork; the prison included pork in her diet at least once a day."[14] Reports on her fight for her "Muslim Sabbath," detailed later, would regularly appear in local newspapers covering the turnpike murder trial. Mention of Shakur's "Muslim name" would also accompany mention of the BLA as a "terrorist" group in newspaper reporting on her trials. And in 1983 the FBI would describe her as wearing "Muslim or men's clothing" on her wanted poster.

The symbols of Islam, when considered in the context of the FBI Most Wanted program and its racial epistemology as traced in chapter 1, facilitate an orientation of Black struggle away from racial concepts and categories that racial science developed for them, toward instead a blackness of their own creation. The "Muslim influence over our struggle," as Assata Shakur calls it in her autobiography, thus militates against race, this chapter argues. The FBI understands Islam as outside of Black people and politics, because the bureau's system of identification and classification can only read Black people on the model of the Negro—the model of what Black revolutionaries were fighting against.[15] My contention is not that the FBI should be able to read and represent Black revolutionaries on their own terms, but rather that it is useful to be more precise about the relation between the Negro and Islam in the FBI's racial order. This chapter shows how the FBI and other state actors materially and representationally try to pull Black politics back into the scientific-rational framework of Quetelet and Bertillon, introduced in chapter 1, as forefathers of state identification practices in which blackness is the Negro. In that framework, Islam is an unnatural, outside influence on the Negro, as earlier FBI records, like one of its training manuals, quite clearly explains.

In 1955, FBI headquarters created a training manual called "The Muslim Cult of Islam."[16] It offered a version of the history of African Americans in the urban north in the early twentieth century, mentioning Noble Drew Ali and Wallace Fard, as well as Marcus Garvey. The manual differentiated between what it thought of as real Islam and the "Muslim Cult of Islam," a reference to the Nation of Islam (NOI); as Sylvester Johnson observes, the manual describes the NOI as "teaching hatred and violence," as "quintessentially a religion of primitivism" that "thereby expressed the atavistic, pristine racial nature of African Americans. The true religion of these Black subjects, in other words, was not an acquired religion of Islam as practiced in the Middle East but an essentially limbic religion of primitivism that stemmed from the racial constitution of Blacks."[17] "Real Islam," in contrast, was peaceful and spiritual rather than political, in the FBI's estimation, making a distinction between the political and the religious, the religious and the nonreligious, and assessing sincerity of belief.[18] Of course, the FBI's determination that this version of Islam is also peaceful would mean little years later following the Iranian Revolution and the development of terrorism discourse focused on that same "real Islam." What is important for this chapter's purposes, however, is Johnson's analysis that racial blackness has a presumed religion.

In the United States, the Negro construct develops in contrast to some notion of what it means to be Muslim, even (or perhaps especially) for African Muslims. Many enslaved Africans were Muslim. Historian Sylviane Diouf estimates that around 15–20 percent of enslaved Africans were Muslim.[19] Policies in the New World to manage the enslaved further attest to the construction of the Negro through a long process of erasing Africans' Muslim history. Upon "discovery" of an enslaved African's Muslim status, enslavers would reconsider whether or not that person was to be considered Negro and if they were, instead, Arab. African Muslims were "culture bearers," in the eyes of their enslavers, Michael A. Gomez notes, and thus faced relatively less degrading treatment than non-Muslim slaves. Along with their propensity to rebel, Muslims were also viewed by their enslavers as noble for their literacy or link to the Moors, resulting in sometimes better treatment; some have gone so far as to argue that Muslim slaves had relative degrees of privilege over non-Muslim slaves based on the idea that they were better in the slave owner's mind for their literacy. But notions of the rebellious Muslim slave and the noble Muslim slave are two sides of the same coin in European settlers' memory of the pre-1492 Muslim control of the Iberian Peninsula in which Muslims were a formidable force, whether as rivals or allies, for various European powers. "The last thing the Spanish wanted was for the New World to evolve into another theater of war in their protracted and costly struggle with Islam," Gomez reasons.[20] The net result was a notion of the Negro outside of Islam, in the eyes of European settlers. The Negro as the "primary referent of racially inferior humanity," as Sylvia Wynter argues, would have race.[21] European ideas about what it means to be Muslim shape the racial hierarchy, since the Negro is not-Muslim. And yet, at the same time, there is no clear or consistent racial position of "the Muslim."[22] In the context of this history, Islam is part of that blackness of Black people's creation, and in direct contradiction to Negro status, as we see quite clearly in the case of the Moorish Science Temple of America and the NOI, two formations critical to the spread of Islam through Black America in the mid-twentieth century. They explicitly responded to this history of the Negro as not-Muslim in their insistence that they were not Negro, colored, and so on but rather were Moors or Asiatic, and that their religion was thus Islam. Sometimes reduced as reactionary, Black engagement with Islam was done on the basis of embracing something historically obliterated in chattel slavery. This possibility of retrieval was what piqued Shakur's interest in Islam. In Shakur's journey through the courts and media, I argue, we see not only continued efforts to reinscribe Black people into the terms of Western race but also Shakur's engagement with Islam as material pushback against this. For the state, Shakur's Islam is a mark of her deviance from her correct (and also deviant) position, her apostasy against "the religion of primitivism," as Sylvester Johnson puts it, which is to say, as deviant relative to Quetelet's average man.

Although most published works on Assata Shakur ignore her years as a Muslim, and only a few briefly mention it, this chapter presents archival material suggesting that her Muslim status influenced her trials and her representation in media and state materials. My goal is not to demonstrate the fairness of her trials, nor to represent them in as much historical detail as possible. Nor is my goal to make an argument about what Islam meant to her but, rather, to show what can be illuminated if her brief relationship with Islam is understood not as a case of racialization, or racialization as Muslim, but as a window into the limits of race that point to alternatives she was part of bringing into the world.[23] The rest of this chapter moves chronologically and analyzes how *Muslim* and *Islam* circulated around her in the 1970s and 1980s, and argues that the state tries to racialize her—to place her in their scientific paradigm—via ungendering and its physical violence. She is ungendered at times through her enemies' invocation of Islam, and she also pushes back against her ungendering via Islam. Importantly, Shakur pushed back not just with representations, although that, too, in a materialist battle of definition in the context of law.[24] Further, Shakur's letters from jail show that she struggles with the theological aspects of Islam even before she calls herself Muslim. Her relationship to Islam points to certain realities of Islam in Black America as an identity that is meaningful to the extent that it represents an epistemology, a different sort of other, and as having its own conception of blackness that is not the same as the West's, in which blackness is the Negro. Offering a look at Islam as epistemological, the chapter puts her struggle in conversation with an essay written retrospectively by another former Black Panther, Safiya Bukhari, who was also Muslim and whose revolutionary and theological dilemmas found resolution in a maneuver in direct opposition to the epistemology of no-god-but-man of racial science. Islam is given meaning to do what it does for Shakur because it represents a rival other and because it is spread in Black America as against that theology of scientific rationality (among other, earlier ways of thinking) that makes the Negro, as Bukhari spells out so clearly.

Competing Orders in the Court

Panthers' trials were among the longest trials to take place in their respective states up until that point. They were record-breaking in length, and this alone was a success for state repression; tying up Panther leadership, literally and figuratively, kept them out of their work. This speaks to the function of the courts in the epic and often romanticized tale of mid-twentieth-century radicals and revolutionaries. Courtrooms were a site in which to make a point, and many others in these years treated them that way: for example, Yippies like Abbie Hoffman arrived in court in costume; a judge ordered that Bobby Seale be bound and gagged in court; and attorney William Kunstler consistently held press conferences and instructed his defendants to ensure that courtrooms would be full of supporters. Likewise, Assata Shakur's Islam came up most consistently in court-related archives.

"THE MUSLIM SABBATH"

In 1976–77, a major issue in Assata Shakur's court cases was having court adjourned on Fridays, an issue about which courts were occasionally sympathetic.[25] "Both Sundiata and Assata were Muslims," Evelyn Williams, Shakur's aunt and attorney, explained in her own autobiography's telling of these events. Williams continued, "In the earlier part of the trial, no sessions had been held on Fridays, their day of worship."[26] For Muslims, the midday ritual prayer on Fridays is to be done in congregation and is colloquially called *jumu'ah*. In prisons, the right to worship in congregation, where Muslims gather and have the opportunity to see one another, however briefly, was a victory of the prisoners' rights movement.[27] In the 1960s, political struggle inside and outside of prisons led to "a beehive of political activity behind the walls," Sundiata Acoli explains, as "prisoners stepped up their struggle for political, Afrikan, Islamic, and academic studies, access to political literature, community access to prisons, an end to arbitrary punishments, access to attorneys, adequate law libraries, relevant vocational training, contact visits, better food, health care, housing, and myriad other struggles."[28] The NOI and its Black nationalism were part of several historical developments that transformed US prisons and how they were run.[29] The prisoners' rights movement pushed courts to cease their hands-off policy that left prisons to prison administrators, and instead expanded from the 1950s to the '70s to make prison conditions a matter of rights. By the late 1950s, particularly in New York, they argued in court that they were being discriminated against as Muslims.³⁰ In December 1959, for example, *jumu'ah* at Clinton prison in Dannemora, New York, was shut down after almost one year of Muslim men having a relatively organized setup in the yard with cooking, a blackboard, and other infrastructure.³¹ Four of them, including William SaMarion, were sent to Attica. In cases like *SaMarion v. McGinnis*, Muslim prisoners at Attica in 1962 made a First Amendment rights case in which the judge ruled that the NOI was a religion. By the early 1970s, litigation had slowed down, and Muslims had the right to hold weekly services, wear religious insignia, have their authorities treated the same as ministers of other faiths, and recruit new members.³²

The right to Islamic practice in prisons was political, a matter of material demands for better conditions from its very institutionalization in US prisons. For Acoli, the "influx of so many captured freedom fighters... with varying degrees of guerrilla experience added a valuable dimension to the New Afrikan liberation struggle behind the walls. In the first place, it accelerated the prison struggles already in process, particularly the attack on control units."³³ One such example of the struggle in prisons, for Acoli, is the push by Shakur and the Center for Constitutional Rights to get her transferred from a control unit out of state in West Virginia.³⁴ Her transfer to that control unit is inseparable from the sequence of events leading up to it, specifically the struggle over her "Muslim Sabbath."

The *Home News* reported as early as February 1976 that Shakur refused to attend court on a Friday.³⁵ During pretrial motions, Judge Theodore Appleby of the Superior Court of New Jersey had no objection to Shakur remaining in her cell during proceedings.³⁶ But with the impending jury selection and trial for the turnpike encounter, he refused to allow court to be adjourned on Fridays. Shakur's legal team then filed a motion to continue not having sessions on Fridays. On March 4, 1976, the National Council of Black Lawyers (NCBL) filed a civil rights complaint and submitted an opinion letter in support of that motion because Friday court sessions would abrogate her First Amendment religious freedom as a Muslim.³⁷ The NCBL cited precedent: trial judges in the criminal and supreme courts of New York previously had ruled such motions by Muslim defendants are a proper application of the First Amendment rights to free exercise of their religion, Lennox Hinds, national director of the NCBL, was quoted as saying in a local newspaper.³⁸ The NCBL alleged her constitutional rights (First, Fourth, Sixth, Eighth, Ninth, and Fourteenth) had been violated. The First Amendment issue was part of how Shakur was singled out, since other Muslim defendants "got their sabbath," the NCBL reports, but she did not, all in the context of facing human rights abuses and imprisonment in a men's facility.[39] The NCBL's support for Shakur focused on her constitutional rights; her attorney William Kunstler, along similar lines, "insisted Mrs. Chesimard's right to observe the Moslem Sabbath [was] 'clear cut' under the First Amendment of the U.S. Constitution."[40]

The motion for adjournment on Fridays was one of many motions her legal defense made at that time. Other motions included removing Appleby as judge, releasing Shakur on her own recognizance, and shifting the trial from New Brunswick to Essex County as there were fewer Black people in the former's jury panels.[41] Shakur's attorneys also motioned for the jury not to be sequestered, and for her to be transferred out of the men's prison. Most of these motions were denied.[42] Appeals flew back and forth and moved through higher courts.[43] "Motions were made and motions were denied," Williams writes, and "among the denials, the most prejudicial, as they affected our right to a fair trial, were [both] the one asking for a free daily copy of the trial transcripts, which were automatically granted to all indigent defendants and for which Assata was eligible, and the motion that court not be held on Fridays to respect Muslim religious practice, also automatically granted in most jurisdictions. Both those motions had been ordered in the earlier part of the [turnpike] trial."[44] The trial start date moved further and further back.

The material stakes of the struggle for Friday adjournment are evident in how it became tied to other issues: sequestering, jury selection, the very white location of Middlesex County for trial, and free copies of trial transcripts. The judge and prosecution cited jury issues as a reason for keeping court on Fridays. In their view, "if the trial recessed each Friday jurors would be 'sitting around' with nothing to do and that the lost day each week would add to the length of the trial."[45] Shakur's side favored the lifting of the jury sequestration order (rather than holding court on Fridays) also because sequestration would result in too many potential jurors being excused due to hardship. Kunstler confirmed to local media that "the defense would have no objection to having the trial on Saturdays 'to achieve Mrs. Chesimard's nonviolation of the Sabbath.'"[46]

The fact that the Friday court adjournment issue was tied to other issues for both the defense and the prosecution makes the question of what Islam meant in the court system a matter not just of representation but of material outcomes in her trial. To be recognized as part of a religion comes with protections from state institutions, and my point here is that it is not just any religion, but the meanings of Islam vis-à-vis US race and the Negro category that matter for Assata Shakur's trial. In other words, it is not just that Islam is a religion and thus can be used to make a case for specific kinds of relief based on religious freedom, but the notion of the specific character of Islam in the United States as a religion that is not for the Negro. For some, like the Philadelphia-based organization MOVE and the earlier Moorish Science Temple, there was an understanding that being defined as a religion could have life-or-death stakes.[47] John Africa and the rest of MOVE called themselves a religion and wanted to be recognized as such but were read as a secular political movement. The material stakes of definition run through debates on what counts as a religion, who belongs to which religion, and what markers must be present to facilitate such identifications.

This host of material stakes considered all together lends support to Williams's claim that the Friday issue affected Shakur's right to a fair trial as one of the "most prejudicial" denials of her defense team's motions. How, then, did Islam and being Muslim circulate in her Sabbath case in her attorneys' statements, the prosecution and judges' perspectives, and her own statements as well? One way was a question of how exactly to understand what Fridays mean for Muslims. Read through the filter of Western Christianity, Friday is called a Sabbath in Shakur's court documents, reflecting in part the extent to which the NOI and later Black Muslim movements and organizations have drawn on Christianity and the Bible toward their establishment of Islam in Black America. Mainstream local newspapers also called it a "Moslem Sabbath." Kunstler translated it as akin to Saturday for Jews and Sunday for Roman Catholics, and local news noted that he pointed out that in New York, court is adjourned on Fridays for Muslim defendants.[48] It was also called a Sabbath in the *Assata Bulletin* and other written works by her supporters. The prosecutor "Barone scored one point during the argument on Friday sessions when he noted a mistake on Kunstler's part. The defense lawyer referred to the Moslem Sabbath as 'Ramadan' and Barone noted that this was actually the Moslem's holy month. After consulting with his associate, Myers, Kunstler conceded his error and said that Friday or the Sabbath was actually 'Goma.'"[49]

Another way Islam appeared was the court's repetition that they recognized Shakur's Islam as authentic. When the motion for Fridays off was appealed, US Circuit Court judge Leonard I. Garth was surprised the judge denied the motion. He said, "The religious issue is the one that gives me the most trouble."[50] Further, he found deplorable "the religious aspect which enters into the case, because it should be given respect."[51] The US Third Circuit Court of Appeals also emphasized the authenticity of her Islam: "Given the nature of Ms. Chesimard's important and sensitive claim, we cannot characterize it as frivolous nor can we assume that the New Jersey Supreme Court would ignore it. The New Jersey Supreme Court is a distinguished tribunal which has been most solicitous of the First Amendment rights of members of the Muslim faith."[52] Kunstler contended that "even Appleby," a judge who clearly did not favor Shakur's side, "recognized Mrs. Chesimard's 'devout belief' in [the] teachings of Mohammed in his opinion rejecting the adjournment of Friday trial sessions."[53]

The court's understanding of religion is based on what Charles McCrary calls "the sincere believer." It is an identity, a secular subject, as McCrary explains, whose "religious belief belongs in its own compartment, on one side of a public/private divide."[54] It is a version of man. Drawing on Wynter, McCrary argues that the US Protestant secular valorization of free choice, individual belief, and an implicitly white and male liberal subject is then universalized or overrepresented. The sincere believer is racial for its overrepresentation of a particular way of being human as a universal way and, importantly, for its understanding of that universal human's relation to a divine figure. This form of piety coexists with the secular and its epistemology in which man replaces God's power and authority as a legitimator of knowledge, operating in the world and making decisions as if God did not exist, often alongside personal, private recognition that God does.[55] Essential to the sincere believer type is a comportment and style of performance of private, quiet, solemn belief that has no relation to the political. This was tested when cases for religious freedom involved an individual whose religiosity did not present this way. The state recognized Shakur's Islam as sincere but not its connection to material questions that both defense and prosecution tied it to. The prosecution and judge were able to maintain symbolic recognition of her Islam while denying her what that meant materially, and, as we see later, punishing her for it. Shakur does not present or read her Islam as the court does, which is as a religion on the model of Western Christianity or Judaism and thus only under the rubric of the First Amendment. While her legal team did present her Islam that way at times, as the terms of legal remedy required, it was not the only way in which her side brought Islam into the picture. Shakur, in contrast, linked Islam to her roots and politics. Assata Shakur joined a powerful history of Black Muslims in prison appealing to the courts as Muslims.[56] Here, Islam restores those read as Negro to a geography and history much closer to the reality of who their ancestors were before the catastrophe of European expansion. This erasure was material via racial slavery, as well as symbolic and epistemological, as the framework attending the Negro construct is fundamental to Western knowledge structures, including its scientific rationality, which codified such historically derived categories as fixed to the body as neutral and natural, as chapter 1 shows.

"CONSCIENTIOUS SCRUPLES," VIOLATION, AND VERDICT

Support for Assata Shakur grew over time. About two dozen people came to support her at her first trial in 1973, but by 1977, two hundred students were attending campus events in support as well as fundraisers with prominent attendees like Amiri Baraka, Yuri Kochiyama, Harry Belafonte, Ossie Davis, and Ruby Dee.[57] The most "spirited and militant" showing of support for Assata Shakur until that point was at her court hearings on March 2, 1977, the *Assata Bulletin* reported. This was during the lead-up to the turnpike trial and the Sabbath issue.[58] Over 150 "Black and Latin" people gathered in front of the courthouse. Inside the court, supporters refused to stand when the judge entered. In the crowd of supporters, a Muslim man was ordered to remove his kufi, a Muslim cap. When he refused, he was ordered out of the court. Shakur protested this, too, and then walked out of the court as well.[59] This was not the first time she refused to stand up for the judge. By this point, Shakur not standing up for the judge had already become an issue in the courtroom, specifically with relation to Islam. Reports from the *New York Times* on major moments in her trial note her defense team's petition to have the trial moved to federal court; this petition was against Judge Appleby, who "directed his clerk to count the number of times Mrs. Chesimard refuses to rise when he enters or leaves the courtroom 'so the matter can be dealt with punitively at a later time.' The defense contends it would violate Mrs. Chesimard's Muslim faith if she followed this courtroom protocol."[60]

There is a tradition of Muslims refusing to respect symbols of American power, in sacred American nationalist spaces ranging from sporting events to classrooms, both before and after Shakur's time (for example, the 1996 NBA suspension of Mahmoud Abdul-Rauf for refusing to stand for the national anthem).[61] Their refusals were acts inseparable from their Islam. As for such refusals that predate Shakur, some precedent is even cited in her case in the federal judges' opinion to deny her appeal to have court adjourned on Fridays. In *Holden v. Board of Education of City of Elizabeth* (1966), also in New Jersey, NOI members successfully appealed the local public school's decision to suspend five of their children for refusing to pledge allegiance to the American flag. School protocols required all students to stand and pledge allegiance except students with "conscientious scruples" or who were the children of "representatives of foreign governments," who were instead required to stand and remove their hats.[62] The students followed the exemption protocol and were still suspended. The court decided that the students were acting appropriately within the school's rules due to "conscientious scruples." Notably, the court's decision recognized Islam as the reason for the students' refusal. While not a one-to-one comparison, this precedent suggests that Shakur's refusal to stand is one moment in a state-recognized history of refusal as a Muslim, and also that Appleby, the judge who oversaw her conviction and recognized her Islam as authentic while undermining its material consequences, knew about this precedent. Despite precedent for Shakur's refusal to stand up for the judge, and the availability of a religious exemption in some moments during her trials, the judge did deal with her refusal to stand "punitively" later as promised. The same judge ordered that Shakur be removed from the Clinton Correctional Institution for Women, where she was to be sent after the verdict, and sent instead to Yardville State Prison. Yardville was an institution for men. No female prisoner had ever been incarcerated there up until that point.[63] Shakur was convicted in 1977 as an accomplice to the murder of a police officer, and one month after she was convicted and sentenced to life imprisonment, the judge added thirty-three years to her life sentence for contempt of court because she would not rise when he entered the courtroom.[64] The issue of whether or not Shakur stood up for the judge is another example of how her Muslim status materially impacted her.

Shakur's Muslim status in the courtroom was important for her trials: it shaped what she could and could not do; it allowed her to do things she might not otherwise be able to, like not go to court on Fridays at some points or remain seated when the judge entered the room; this is a case of how "law both opens up and closes down forms of representation, spaces of accommodation and transformation, possibilities of expression, truth claims, and legitimation."[65] Islam was a source of power. It sent a message to the court that they were not wholly in possession of her even if they thought they were. It was also something that worried her attorneys the day of her guilty verdict because of another major event that took place around the same time. On March 11, as the jury was preparing to deliberate in Shakur's murder trial, the five-hour-long "Hanafi Siege" or "Moslem Siege" took place at an office building in New York City. Several gunmen took over the small office building and released a set of demands including a loan from a bank to build a mosque, a day care center, and housing for fourteen Sunni Muslim families, and a demand for "more recognition of the Muslim faith by government officials," according to the *Daily News*.[66] The *Home News*, a small local New Jersey newspaper that steadfastly reported on Shakur's trials, ran the headline: "Chesimard Judge Says Jury Unaware of Moslem Siege."[67] Kunstler is quoted in the article saying that it would have a "catastrophic effect" if the jurors were to know about the siege. The article concludes that Kunstler "conceded that Mrs. Chesimard is a Muslim but a member of the orthodox religion and has no connection with the Hanafi Muslims, who killed one man, wounded others and held 100 persons as hostages before last night's release."[68] The deployment of Islam as a symbol of power does not mean it cannot be a liability. As chapter 3 on raceless Muslims on the FBI Most Wanted Terrorist list also shows, being marked as powerful by the United States, as raceless, is not a guarantor of better treatment. It is a particular pathway to experiencing violence.

Prison Escape: "Muslim or Men's Clothing"

Assata Shakur escaped prison in 1979, making her one of the only Panthers to have escaped prison alive.[69] Her escape signaled a victory for the BLA in the eyes of both the police and her supporters. Three days later, anywhere from hundreds to up to five thousand people—estimates range—marched from Harlem to the United Nations building as a show of support.[70] On the tenth anniversary celebration of Black Solidarity Day, their signs read "Free the Land," "Black People Charge Genocide," "Human Rights Is the Right to Self-Determination," "Take Command: Fight for Human Rights," and also, "Assata Shakur Is Welcome Here."[71] At the rally that day, a statement was read from the BLA, and a statement written by Shakur a few days before her escape was also circulated. She condemned US prison conditions, called for freedom for political prisoners, and expressed her support for human rights and an independent New Afrikan nation-state.[72] For the next few years, little would be heard publicly from Shakur as she remained in hiding. New York State and federal law enforcement joined together to form the first-ever Joint Terrorism Task Force, an important law enforcement formation for the twenty-first century's war on terror. Its earliest task upon its 1980 creation was pursuing the BLA members, May 19th Communist Organization members, Panthers, and others who they believed had helped Shakur escape.[73]

As Shakur was wanted by both the federal government and the state of New Jersey, the FBI were not the only ones to circulate wanted posters after her 1979 escape from prison. The New Jersey State Police circulated several different posters. One such poster featured a dozen images, mostly photographs but also a sketch, and identifying information in list form per the Bertillon model. The New Jersey State Police's 1980 poster has a line in bold that reads: "ATTENTION: Subject may be dressed in Muslim clothing or in men's clothing." This state police poster may have influenced the FBI's poster dated three years later, which features similar phrasing. The FBI's 1983 poster (figure 2.1) shortens this to "Muslim or men's clothing." The phrase "Muslim or men's garb" would appear in advertisements for Shakur's capture (figure 2.2) as late as 1985 in popular pub-

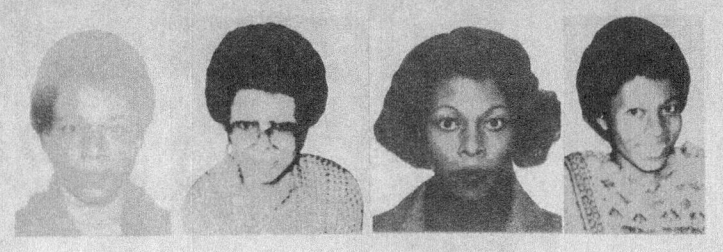

FIGURE 2.1. FBI wanted poster for Assata Shakur, 1983. Source: FBI.

FIGURE 2.2.
Official Detective 55,
no. 5 (May 1985): 52.

THE MANY FACES OF JOANNE CHESIMARD

Joanne Chesimard, 36, was serving a life term plus 26 to 33 years consecutive for the murder of a New Jersey State Trooper on May 2, 1973. She has been a fugitive since November 1979, when she escaped from Clinton Reformatory for Women with the aid of three black males and one white female. The breakout was described as a commando-style jailbreak.

Chesimard was once known as "the soul" of the Black Liberation Army, and is believed to have helped plot the Rockland County Brink's robbery in New York. In this heist, two police officers and a guard were killed.

The subject is also known as Assata Shakur, Justine Henderson, Joanne Byron, Barbara Odoms, Joanne Chesterman and Joan Davis. She may be dressed in Muslim garb or men's clothing. She has a round scar on her left knee and bullet wounds on her left shoulder and the underside of her right arm.

Chesimard has allegedly been sighted several times in New York City, but managed to slip away. Authorities say that she may be moving about in New Jersey and surrounding states in an effort to locate places of refuge. If you have any information on this subject, notify:

New Jersey State Police
Fugitive Unit
West Trenton, New Jersey 08625
Telephone: (609) 882-2000, ext. 440

lications like *Official Detective*, a magazine of true crime and crime fiction. In the May 1985 issue of the magazine, Shakur's mug shot and side profile appear on a corner of the front cover under the heading "WANTED FOR ESCAPE" followed by "JOANNE CHESIMARD" with directions to see page 52 for more.

The wording of the description on the respective posters of the FBI and the New Jersey State Police can be interpreted in several different ways: it may suggest that Muslim clothing is distinct from men's clothing, and that she could be wearing one or the other, or it could suggest that the same clothing can be characterized either as Muslim or as men's. Little description is given as to what this means, and "Muslim" and "men" are left to do the signifying work in the context of the time.

Archival materials provide more description of her actual clothing and what these terms could signify. Direct references to masculinity appeared in state and media documents and, again, especially in court. In the early 1980s, prior to her surfacing in Cuba, police reported that they saw Shakur in New York "accompanied by six black males wearing Muslim attire."[74] Her association with Black men and robberies with reference to Muslim clothing was well worn by that time. In one of her 1970s trials for bank robbery in the Bronx for which she was ultimately acquitted, Avon White, an informant who participated in the robbery, said that she was the one woman involved. He testified that she attached a mustache and a goatee to her face and wore overalls and a rain hat.[75] At the urging of the judge and prosecutor, the informant went into some detail in his testimony on how she created a beard and mustache using spirit gum. The testimony from two informants who pleaded guilty to the robbery was the state's main evidence against Shakur; no other evidence such as fingerprints, weapons, photographs, or surveillance video was available. Her dressing "as a man" was therefore significant for her trial even as it was weak evidence of her participation in the robbery.

This accounting of her clothing so far may suggest that "men's" is the most important adjective in "Muslim or men's clothing," and that the FBI is simply conflating Muslim and men's clothing with each other; indeed, this would resonate with the association between Black masculinity and Islam, and thus our question on how to interpret the FBI's representation of Shakur's clothing would appear to be answered. But the picture is not so neat. At the same time, the clothing Shakur wore in court for her trials was both feminine and Muslim by many accounts. For example, the *New York Times* reported that she wore a "flowered Muslim peasant dress."[76] What is identified here as Muslim clothing— a dress—is decidedly feminine in the US context. Evelyn Williams recalled when Shakur "had asked her mother to buy ankle-length African dresses and

FIGURE 2.3. Ida Libby Dengrove, "Untitled," c. 1976–77. CC BY Image courtesy of the Courtroom Sketches of Ida Libby Dengrove, University of Virginia Law Library.

geleis (African head wraps) to match, and they were so beautiful and colorful that each time she appeared in court every newspaper described what she wore as if the trial were an item on the fashion pages."[77] What Williams calls African, the *Times* calls Muslim—together a testament to how Islam functioned as an expression of Black Power. As for how Shakur wore the *geleis* her mother bought her, she sometimes appeared in court with her hair covered in different styles. Three of sketch artist Ida Libby Dengrove's courtroom drawings of Shakur from 1974 to about 1977 show at least two different styles. The style in figure 2.3 is common to Muslim women across many contexts, while the style in figure 2.4 matches the unmistakable style of the women of the Nation of Islam: the covering is pinned behind the head at the nape of the neck, and the hanging sides of the covering are pulled forward. The hijab style of the women in the NOI is also unquestionably feminine inside the gendered order of the Nation and, arguably, in many places outside it as well. Shakur was never part of the Nation, but the image remains to be dealt with here. Of course, sketch artists take liberties, and their drawings do not reveal neutral truths of court-

FIGURE 2.4. Ida Libby Dengrove, "Chesimard," c. 1974. CC BY Image courtesy of the Courtroom Sketches of Ida Libby Dengrove, University of Virginia Law Library.

room happenings; they are to be read critically, like all other court materials. Nevertheless, the very fact of the head covering and its general style do suggest an overwhelmingly feminine kind of clothing. It likely suggests "Muslim clothing" as well, though not necessarily, since the style in figure 2.5 is a common way for non-Muslim Black women to wrap their hair as well.[78]

In sum, between masculine and feminine clothing, the use of masculinity to incriminate her, and the other various social meanings of different styles of hair coverings, the FBI's description of "Muslim or men's clothing" could mean just about any style of dress. This wide range would seem to limit the utility of such a description, which suggests that the purpose of the poster is not only to facilitate expedient capture but to advertise deviance and announce policing priorities. What do these particular signifiers of *Muslim* and *men's* accomplish or allow? For this, we must turn to the race category the FBI gives her on her poster. The FBI used the word *Negro* as a race category on its posters until about 1980, when it switched to *Black*, which was late compared to many other American institutions.[79] Shakur's 1972 FBI identification order labels her as "Negro,"

ASSATA, THE MUSLIM   69

FIGURE 2.5. Ida Libby Dengrove, "Mrs. Chesimard," c. 1974. CC BY Image courtesy of the Courtroom Sketches of Ida Libby Dengrove, University of Virginia Law Library.

and her 1983 FBI poster labels her as "Black."[80] *Negro* is a fabricated category given to most Africans that Europeans brought to the Americas as slaves; it is a category as property. After the end of chattel slavery, the property relation of the Negro was defined not always by legal ownership but through other economic mechanisms and meanings that reproduced the Negro category as a lesser form of humanity in the racial order of man. Although the word *Black* certainly existed as a way to refer to this category, often as a derogatory term, it was reappropriated in the mid-twentieth century as an identity tied to a politics against the Negro construct. Early- to mid-twentieth-century Black movements generated a politics against the social structures that made them in the legacy of that property relation as controlled and determined by Western capitalism after emancipation. For Black politics, this was not simply (or at all) a swapping of one word for another for the exact same group understood in the exact same terms. But this sort of swap is precisely how the FBI understood it when it adopted the word *Black* in place of *Negro* in 1980. The FBI's change from printing

Negro to *Black* on their posters was the bureau's way of preserving the categorical Negro in newer terms as a concession of sorts after decolonization movements and a mid-twentieth-century Western consensus against racism, in line with how other state and corporate institutions interpreted and incorporated the aesthetics of Black politics and put them toward purposes directly opposed to the politics from which the aesthetics came.

Europeans made peoples into property in the New World through what Hortense Spillers calls ungendering. The "socio-political order of the New World" is "marked by a *theft of the body*—a willful and violent (and unimaginable from this distance) severing of the captive body from its motive will, its active desire," Spillers writes. "Under these conditions, we lose at least *gender* difference *in the outcome*, and the female body and the male body become the territory of cultural and political maneuver, not at all gender-related, gender-specific."[81] Enslaved Africans came from worlds with gendered social orders, but the theft of the body in chattel slavery made the body of the slave the property of the slave owner and did not allow for the preservation of the gendered meanings and orders from which Africans came. The body cannot have its own will or desire in a societally recognized sense in the social order of the New World. The bodies of enslaved people are commodified into whatever serves the interests of slave owners, which did not map onto white Western gender difference, for example, such that enslaved women were treated more delicately than men, or consigned to the domestic. This historical process of ungendering and these meanings inform the state's approach to Black people after the end of slavery, codified and fixed through scientific rationality and its categories, which gain purchase in policing via Bertillon in the late nineteenth century after chattel slavery ends.

While pregnant in jail during her trials, Shakur was kept under twenty-four-hour solitary confinement in a cell with no natural light, poor ventilation, and no opportunity for fresh air, recreation, physical exercise, or contact with other people.[82] She was given food she could not eat, as "a Black Muslim subject to the sect's dietary laws that prohibit eating pork," as local news reported.[83] To apply Spillers's words to Shakur's case, Shakur was "the target of torture that we imagine as the peculiar province of male brutality from other males."[84] Perhaps most dramatically suggesting ungendering, which cares little for the preservation of gender difference that does not serve capital or its vengeful whims, Shakur was the only woman in several men's facilities.[85] The National Council of Black Lawyers reported that she was the "first woman to be incarcerated in a male prison in the history of New Jersey and possibly the United States"; they "[saw] her as a victim of racism, political repression, and sexism unique in the history of the United States."[86] Shakur's ungendering is not exclusive to her, but, like Spillers's concept of ungendering, it signals the structural; gender is formed and manipulated in ways that serve broader purposes. CHESROB is an example: the FBI named Shakur as a suspect in whichever local robberies it was believed a woman was involved in. CHESROB was an FBI effort to investigate these robberies, and it was even named after her (Chesimard). On the one hand, it is a move that targets Shakur very directly, but on the other hand, as others have noted, CHESROB had broader goals to repress Panthers and BLA members.[87] It cannot and should not be denied that Shakur had choices she could make around gendered presentation. To the extent that Shakur dressing "as a man" can provide cover, it may be called a case of what Simone Browne calls "dark sousveillance," in which tools of surveillance and control are repurposed and appropriated to facilitate escape or survival.[88] The primary point here, however, is to notice that ungendering and, paraphrasing Marx, to note that she did not choose this ungendered context in which her gender-related choices operated.

Ungendering is rightly understood as a racial, capitalist, structural process, but Shakur's ungendering here clarifies how it is also wrapped up in her Muslim status as well. What ungendered Shakur in explicit terms on her 1983 wanted poster is the word "men's" next to "Muslim," a religious word that suggests a material, civilizational, theological threat to man, to Western dominance. The "Muslim influence over our struggle," as Shakur puts it, is what made Islam associated with Black resistance in the mid-twentieth century.[89] The history of Islam in Black America suggests that Islam could be a deep epistemological challenge and remaking for Black people in part because it suggests dominance and a powerful rival in the view of the West, in contrast to the weakness or abjection of the West's Negro construct. The material and discursive separation of enslaved Africans from Islam is important for the creation of the Negro category, which makes Black engagement with Islam powerful and restorative. This attempted separation carries over, as ungendering does, in efforts to preserve that categorical Negro, which is to say as by, of, and for the West. Naming Shakur's clothing as Muslim, as something other than what she should be for them (Negro), thus names her deviance, again, a concept that recalls volumes of scientific racist thought and policy.

To Cuba: "but i had never practiced it"

Shakur was underground for several years after her escape and surfaced in Cuba in 1984, where she has remained while New Jersey state officials, police organizations, and the federal government continue to pressure the Cuban government and related actors to extradite her. She was granted formal political asylum in Cuba like several others before her, including Huey Newton (1975), Eldridge Cleaver (1968), and Mabel and Robert F. Williams (1961).[90] Since 1968, nearly a dozen Panther, Republic of New Afrika, and affiliate members have hijacked planes to go to Cuba. Cuba served as a sanctuary for its allies—Third World left-wing dissidents, African Americans, and war refugees—which tied in with Cuba's Cold War anti-imperial aims. The United States designated Cuba a "state sponsor of terrorism" in 1982 based in part on its role as a safe harbor for American dissidents and hijackers, and the United States has since ping-ponged Cuba in and out of this status in order to isolate Cuba in the world system. It is no coincidence that the specific framework of terrorism was used in the 1980s to malign Cuba as the only sovereign communist nation in the hemisphere. This framing would be renewed in the twenty-first century with the FBI's representation of Shakur as a key terrorist of interest.

Upon her arrival in 1984, the Cuban government provided her an apartment in Havana and a living stipend. Her daughter joined her. Her family visited several times. Her phone number was even listed in the Havana phone book.[91] She attended school, studying social sciences and philosophy.[92] As her autobiography was about to be released, her whereabouts and a glimpse into her life in Cuba were also made public. It was an October 1987 *Newsday* report based on an interview with Shakur that revealed that she was living in Havana as an asylee. Although the FBI heard that she might be in Cuba, they did not reveal it to the public. By the mid-1990s, she was a regular attendee at cultural and political events in Havana. She also worked as an English language editor for Radio Havana Cuba. She granted interviews to foreign journalists and activists, and met with delegations, including academic ones.[93] She served as an intermediary between the Cuban government and representatives of American left-wing movements. Her Muslim status, so important to her courtroom experiences, lost relevance. The word *Muslim* arrived in the 1970s and departed in the 1980s from state records and documents, including Shakur's subsequent wanted posters, as well as from her published statements. The signifier would soon fade from much public and popular memory of Shakur's journey through the carceral system in the 1970s. Interestingly, it is also noticeably absent in most scholarly and biographical treatments of her story, despite the availability of sources on Shakur and Islam, including the writings and speeches of other former Panthers.[94] One possible reason for this absence may be her autobiography, published in 1987 while she was in Cuba.

Her autobiography would serve as the final word on her engagement with Islam, and the word *Muslim* would then recede from media and state documents where it once appeared.⁹⁵ The only direct reference to her relationship with Islam in her autobiography is just several sentences long:

> I had always said that if i had any religion, it was Islam, but i had never practiced it. Because of Elijah Muhammad and Malcolm X, the Muslim influence over our struggle has been very strong, but it had always been difficult for me to accept the idea of an all-powerful, all-seeing, all-knowing god. And, i reasoned, how could i be expected to love and worship a god whose "master plan" included the enslavement, torture, and murder of Black people?⁹⁶

The Panthers are often understood biographically (and autobiographically), and perhaps because Shakur "never practiced it," Islam is deemed not important in a biographical approach. But the biographical approach and its typical narrative structure has its limits and can obscure the role of factors that were important enough to shape an outcome but not important to the (auto)biographized individual themselves. The primacy of (auto)biography is one possible reason among any number of possibilities as to why little is written on her connections with Islam. This autobiographical form lends itself to iconography. As Joy James writes, "Assata Shakur's power as a narrator of black struggles and freedom movements would become eclipsed itself as she evolved, along with the BPP, into an icon. The reified thing, the icon, replaces the dynamic human being who changes her mind, her practices, her desires as a living entity."⁹⁷ As far as Islam goes, it is clear that in one way or another, at some point or another, Shakur changed her mind.

The short reference to Islam in her autobiography continues, recounting her conversations about Islam with Kamau Sadiki, her codefendant in the Bronx robbery trial and the father of her child. Both Sadiki and Shakur had been cited for contempt of court for disrupting court proceedings. For pounding her fist on the counsel table and refusing to be quiet, they were both removed to a room next to the courtroom while their trial continued without them in late 1973 and early 1974. As she wrote in her autobiography, "Kamau argued that Islam was a just religion, opposed to oppression. 'Oppression is worse than slaughter,' he quoted from the Holy Koran. 'A true Muslim is a true revolutionary. There is no contradiction between being a Muslim and being a revolutionary.' I didn't know much about it, but i agreed to seriously check it out. Muslim services were held regularly on Rikers Island, and Simba [another prisoner in Rikers] and i began to attend."⁹⁸

This final statement on Islam—a promise to explore with no reporting back on the findings—is fruitful for thinking about how Islam functions for Shakur by setting up what may appear as a contradiction: her self-identification as a Muslim being important for her trials in the 1970s, as this chapter has shown, while Shakur also stated in her 1987 autobiography that she "never practiced it." What is observable based on available materials returns to one of the main themes in this chapter and the next: Islam was a symbol of strength and power in much of Western memory, whether threatening or not, and not always or only a symbol of racial abjection, thus making it available for Black political claims like Shakur's. Islam is an external, adopted, unnatural thing for the Negro in *race*; and Islam can serve the role she has put it to because Islam is sometimes *not-race* in the very same order that makes the Negro construct. I am not arguing that this is a case of the selection of an identity that is less demeaned in that Western racial order and thus adopted to challenge it; rather, the point is that it is possible for Islam to mean something theologically and epistemologically in this context that makes Shakur's "never practiced it" possible.

A story from another former Panther and BLA member who was also part of the Republic of New Afrika, Safiya Bukhari, illuminates that epistemology and its theological dimensions in a similar context. She was born in the Bronx in 1950 and passed away in 2003. In 1975, she was sent to prison and experienced terrible conditions there, including being denied medical care for serious, potentially fatal, health problems. She was in solitary confinement for long stretches of time. She escaped and was recaptured, and then released on parole in 1983. She became a social worker and a leader in the movement to free political prisoners. Bukhari converted to Islam in prison in the 1970s. There are important parallels between Shakur and Bukhari in their complex experiences of motherhood and in how both escaped prison. Both were also Muslim, in some way, but Islamic practice was important to Bukhari, and Islam continued to be important to her after leaving prison.

Safiya Bukhari repeats "Allah alone makes Muslims" several times in her essay "'Islam and Revolution' Is Not a Contradiction." This phrase appears first in her essay as an insight she gained from reading *Islam: The Misunderstood Religion* by Muhammad Qutb, the brother of Sayyid Qutb. Another former Panther, Albert "Nuh" Washington, told Bukhari about the book, and she says it answered many questions she had about Islam. "As I studied, I learned that Allah makes Muslims, man does not. Which to me meant that simply declaring, 'There's none worthy of worship but Allah,' does not make you Muslim. It is the intentions of your heart and your determination to struggle in the way of Allah that makes you Muslim."[99] In this understanding, Allah is the only power that can make. And worship of Allah—a matter of Islamic theology, not only or mostly Muslim identity—is intertwined with being a revolutionary. "There was one more thing I had to learn as a Muslim—and as a revolutionary," Bukhari begins, noting the tension between "Muslim" and "revolutionary" while arguing against that tension:

> From the day I became Muslim, I had been told about *shirk*. ... There is no greater sin than *shirk*—believing that there is someone or something more worthy of worship or fear than Allah. I thought I had that one down pat.... The problem was that I also had an overwhelming fear, an uncontrollable and irrational fear. This fear superseded and overshadowed even my faith in Allah.... I was scared beyond reason of snakes.[100]

The fear of something other than or in greater magnitude than fear of Allah had implications for Bukhari's revolutionary politics and Islamic faith: "What worried me was how I would handle it if they attempted to use my fear of snakes to obtain information about my comrades and activities in the Black Panther Party or Black Liberation Army.... I never thought about that kind of fear being *shirk*."[101] The concern that her fear of snakes could be used to torture information out of her was soon resolved. While in prison, Bukhari encountered a snake that had found its way into the recreation room. Her reaction was "so elemental that there was no way anyone could use it to extract information."[102] But this did not resolve another difficulty with her fear of snakes, she writes, because of the questions it raised that she regarded as a much greater problem: "My reaction to this fear made a lie of my statement of belief, that there is nothing more worthy of worship or fear than Allah.... How could I rationalize this fear of snakes without ascribing a partnership to God in this snake, or without deifying this snake itself?"[103] This question found resolution over the next month as she prayed and reflected, leading her to conclude

> that nothing happens to us without the permission of Allah. This may sound simple and matter of fact, but it's not. There was an entire analysis and process I went through before this became real to me. For me as a revolutionary, death was something I lived with daily and constantly.... In dealing with the government of the United States of America, I was very clear that they were just men and women, while Allah was God. Him alone should I fear.[104]

The snake, she concluded, as well as the US government are all created by God and thus not worthy of fear to those who "had already conquered the fear of death and in fact welcomed it on the battlefield."[105] Over many years she went through a process of, she said, "killing off those things within me that undermined my ability to submit myself to the will of Allah—as well as to learn what

Che Guevara knew early on, that 'a true revolutionary is motivated by great feelings of love,'"—a quality of Bukhari's that Assata Shakur honors in her eulogy for her.[106]

Fear and worship are deeply entangled as acts that recognize power, as the concept of *mysterium tremendum*—that trembling before God, the First Creator—would suggest.[107] That First Creator, Sherman A. Jackson writes, loses its (socially recognized) monopoly on divinity when the second creator (man) organizes the world in his image. False *mysterium tremendum*, then, is trembling before that second creator who goes by many names: the West, (average or noble) man, whiteness, and so on. This *mysterium tremendum et fascinans* is "inscribed within the oppression of colonialism" in its no-god-but-man epistemology that exceeds the obviously theological and extends, as chapter 1 shows, into the basic structure of knowledge production in social science and into identification practices in policing.[108] A contemporary example is Palestinians' repeated recitation of part of the following verse from the Qur'an in the context of the Israeli war on Gaza in 2023: "Those who were warned, 'Your enemies have mobilized their forces against you, so fear them,' the warning only made them grow stronger in faith and they replied"—*Ḥasbunallahu wa-niʿmal wakil*—"'Allah alone is sufficient for us and is the best Protector.'"[109] It reminds them that Allah is greater than their enemies, who are not worthy of fear.

Bukhari's story of the snake narrates the killing of ownability by anything but God. The Negro construct as property, as ownable/determined by man, is killed via the rejection of man for Allah in a process that cannot be reduced to the symbolism of Muslim identity (i.e., self-identify or recognition as a Muslim) but rather is battled out in the arena of epistemology—which is also what makes Islam and revolution not a contradiction per the title of her essay. Of course, these two are not neatly separate nor static across time and space; the significance of that epistemology, particularly in these years, made Islamic identity available as a powerful symbol of the rejection of capitalism, whiteness, and its divinities. In such a context, Black Islam can be said to be about destroying the Negro as property. That has an unmistakably religious dimension of course, and primarily so, for many Muslim Panthers. The social role of the theological dimension influences the less overtly theological approach of Shakur; in other words, the religiosity that is essential to Islam for Muslims in the BPP influenced what Islam would mean in Shakur's case, whether or not theology and the practice of religion was important to her at any time.[110]

For Sherman A. Jackson, Jamil Al-Amin (H. Rap Brown), and many others, Islam cannot be reduced to confrontations with whiteness, or with man.[111] If it were, then Islam is a this-worldly symbol of that which is not-man. To be reduced this way is to continue to be defined in relation to man. In terms of the argument of this book, to do so is to try to make Islam fit the terms of race, which is to say, to mold it into something that would make it consistent with the terms of race (see chapter 4). In all of these positions, whether different or the same, all are nevertheless defined in relation to man, as more or less deviated from him, per the general approach of Quetelet in chapter 1. In some more recent iterations of man, there is a continuation of being defined as man's opposite, but with a meaning that one can regard as positive. Wynter writes that the Negro cannot be valorized in a Western order of knowledge; positive meanings sit superficially and tenuously atop an epistemological order based on systematic de-valorization.[112] More than an identity with an inverted (negative to positive) meaning in the same epistemological order, Islam offers an alternative epistemological world for those incorporated into the Western world system, into the Negro construct, as Islam proliferates in Black America as being about living a life not defined on man's terms. Al-Amin provides a retrospective on Third World politics that suggests this point. "It is Allah who defines," he begins, and "it is important for Muslims to know that it is Allah who defines. Because, when we accept any other definition, then there is a certain inadequacy, a certain deficiency in it, even when we try to define it for ourselves.... A good example would be the concept of the Third World."[113] He points out that the concept comes from the Cold War context and its binary order of First World and Second World. In this context,

> people of color ... attempted to define their reality for themselves. They acquiesced and said that, "OK, Since you're the First World and you're the Second World, we'll be the Third World." And thereby, they defined themselves in [an] inferior position.... In ignorance, we have defined a position of subordination for ourselves. When we define for ourselves, without using that which Allah has given us, we perpetuate the insinuation of subservience. Such things will not benefit us in struggle.[114]

Further, "We must begin to examine the tools that were produced for us. We must become aware of other people defining for us our reality. We must be able to detach ourselves from man-made concepts of right and wrong, good and evil, individuality and equality ... in order to see our problem, objectively, and define our struggle," he concludes.[115] Bukhari and Al-Amin articulate a notion of freedom that cannot be captured by the model of the liberal subject, the same subject that Saba Mahmood's work critiques.[116] Questioning the assumptions of the liberal subject, Mahmood argues for a need to move beyond a simple binary between resistance and subordination, as Al-Amin articulates here. Al-

Amin and Bukhari rely on a type of authority and a model of subjectivity that not only refuses to map onto the model of the liberal subject but actively seeks, as its highest goal, pleasing an authority through a notion of submission that, on man's terms, is precisely unfreedom. At this point, that epistemology of man, and especially its progressive feminist version, fails completely at the task of explanation or interpretation.

Shakur cites Elijah Muhammad and Malcolm X in her autobiography as part of why she was attracted to Islam. Their understanding of blackness not being race, of fighting against the Negro construct, and against the notion of Black Muslim to describe them, are all relevant here. Elijah Muhammad masterfully "appropriated" Black religion, as Jackson puts it, thus making Islam the basis for "an alternative modality of American Blackness."[117] This is what Shakur went on to call the "Muslim influence over our struggle," as this alternative modality had an influence on Black political thought generally and not only on practitioners of Islam particularly.[118] To understand Islam as the basis of another way of being Black is to have a definition of blackness that departs from the Western construct of the Negro.[119] Malcolm X viewed the term *Black Muslim* as an effort to undermine such a definition. The term was largely used in the mid-twentieth century to refer to the NOI, as suggested by works such as C. Eric Lincoln's *The Black Muslims in America* and E. U. Essien-Udom's *Black Nationalism: The Rise of the Black Muslims in the U.S.A.* Black practitioners of other sects of Islam were not assigned this term as much. The NOI heavily contested this phrase that was reserved for it, for several reasons. They argued that it suggested their Islam was inauthentic or derivative, matching the federal government's early characterization of the NOI.[120] Further, the term did not reflect their internationalist understanding of blackness, evidenced in Malcolm X's famous "Message to the Grassroots" speech in which he cites anticolonial movements in Africa and Asia as examples of "Black revolution." This is not a racial blackness, which is to say in the fixed, biological sense guaranteed in Western scientific terms, but a political one. Malcolm X, Elijah Muhammad, and the NOI made a geographic and historic claim that, even as it drew on some structural aspect of Western race, challenged its narrative of history.[121] They understood themselves not as products of Western obliterations whose history begins with the rise of the West, but as peoples with rich histories prior to Western obliteration and the colonial characterization of the Negro as lacking history and civilization per the arguments of philosophers like David Hume and historians like Arnold Toynbee.

Although Black Islam cannot be limited to its utility in challenging Western man, it certainly operated at least on that level for Assata Shakur in courtrooms and media. It is a testament to the embeddedness or indigenization of Islam in Black America that the use of Islam to kill the Negro fabrication need not be explicitly theological nor based on religious practice as in the case of Shakur, while this reality is also possible because of the theology of Islam. Just as the theological dimension of race is present even if it goes unnamed and unrecognized, so too does a theological, Islamic dimension of Black Power animate Black radicalism even when it goes unnamed and unrecognized. Shakur's courtroom resistance has theological implications even as the theodicy question remains unresolved for her by Islam, as we will see in a moment. The observably theological dimension in her case is the expulsion, the nonworship, of man who is rejected as a god through her sending of the message that she is not controllable. It seemed to give her solace and strength on some level; as she said in an Assata Shakur Defense Committee report, "I can't think of one logical reason why I haven't gone crazy ... except for my Islamic faith, my many supporters and the fact that I know the state is trying to crush my being, to destroy me—mind and spirit—and I just can't let that happen. I refuse to imitate a dog—I will live free or I will truly not live at all."[122]

In vignettes from her autobiography, she projects fearlessness at times that could be attributed to the nature of the autobiographical form (hindsight, dramatization, heroics), but that can also be read in relation to Islam as a symbol of power connected to fearlessness (defined not as the lack of a human instinct or emotion but as an interpretive choice, or a political-theological position per Bukhari).[123] Reports from the 1970s also emphasize Shakur's will; this is not only an observation based on autobiographies written years later. For example, when the verdict of her guilt was announced, she expressed anger that she allowed the trial to continue. This spirit resonates with the spirit of Islam in Black America in these years as a modality of blackness. This is what helps us answer the question of how it is possible that there is extensive evidence of her self-identification as a Muslim—particularly with regard to the question of the practice of Friday ritual prayer—alongside her statement years later that she never practiced Islam. The position of Islam as an alternative modality of blackness makes these two things possible and not an obvious contradiction. She is operating in the terms of that alternative modality of blackness, both when it is signified by Islam and when it is not.

She was consistent in the issues she took with Islam from the 1970s to her autobiography. Shakur wrote to Nuh Washington while in prison awaiting trial. He was Muslim and instrumental in several other Panthers becoming Muslim, including Bukhari. Shakur's correspondence with Washington is worth an extended discussion here. "Where did you hear that i have become a Muslim?"

she wrote to him, in a letter dated July 2, 1973. "i am curious to know I am very anxious to know more about Islam mainly because so many Black people are embracing it."

> The thing that i relate to about Islam is the feeling of unity, love, and strength that i have felt from the brothers and sisters that i know who relate to Islam. In a way i think Islam brings about the kind of life style that is conducive to revolutionary struggle. And i think that Islam teaches discipline, strong sense of family, unity and pride which are necessary in our struggle for freedom. Much of our former life styles is negative, gets in the way, and we have got to create a new one. If Islam will help our struggle for liberation then i will embrace it with open arms. But i have got a lot of questions.[124]

Her questions are about jihad (struggle), and then about what Islam would mean to her as a revolutionary woman who does "not believe in submissiveness because i think it is a dangerous attitude for a revolutionary woman to have."[125] She continues in this letter to say that she received another letter from a mutual contact who asked her, she writes, "if i am a Sunni however i do not really know just what that is exactly. Do you know what Sunnis believe?"[126]

She then points out several aspects of Islam that she does not "relate to": the idea of an unseen divine, "you know, like from out of the sky and stuff like that because only the things that i can see, hear, touch, and conceive of seem real to me"; and the concept of an "all powerful all knowing god" is also unappealing "because to me they would have to be some kind of sadists to permit all this suffering." The theodicy question stays with her, formulated as a question about Black suffering, as it has also been for James Cone, William R. Jones, and Sherman A. Jackson.[127] Printed in the Assata Shakur Defense Committee newsletter in March 1977, a couple weeks before her conviction, and again in her autobiography, Assata Shakur's poem "What Is Left?" repeats this question every three or four lines.

> WHAT IS LEFT?
> I MEAN, LIKE, AFTER YOU KNOW THAT GOD CAN'T BE
> TRUSTED[128]

She can have Islam as a signifier alongside distrust of divinity because the negation remains—that man is not God, and the rest of it is an ongoing question. She asks Nuh Washington this theodicy question in 1973, at least three years before references to Islam appeared in her trial. The theodicy question was also there during and after her trial. Unresolved as this question was for her by Islam, the mode of asking the question, and what her answer rules out—man's divinity—shares a space with much of the Islamic tradition that spread through Black America in the twentieth century.

Deeper engagement with Shakur's story of Islam here is valuable, not only in an archaeological or historical sense of unearthing and reconstructing an infrequently told story, but more so, in my view, for questioning reigning racial epistemology in ways that suggest a glimmer of alternatives, not only critiques leading to dead ends. The epistemology of Quetelet's average man, for example, as one version of man, like that noble man R. A. Judy critiques or Sylvia Wynter's *Man2*, as a god-figure, is the basis of the order against which Black Islam mounts a critique, as Shakur's challenge to the courts illustrates. The courts try to pull Shakur into the terms of the Negro construct, and Islam is employed to play a role in moving against this effort. Several key moments in Shakur's 1970s courtroom experiences, specifically her "Muslim Sabbath" and not standing up for the judge, suggest that her Muslim status was important for shaping an outcome, even as the words *Muslim* and *Islam* did not follow her after this time. While the words vanish, they are signaled in other ways, such as when the FBI adds her to their Most Wanted Terrorist list in 2013, placing her poster alongside the posters of the raceless Muslims who are the subject of chapter 3.

3

THE RULE OF RACELESSNESS

The Rewards for Justice program is a "formidable weapon in the U.S. arsenal for combatting international terrorism" according to the State Department in which it is housed. The Rewards for Justice program was established by the 1984 Act to Combat International Terrorism.[1] It contributes the money for rewards for information leading to the capture of wanted fugitives, and in the past, the program has distributed posters, matchbooks, flyers, and newspaper advertisements to capture terrorism suspects.[2] After 9/11, in collaboration with Rewards for Justice, the FBI Most Wanted program created its first terrorism-specific wanted list. George W. Bush unveiled the new list of "22 most wanted terrorists" to photographers, journalists, and news media at FBI headquarters on October 10, 2001. This list of twenty-two would go on to be called the FBI Most Wanted Terrorist (MWT) list. The MWT list is now well established in the program, and it stands out from the rest of the program in a few ways. Reward amounts are one way in which this new list emerged as unique compared to other FBI crime-specific wanted lists, such as the Cyber's Most Wanted and Parental Kidnapping lists. Rewards for information leading to capture listed on posters are typically in the thousands, although sometimes no reward is included at all on posters on other FBI lists. Some posters for the twenty-two also did not include rewards immediately in October 2001. But by the end of the year, all those on this new terrorism list had $25 million rewards for capture.

The dollar amounts on the MWT list remain in the millions; they even exceed those on the FBI's famous Ten Most Wanted list, which has existed since the very creation of the program in 1950. If reward amounts signal the FBI's priorities, then the people on this list are truly the most wanted of the most wanted.

Although the bureau created this terrorism list just one month after 9/11, and with 9/11 as the stated impetus for creating it, none of the twenty-two men who were placed on it were connected with 9/11 at that time. Senior law enforcement officials said some might be linked to 9/11 but did not specify which of the twenty-two.[3] Over half were indicted by federal grand juries and associated with earlier attacks in Kenya and Tanzania in 1998, the 1993 attack on the World Trade Center, and a 1995 effort to blow up US airliners.[4] Osama bin Laden was one of the original twenty-two. He had already been on the FBI Ten Most Wanted list since 1999 in connection with the 1998 bombings of US embassies in Tanzania and Kenya. After 2001, he remained on both lists for the next decade as one of few people in the FBI's program to have ever been on two types of wanted lists at the same time. It is difficult to overstate the US government's appetite for bin Laden, specifically; he was high priority in the late 1990s and then only increased in importance after 9/11. Some significant antiterrorism efforts under the Clinton presidency sought to assassinate him, such as the bombing of one of bin Laden's camps in Afghanistan, a camp that the United States had in fact set up to train fighters against the Soviet Union.[5] In the intervening years, from the Clinton to Bush to Obama presidencies, the $5 million reward listed on bin Laden's 1999 poster went up to $25 million.[6]

Bin Laden may have been singularly high priority for the bureau and the US government in general, but his wanted poster would inaugurate a rather steady pattern on the MWT list. The pattern, reserved for those who fit the Muslim terrorist archetype like him, was that the wanted poster lacked a race category. His poster was otherwise ordinary enough in most ways, matching the wanted poster conventions whose history was introduced in chapter 1. Like other posters, which come out of the tradition of scientific rationality and anthropometry as a product descended from Adolphe Quetelet's *l'homme moyen* and Alphonse Bertillon's anthropometric method, bin Laden's poster had the standard list of fill-in-the-blank attributes: height, weight, sex, date of birth, eye color, and so on. Each of these categories had an entry on all official versions of bin Laden's wanted poster, but race was singularly missing as an attribute.[7] Prior to this unique pattern of racelessness starting with bin Laden, if race was absent on a poster, it was usually one of many missing attributes, which suggests that the FBI simply could not or would not produce much descriptive information about that person to begin with. This is still the case on some posters. But in the case of bin Laden and most other Muslims on terrorist lists in the Most Wanted program for the first two decades of the war on terror, race is a consistently absent attribute on posters with other consistently present attributes.[8]

Posters with this pattern of racelessness are unique not only compared to their contemporaries but also over time. Under the race category on FBI wanted posters, the labels "White" and "Negro" were the most common entries for decades in the program since its beginnings in 1950, with "White" as the most common race across the life of the program. In the 1960s and 1970s, "Negro" would begin to appear more often on FBI posters. Former Student Nonviolent Coordinating Committee chairman H. Rap Brown, now Jamil Al-Amin, as well as communists like Angela Davis, were both on the Ten Most Wanted list in 1970 with posters that read "Race: Negro." Theirs would be among the 14 percent of posters with this label on the Ten Most Wanted from 1950 to 1980. In 1980, the FBI replaced it with Black instead. For Assata Shakur, for example, her race is listed as "Negro" on her identification order from 1972, then as "Black" on her wanted posters from 1983 onward. This change in label for the same person is just one example of a broader transition from using the word *Negro* to using the word *Black* to describe the very same people. Her example suggests, further, in the context of identification in crime and policing, that the categories and labels of identification used reflect more about the culture and politics of a time than any sort of neutral realities about the body of the wanted person. It is also important to note that Black revolutionaries and antiwar protestors of the Vietnam War era, including those still on a wanted list, have had posters including the word *terrorist*, but they have also consistently had a race (typically one of the most common race categories—white or Negro, then Black). This suggests that racelessness is not simply a proxy for *terrorist*. Along similar lines, as this chapter demonstrates in detail, racelessness is also not a proxy for Muslim identifiability, since Muslims on other sorts of crime lists in the Most Wanted program do have race categories. This pattern of racelessness, stable over the first two decades of the war on terror, is largely limited to the archetypal Muslim terrorist. In contrast, the Muslims associated with nonterror crimes in the rest of the program do have race, as a rule.

The ability to come up with a race category for Muslims therefore exists for the bureau but suddenly disappears for the MWT list. Islam has been so deeply imbricated in the very meanings of the word *terrorism* as its lone ideological impulse or cause that it is reasonable to conclude here that the raceless terrorist represents Islam for the Most Wanted program; the others are indeed Muslims, but they are not functioning as embodiments of Islam for the FBI in which Islam is the cause of terrorism. Based on this and other findings detailed in this chapter, I argue that racelessness distinguishes the extreme deviance of the post-9/11 Muslim terrorist, where deviance is a matter of distance from the norm, or what was earlier called *average man* for Quetelet, an important figure for the development of identification practices in policing. Perhaps this means that the distance of Muslim terrorists from the norm is farther than all the other deviants in the Most Wanted program in the first two decades of the war on terror. Examples from terrorism studies of explanations for terrorism draw on notions of sexuality and family and employ classic notions of deviance: troubled relationships with parents, negative childhood experiences, and a poor sense of self. Jasbir K. Puar and Amit Rai argue, "What all these models and theories aim to show is how an otherwise normal individual becomes a murderous terrorist, and that process time and again is tied to the failure of the normal(ized) psyche."[9] That failure, which we may put in social scientific Queteletian terms as a deviation from the normal, is advertised on the MWT list, along with another element recalling a theological enemy that is also a rival. It is useful, then, at this point to bear in mind what race categories reflect: race categories are the fixing of history as if it is nature—histories of domination, slavery, dispossession, and conquest, told from the perspective of the idealized human. However, this fixing of history as nature also involves fabricating and erasing history, reflecting aspiration and desire. The racelessness of the Muslim terrorist recalls Muslim rule of the Mediterranean and Christendom's desire to defeat it while being far away from doing so. What remains is a group that has been given a place in Western memory that both deviates from man and also is comparable to him as a rival. The paradox of deviance and rivalry, with a theological gloss, is expressed in scientific terms as racelessness.

Much social scientific scholarship critical of the violence of the war on terror has argued that the war racializes Muslims.[10] This literature has been successful in feeding the increased appetite in public debates for understanding the experience of Muslims in the war on terror as a racial justice issue. But a closer look at Muslims and those associated with them across the entire Most Wanted program shows that they are not all (or even mostly) lumped together into one big racialized category, as this literature and perhaps post-9/11 common sense would lead one to expect. The Muslim racialization argument holds that the state is the central racializing force of Muslims, which makes the missing race of the FBI Most Wanted program—at the intersection of law enforcement and media representation—something that should be explainable as a case of the racialization of Muslims, but it is not. The argument that the war on terror racializes Muslims is unable to account for cases like the MWT list in which the state is focused on Muslims as terrorist threats but actively avoids racializing them.

Research on the racialization of Muslims documents violence and discrimination to demonstrate racialization. Posters threaten violence and may thus appear as evidence of racialization. However, here we see the promise of extreme violence (like extrajudicial killing), rationalized as part of fighting an extreme enemy, alongside racelessness, leading to my conclusion that racelessness is not accidental to the promise of violence. The racelessness of Muslim terrorists helps to make the case for the extreme violence of the war on terror. This case suggests that the representation of Muslims as powerful, drawing on older ideas of Muslims as a competing force capable of colonizing Europeans, makes material reality possible: that Muslims are colonized and killed in droves in the war on terror, to the point that we do not even have a count of how many have been sacrificed at its altar. Critics of the war on terror may operate under false assumptions and inaccurate understandings of how the war on terror works if we miss this critical role of racelessness by reading racialization into it ourselves.

Based on analysis of the missing race, it is necessary, I argue, for a shift in the questions asked and the theories used to understand the relationship between Muslims and race. I argue that a more promising pathway for understanding this relationship is in drawing on and contributing to theoretical frameworks that take the limits of race seriously and emphasize its obliterative work rather than social constructionist frameworks seeking an expansive definition of race.[11] Rather than to immediately reroute racelessness back into race, the fact of racelessness is something to think with. There is analytical benefit in not trying to make the raceless fit into a race framework, and, notably, homogenizing observations to make them fit is the epistemological work of race making that the sociology of race and similar fields otherwise position themselves against. Rather than trying to situate Muslims characterized as terrorists in race, then, I argue they are better understood as indicators of the defects in race, which would then analytically be left as such rather than repaired by redefining race to make Muslims fit inside its terms. The analytical task shifts from an attempt to make a space for Muslims in order to make an appeal to race-based redress, to instead seeking a more accurate understanding of race with broader potential.

The Archetypal Muslim Terrorist

This chapter is centrally concerned with a subgroup of the Most Wanted program. This is a group I have not predetermined but rather delineated through making comparisons across the categories put forth by the FBI in order to excavate their racial logic. FBI wanted posters were collected for the period from 1996, the earliest available through the Internet Archive with old versions of the FBI website, until 2021, constituting a nearly comprehensive archive of FBI posters of the first two decades of the war on terror and an incomplete archive pre-1996.[12] From there, I compare the text across posters: the category labels and their content. A battery of demographic charts, graphs, and summaries are possible and some are offered in the pages that follow, but comparisons between present and absent categories and labels are especially revealing, beginning with the presence of race categories on the posters of Muslims on nonterrorism lists.

MUSLIMS ON NONTERRORISM LISTS

Whether marked by their names or their affiliation with Al-Qaeda or Al-Shabaab, every single one of the raceless most wanted terrorists are identifiably Muslim.[13] However, they are not the only identifiably Muslim fugitives in the Most Wanted program overall. The majority of Muslims across the rest of the program, which is to say on nonterrorism lists, do have a race category, and it is typically "White" with some sort of modifier in parentheses, most commonly "(Central Asian)" and "(Middle Eastern)," though there are other categories as well.

The consistent use of race categories for Muslims and those associated with them across the rest of the program remains both before and after 9/11, as the next few examples show. For example, Yaser Abdel Said was born in Egypt and was on the Ten Most Wanted and Violent Crimes—Murders list for killing his daughters. It is a crime that fits easily in the frame of honor killings, a gendered crime represented as unique to Muslims, Arabs, and other presumably uniquely misogynist groups. He was added to this list in 2008 and removed some time after his capture in 2020. His race is "White." Hilal Hasan Ali Jaafar wears a white turban or cap in all the headshots on his wanted poster. His thick beard and mustache are also consistent across all the photographs. He is the imam for a mosque in Oman, according to the occupations section on his wanted poster (figure 3.1). Commentary on the rest of the poster says he is "a religious person and a member of the Al-Lawati tribe." It continues, "He may be dangerous and have violent tendencies." Jaafar has been on the Parental Kidnapping list since 2010. His poster explains that he kept his child in Oman rather than releasing the child to the mother upon her return to the United States from Oman. The rest of his poster informs the viewer that he was born in Kuwait and that he speaks several languages, including Arabic, Turkish, Farsi, and English, as well as "Indian," though no such language exists. Perhaps it refers to Hindi or something else entirely. In terms of word count, the race category on his poster is the longest one I have encountered in my research on FBI wanted posters. His race

HILAL HASAN ALI JAAFAR

International Parental Kidnapping

Photograph taken in 2006   Photograph taken in 2004

DESCRIPTION

Aliases: Hilal Hassan Ali, Hilal Hasan Ali, Helal Hasan Jaafar, Hilal Jaafar Al-Lawati, Helal Hasan Jaefer, Hilal Jaafar, Helel Hasan Jaafar, Hilal Hasan Ali Jaafar, Helal Hasan Ali Jaafar, Hilal Hasan Al-Lawati, Hasan Ali Al-Lawati, Hasan Ali, Abu Ali, Hilal bin Hasan Al-Lawati	
Date(s) of Birth Used: September 2, 1967	**Place of Birth:** Kuwait
Hair: Black (slight gray coloring, mostly bald on top of head)	**Eyes:** Brown
Height: 5'10"	**Weight:** Approximately 200 pounds
Sex: Male	**Race:** White (Kuwaitian with darker complexion than photographed above)
Occupation: Jaafar is the Imam for a mosque near Muscat, Oman: Masjid Ibrahim Al-Khalil, Ghoubra, Muscat, Oman.	

FIGURE 3.1. FBI wanted poster for Hilal Hasan Ali Jaafar, 2017. Source: FBI.

category reads "White (Kuwaitian with darker complexion than photographed above)." It does not fit on one line on his poster.

Flora Mahmood, born in Pakistan and on the Parental Kidnapping list from 2007 to 2016, is "White (Central Asian)." Some other Pakistanis are "White (Middle Eastern)" on the Cyber's Most Wanted list, such as Noor Aziz Uddin and Farhan ul Arshad. Zahidul Islam is on several FBI wanted lists from 2001 to 2016, including Fugitives and Additional Violent Crimes. In 2012, his poster changed from saying he was born in Pakistan and of Pakistani nationality, to born in Bangladesh and of Bangladeshi nationality. His race remains the same in all posters: "White (Central Asian)." Shafiuddin Syed was labeled "White (Indian)" while on the Seeking Information list for bankruptcy fraud, 2000–2002 and 2004–2006. It is worth considering not only those who are identifiably Muslim but those who are associated with Muslims in post-9/11 color logic, and we find that they, too, are generally raced in the rest of the Most Wanted program, with a few exceptions.[14] Also identifiably South Asian but not Muslim is Shaileshkumar P. Jain, who was on the Cyber's Most Wanted list from 2011 to 2016 and labeled "White (Indian)." Gautam Gupta, born in India and speaking the languages English and Hindi, is labeled "White (Indian)" on the White Collar Crime list from 2011 to 2013. All are on different crime lists, born in India, and of Indian nationality according to their posters. A similar

THE RULE OF RACELESSNESS   89

racial identification is attached to non-Muslim Arabs: George and John Silah, born in Syria and on the Parental Kidnapping list, are "White." Muslims on nonterrorism lists certainly have markers that make them identifiably Muslim: Jaafar's poster even says that he is an imam, and he is still "White" (with a long parenthetical note following it). To be sure, identifiability as a Muslim is an important aspect of the raceless on the MWT list; however, that identifiability is insufficient on its own to merit the absence of a race category in FBI race logic.

MUSLIMS ON TERRORIST LISTS

Some description of this raceless group's features in the context of terrorism lists and the Most Wanted program is necessary. There are three terrorism lists in the Most Wanted program: Domestic Terrorism (DT), Seeking Information—Terrorism (SI-T), and, of course, MWT. The rule of racelessness that characterizes Muslim terrorists is limited to the MWT list, specifically. One indication of this is that Ishmail Muslim Ali of the DT list even has the word *Muslim* in his name and he is raced as Black.

The DT list was created in 2006. It is largely composed of leftists and antiwar activists, with lower rewards for capture than the MWT list, and every single one of them has a race. Aside from an indication of priority, the difference between the DT and the MWT lists does not appear to be domestic or foreign birth, nationality, citizenship, or location of alleged crime. In fact, there are several people with Canadian birth and citizenship whose posters describe their participation in "a French Canadian Separatist Movement" who are on the DT list. Identifying a similar logic, legal scholar Shirin Sinnar compares the prosecution of domestic versus international terrorism and finds that the prosecution of Muslims as terrorists is usually in the framework of international terrorism, even when they have meager international connections.[15] As for the SI-T list, it is defined by a lack of information—and every single person on this list is lacking a race along with most other identification categories on their posters. Though it is also a terrorism list, and was created in 2002, and there is a strong pattern of missing race, I omit it from my analysis because race is not a uniquely missing category on SI-T posters. Most information is missing, which is also the case for the program's Seeking Information list that is not specific to terrorism.

The MWT is of interest because it has such high priority; it stands out from the rest of the program; and because a whopping 90 percent of its posters have most possible identifiers on them, while uniquely missing race. The MWT list comprises mostly Muslims reportedly affiliated with foreign terror organizations. For these reasons, this list is a window into twenty-first-century developments. From 2001 to 2021, about three-quarters of people on any of the

TABLE 3.1. Race Categories on Terrorism Lists, 2001–21

	Most Wanted Terrorist (MWT)	Domestic Terrorism (DT)	Seeking Information— Terrorism (SI-T)[1]	Total
Asian	1	0	0	1
Black	2*	5	0	7
White	2**	11	0	13
White (Hispanic)	0	5	0	5
[MISSING]	46***	0	30	76
Total	51	21	30	102

The individuals named below appeared on one terrorism list initially and then were moved to another terrorism list. To avoid duplicates in the table, such individuals are represented above only on the list on which they most recently appeared.

*Joanne Deborah Chesimard (DT, MWT)
**Daniel Andreas San Diego (DT, MWT)
***Adnan G. El Shukrijumah (SI-WOT, MWT), Fahd Mohammed Ahmed Al-Quso (SI-T, MWT), Adam Yahiye Gadahn (SI-T, MWT), Jaber A. Elbaneh (SI-T, MWT), Jamal Ahmed Mohammad Ali Al-Badawi (SI-T, MWT)

1. This includes variations on this list's name over the years: Seeking Information—War on Terrorism, Seeking Terror Information, etc.

three FBI terrorist lists at any given time are raceless (see table 3.1).[16] This pattern stands in stark contrast to the rest of the Most Wanted program. In 2017, for example, roughly 83 percent of posters in the program overall had a race category. That proportion is based on including terrorism lists as part of the total. If we take all three terror lists out of consideration, the proportion jumps up: 92 percent of (nonterrorism) posters include race. The rule of racelessness is associated with other features on the MWT list: instead of race, those on the MWT list tend to include complexion, and the most common entries are "Olive" or "Light." The raceless also tend to have a citizenship category rather than nationality. This is rather inverted compared to the rest of the program, in which nearly everyone has a race and nationality, and very few have a complexion. In the context of the Most Wanted program as a whole, complexion and racelessness function as the marks of the archetypal Muslim terrorist.

The MWT consists of a perhaps surprisingly diverse assortment. Those who fit the pattern of racelessness are listed as having birthplace and citizenship categories from all over the world. If one had to categorize them racially based on proxies like citizenship, skin color, hair texture, and so on, those racial categories would cover much of the color line. This raceless cohort includes people

HAKIMULLAH MEHSUD

Aliases:
Hakimullah Mahsud, Zulfiqar Mehsud, Hakeemullah Mehsud, Hakimullah Masoud, "Mehsud"

DESCRIPTION

Date(s) of Birth Used:	January 1, 1980; circa 1978 - 1981	**Hair:**	Black
Place of Birth:	Kotkai Region, South Waziristan, Pakistan	**Eyes:**	Brown
		Complexion:	Olive
		Sex:	Male
Height:	6'0"	**Citizenship:**	Pakistani
Weight:	200 pounds	**Language:**	Pashto
Build:	Medium		

FIGURE 3.2. FBI wanted poster for Hakimullah Mehsud, 2012. Source: FBI.

easily classified as South Asian and Arab, as the examples on the next few pages illustrate, as well as those who could easily fit into more consistent US race categories like Black, white, and Asian, based on US epidermal logic.

South Asians, North Africans, and Arabs from the Levant are well represented on the MWT list, so the following are just some examples of a larger whole. Hakimullah Mehsud, second in command of the Pakistani Taliban, was on the MWT list from 2011 to 2013, when he was killed by a US drone strike. Mehsud's poster (figure 3.2) reports that he was born in Pakistan, is a Pakistani citizen, and that his complexion is "Olive." He appears with a beard, mustache, and a tan Peshawari cap in each of the four photographs on his poster. His poster reports he was wanted for his involvement in a 2009 bombing of a US military base near Khost, Afghanistan. His poster lacks a race category. Adnan Shukrijumah also has connections to the subcontinent and lacks a race category. Born in Saudi Arabia and with Guyanese citizenship, he was wanted in relation to an alleged plot to target the New York City subway system, directed by Al-Qaeda leadership in Pakistan. Anas Al-Liby was wanted in connection with the embassy bombings in Kenya and Tanzania in 1998. His poster notes Libya as his place of birth and citizenship. His languages are Arabic and English. He has no race, and his complexion is "Olive." Ahlam Ahmad Al-Tamimi was the second woman to be added to the MWT list. The first was Assata Shakur (see chapters 2 and 4). Al-Tamimi, whose poster (figure 3.3) says she was born in Jordan and is of Jordanian nationality, was on the MWT list from 2017 to 2020. With

92 CHAPTER THREE

AHLAM AHMAD AL-TAMIMI

Conspiring to Use and Using a Weapon of Mass Destruction Against a United States National Outside the United States Resulting in Death and Aiding and Abetting and Causing an Act to be Done

DESCRIPTION

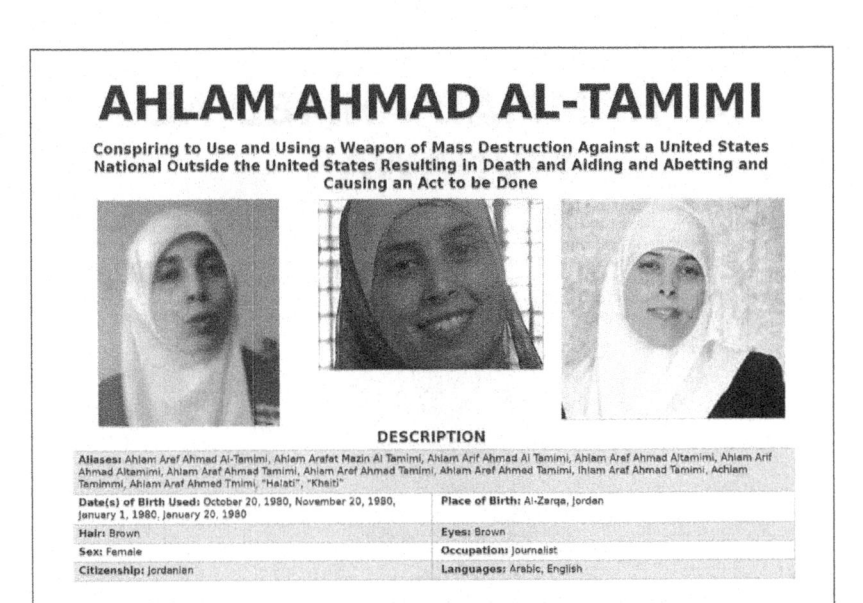

Aliases:	Ahlam Aref Ahmad Al-Tamimi, Ahlam Arafat Mazin Al Tamimi, Ahlam Arif Ahmad Al Tamimi, Ahlam Aref Ahmad Altamimi, Ahlam Arif Ahmad Altamimi, Ahlam Araf Ahmad Tamimi, Ahlam Aref Ahmad Tamimi, Ahlam Aref Ahmed Tamimi, Ihlam Araf Ahmad Tamimi, Achlam Tamimmi, Ahlam Araf Ahmed Thimi, "Halati", "Kheiti"	
Date(s) of Birth Used: October 20, 1980, November 20, 1980, January 1, 1980, January 20, 1980		Place of Birth: Al-Zarqa, Jordan
Hair: Brown		Eyes: Brown
Sex: Female		Occupation: Journalist
Citizenship: Jordanian		Languages: Arabic, English

FIGURE 3.3. FBI wanted poster for Ahlam Ahmad Al-Tamimi, 2019. Source: FBI.

no mention of the word *Palestinian*, her poster reports that she was a journalist and on the list for facilitating a suicide bombing in Jerusalem. Unlike most other posters on the list, hers does not name a group or organizational affiliation. Muhammad Ahmed Al-Munawar was added to the program in 2012. Al-Munawar is wanted for a 1986 hijacking. His poster notes that he "is most likely residing in a Middle Eastern country" and that he is "believed to be a member of the Abu Nidal Organization." The lone photograph on Al-Munawar's poster (figure 3.4) is blurry. Facing the camera for a photograph that includes half his torso, he appears of slight frame in a light blue polo shirt with a beard and mustache. His complexion is "Light" on his poster.

Based on what is widely known of the racial logic of the war on terror beyond the FBI alone, it is not surprising that Arabs and South Asians are well represented as terrorists or that they occupy an unsteady place in the US racial order such that they would lack a race category.[17] Nor is it surprising that the racial categories assigned to these groups are unstable across contexts. However, also lacking a race on the MWT list are some who have likely been classified as white quite easily at some point in their lives. Adam Yahiye Gadahn, who is US-born and has US citizenship according to his poster, has no race on any of his posters: not when he was on the Seeking Information—War on Terrorism list in 2004 and 2005, and not when on the MWT list from 2006 until

MUHAMMAD AHMED AL-MUNAWAR

Damaging an Aircraft; Unlawful Placing of a Destructive Device on an Aircraft; Performing an Act of Violence Against an Individual on an Aircraft; Hostage Taking; Murder of United States Nationals Outside of the United States; Attempted Murder of United States Nationals Outside of the United States; Causing Serious Bodily Injury to United States Nationals Outside the United States; Assault on a Passenger; Malicious Damage to an Aircraft; Use of a Firearm During a Crime of Violence; Aircraft Piracy; Aiding and Abetting; Conspiracy to Commit Offenses Outside the United States

Photograph taken in 2000
DESCRIPTION

Aliases: Abderhman Al Rashid Mansour, Ashraf Naeem Mansoor, Zubair, Shamed Khalil Zubair, Abdul Rahman Al-Rahid Mansoor, Al Rashad Mansur, Ahmed Khalid Zubair, Abdur Rehman Rashad Mansar	
Date(s) of Birth Used: May 21, 1965	**Place of Birth:** Kuwait
Hair: Black	**Eyes:** Dark
Height: 5'9" (177 centimeters)	**Weight:** 132 pounds (60 kilograms)
Build: Medium	**Complexion:** Light
Sex: Male	**Citizenship:** Palestinian and possibly Lebanese
Languages: Arabic	**Scars and Marks:** Al-Munawar has a scar on his left hand near his thumb.

FIGURE 3.4. FBI wanted poster for Muhammad Ahmed Al-Munawar, 2017. Source: FBI.

2015, when he was killed by a US drone strike at the Afghanistan-Pakistan border. Mainstream media reporting on his killing in 2015 drew attention to the white American features of his biography: a *New York Times* headline reads, "Adam Gadahn Was Propagandist for Al Qaeda Who Sold Terror in English."[18] CNN reported, "Adam Gadahn, American Mouthpiece for Al Qaeda, Killed," with a subheading "No Pizza Dinner in Pakistan."[19] The *Guardian*'s headline proceeded similarly: "Adam Gadahn: California Death Metal Fan Who Rose Quickly in Al-Qaida's Ranks."[20] Each article described his transition from a recognizably American life to an Islamic one; a fall from grace. A 2007 *New Yorker* article is bewildered at the transformation, representative of the big questions raised by "homegrowns" like Gadahn for major news outlets: "Because of their cultural literacy, and because of the mobility that their citizenship provides, they are potentially the most dangerous of terrorists."[21]

Both of Gadahn's posters read "Complexion: Light" (figure 3.5). But some relevant changes materialize for him when moving from one list to another. His

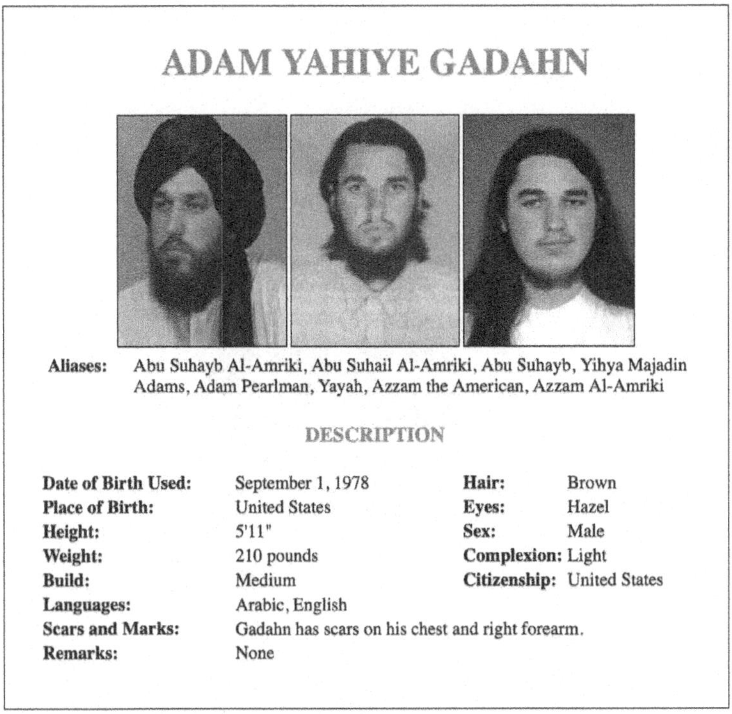

ADAM YAHIYE GADAHN

Aliases: Abu Suhayb Al-Amriki, Abu Suhail Al-Amriki, Abu Suhayb, Yihya Majadin Adams, Adam Pearlman, Yayah, Azzam the American, Azzam Al-Amriki

DESCRIPTION

Date of Birth Used:	September 1, 1978	Hair:	Brown
Place of Birth:	United States	Eyes:	Hazel
Height:	5'11"	Sex:	Male
Weight:	210 pounds	Complexion:	Light
Build:	Medium	Citizenship:	United States
Languages:	Arabic, English		
Scars and Marks:	Gadahn has scars on his chest and right forearm.		
Remarks:	None		

FIGURE 3.5. FBI wanted poster for Adam Yahiye Gadahn, 2008. Source: FBI.

MWT poster gains a third photograph of him in a black turban alongside existing photographs of him clean-shaven with long, dark hair that continues past the bottom border of the photograph, and another in which he has shoulder-length hair and a full beard. The Seeking Information poster notes that he is "being sought in connection with possible terrorist threats against the United States." It continues, "Although the FBI has no information indicating this individual is connected to any specific terrorist activities, the FBI would like to locate and question this person." His MWT poster is more specific and involves charges, along with some awkward description: he was indicted in California for treason and material support to Al-Qaeda, and the charges are related to "providing aid and comfort to Al Qaeda and services for Al Qaeda."

Some of the earliest additions to the MWT list in 2001 who could easily be classified as Black based on US epidermal logic, per the rule of hypodescent, were instead raceless. This is clear on the posters of three men who are wanted in connection with the 1998 bombings of US embassies in Kenya and Tanza-

FAHID MOHAMMED ALLY MSALAM

Aliases: Fahid Mohammed Ally, Fahid Mohammed Ali Musalaam, Fahid Mohammed Ali Msalam, Fahid Muhamad Ali Salem, Mohammed Ally Msalam, Usama Al-Kini, Fahad Ally Msalam

DESCRIPTION

Date of Birth Used:	February 19, 1976	Hair:	Black, curly
Place of Birth:	Mombasa, Kenya	Eyes:	Brown
Height:	5'6" to 5'8"	Sex:	Male
Weight:	160 to 170 pounds	Complexion:	Dark
Build:	Unknown	Citizenship:	Kenyan
Languages:	Arabic, Swahili, English		
Scars and Marks:	None known		

Remarks: Msalam sometimes wears a light beard or moustache and has, in the past, worked as a clothing vendor.

FIGURE 3.6. FBI wanted poster for Fahid Mohammed Ally Msalam, 2001. Source: FBI.

nia. Fazul Abdullah Mohammed was on the MWT until 2011. His poster listed the languages he speaks as French, Swahili, Arabic, English, and "Comoran." His citizenship category reads "Comoros, Kenyan," and he was born in the Comoros Islands. Fahid Mohammed Ally Msalam was on the MWT list until 2009 (figure 3.6). He speaks Arabic, Swahili, and English, and has Kenyan citizenship and place of birth, no race, and "Dark" complexion. Sheikh Ahmed Salim Swedan has the same citizenship, place of birth, and (no) race. It is striking for them to lack a race category because blackness has long served as a proxy for race. In this case, however, the rule of racelessness reigns, and though they could be classified as Black, they are not. This further supports an argument of this book that blackness does not always, necessarily, automatically, fit inside the bounds of race, even for those invested in making race.

Because most of the MWT list is Muslim (and non-Muslims on the list are such a minority, at 4 percent), it may appear that the FBI's racial logic is that visibly/externally identifiable Muslims (and those associated with them) tend to lack race. There would even be some evidence to support this interpretation since the raceless on the MWT are visibly Muslim. So far, this pattern of racelessness may appear to be a case of a diverse range of Muslims across the program being lumped together—a hallmark of racialization—and are then marked differently from everyone else in some way.

As Junaid Rana articulates the Muslim racialization argument, "the internal logics of racialization figure Muslims as a broad population that encompasses multiple nationalities, ethnic groups, and cultural experiences" like we see above.[22] However, the previous section on Muslims and those associated with them across the entire Most Wanted program shows that Muslims are not all lumped together into one big, racialized category, as the literature and post-9/11 common sense would suggest. Of course, the burden of proof for the Muslim racialization argument is not that every single Muslim must be characterized in the same way; however, the pattern in the Most Wanted program does not have a racialized category that most Muslims fall into as Muslims. Instead, the labeling of Muslims is organized along different lines: highest-priority terrorists, on the one hand, versus mostly nonterrorists (and to some degree lower-priority terrorists) on the other hand. The Muslim racialization argument further considers how "the Muslim" is a composite that includes non-Muslims like Hindus and Sikhs, for example, and others who "look Muslim." The above examples of Muslims on the MWT list who are marked as raceless certainly do form a composite and are imagined in many of the ways that the literature on Muslim racialization describes perceptions of terrorism. For an example of an observation of this lumping, Rana reads FBI alerts, close enough to wanted posters, along these lines, as demonstrating

> how the Islamic world and Muslims are homogenized as a single group to fit the needs of the U.S. security apparatus. Muslims, as embodied in the religious practice of Islam, are figured as ideological opponents to the United States. Such a representation seems to translate religious difference not only into cultural difference, but also into innate and essential differences between the United States and Islam. Going against the logic of the U.S. racial formation that generally assigns race according to phenotypic characteristics, the War on Terror broadly defines racial phenotype in terms of Islam as a religion that is naturalized and biologized into Muslims' bodies.[23]

In my view, the MWT list displays thinking on Muslims that is no more inconsistent with US race and its scientific, biologistic, phenotypic organization than anything else that is drawn into this racial order. From 2001 to 2021, there are five people who do have race on the MWT list, out of the total of fifty-one who have ever been on this list (see table 3.1). They are so few in number that they can all be named and discussed quite easily: Omar Shafik Hammami (White), Raddulan Sahiron (Asian), Liban Haji Mohamed (Black), Daniel Andreas San Diego (White), and Assata Shakur, as she appears on her poster, Joanne Chesimard (Black). Of these, the first three are Muslim. The remaining two are not indicated as Muslim in any way, though as chapters 2 and 4 discuss, this matter is not straightforward in the case of Shakur. They are the only people on the MWT list whose posters do not indicate that they are or were Muslim, nor that they have any connection to Muslim organizations, as San Diego is an "eco-terrorist" and Shakur represents the Black liberation movement. These exceptions ultimately demonstrate the strength of the rule of racelessness for the archetypal Muslim terrorist because (1) these exceptions are so few in number, but also because (2) they show that the raceless could have easily been raced as White, Black, or Asian, but they are not, suggesting that what I call the rule of racelessness is not haphazard, nor is it a complete exception for which no racial logic is employed.

Hammami, for example, was on the Crime Alert list 2010–12, and then the MWT 2012–13. There are some differences between his posters when on each list. When he is moved to the MWT list, his poster (figure 3.7) gains a few categories: it begins to list languages he speaks (Arabic, English, and Somali), and it lists his complexion as "Light." His poster also loses the category of nationality (American) when he is moved from the Crime Alert list to the MWT list, and he gains a citizenship category that says "United States." Both posters note he was born in Alabama and is wanted for traveling to Somalia to join Al-Shabaab. One of his aliases is Abu Mansour al-Amriki, matching the naming conventions used in the context of jihadi movements in which people are identified by where they are from.[24] The race on both of his posters is White, making him a rare individual with an identifiably Muslim name as well as a race on the MWT list. Like Gadahn before him, he was the subject of extended profiles in media outlets like the *New York Times Magazine* and *Foreign Policy*, as well as a podcast called *American Jihadi*. All circle around the same question, again, like Gadahn: How and why would an American become a jihadi? Hammami's family and upbringing differed significantly from Gadahn's in one way especially. Hammami's father is a Syrian Muslim immigrant to the United States, and his mother is a white American Christian from Alabama, where Hammami was also raised. Still, Hammami is white on FBI terrorism lists, while Gadahn (with two white American parents and possibly some Jewish roots) has no race whatsoever.

OMAR SHAFIK HAMMAMI

Aliases: Abu Mansour al-Amriki, Farouk, Farouq

DESCRIPTION

Date(s) of Birth Used:	May 6, 1984	**Hair:**	Brown
Place of Birth:	Alabama	**Eyes:**	Brown
Height:	5'11"	**Complexion:**	Light
Weight:	160 pounds	**Sex:**	Male
Build:	Medium	**Race:**	White
		Citizenship:	United States
		Languages:	Arabic; English; Somali

FIGURE 3.7. FBI wanted poster for Omar Shafik Hammami, 2013. Source: FBI.

Liban Haji Mohamed is an identifiably Muslim man, also wanted for ties to Al-Shabaab, and he has a race on his MWT poster: "Black." The FBI added him to the MWT list in 2016. Mohamed's poster (figure 3.8) signals his status as Muslim through several markers, aside from his name: he was wanted for providing material support to Al-Shabaab and Al-Qaeda; and he speaks English, Arabic, and Somali. In addition to these markers of his Muslim status, Mohamed has a complexion category, and it reads "Dark." The majority of the MWT list has complexion instead of race, but Mohamed has both. So if, in the case of the three men wanted for the 1998 US embassy bombings in Kenya and Tanzania, the rule of racelessness trumped the rule of naming phenotypic blackness as such, such that they had complexion categories and no race categories, then for Liban Haji Mohamed, there was no replacement of one set of markers with another. Instead, he has some of the mark of raceless Muslim terrorists—the complexion category—and some of the rules that apply to everyone else—the race category. Raddulan Sahiron is also identifiably Muslim and on the MWT list with a race category: Asian. He has been there since 2012. He was born in the Philippines and has Filipino citizenship. His Muslim status is indicated on his poster (figure 3.9) via the languages he speaks—Tausug and Arabic—as well as through being wanted by the FBI for his participation in the kidnapping of a US citizen as part of Al Harakat al Islamiyyah or the Abu Sayyaf Group. At the same time, another Filipino is among the raceless. For example, Khadafi Abubakar Janjalani was on the MWT list for 2006 and 2007 (figure 3.10). His languages: Tausug, Tagalog, limited Arabic and English, complexion "Tan." He

THE RULE OF RACELESSNESS 99

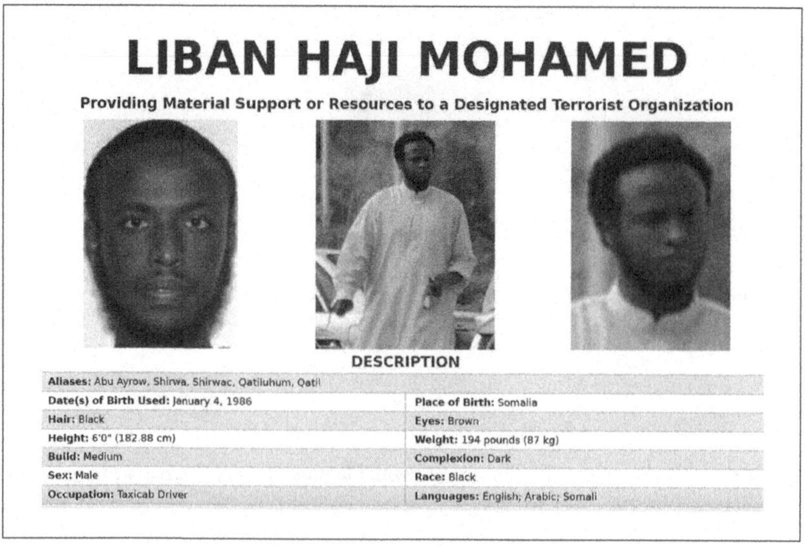

FIGURE 3.8. FBI wanted poster for Liban Haji Mohamed, 2017. Source: FBI.

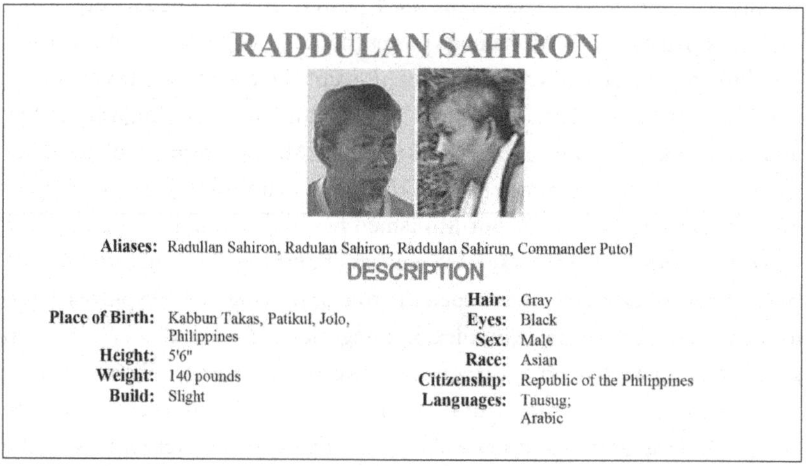

FIGURE 3.9. FBI wanted poster for Raddulan Sahiron, 2015. Source: FBI.

KHADAFI ABUBAKAR JANJALANI

Aliases: Khadafi Abubakar Janjalam, Khaddafy Abubakar Janjalani, Abu Muktar, Amir Khadafi Abubaker Janjalani, Khadafi Abu Muktar, Jimar Manalad Montanio, Khadafi Montanio, Abu Mochtar ("The good-hearted"), "Daf", Omar Bin Salik

DESCRIPTION

Date of Birth Used:	March 3, 1975	Hair:	Black
Place of Birth:	Isabela, Basilan, Republic of the Philippines	Eyes:	Brown
Height:	5'4"	Sex:	Male
Weight:	120 pounds	Complexion:	Tan
Build:	Thin	Citizenship:	Philippine
Languages:	Tausug, Tagalog, limited Arabic and English		
Scars and Marks:	None known		

FIGURE 3.10. FBI wanted poster for Khadafi Abubakar Janjalani, 2006. Source: FBI.

was also born in the Philippines and has Filipino citizenship. According to his poster, he "allegedly served as the Amir or spiritual leader of the foreign terrorist organization, Abu Sayyaf Group."

These last few examples show that it is possible for the FBI to select a race for people otherwise comparable to the raceless along the lines of national origin, complexion, birth place, languages spoken, and so on, if these were the only considerations, as much contemporary race theory might suggest. There is more to the FBI's racial calculus than phenotype and geographical markers as considerations in the selection and rejection of a race label.

A Muslim Race?

If the perception of a phenotypic Muslim marker guided the racial categorization in the program, perhaps those who share nationality, place of birth, citizenship, and other proxies for race would share a race category; perhaps Kuwaitis on terror and nonterror lists would have the same category.[25] Perhaps Pakistanis

THE RULE OF RACELESSNESS   101

would, too, but that is not what happens in the FBI Most Wanted program. Instead, there are Arabs with and without race categories; there are South Asians, Filipinos, and (presumably) Black and white people also with and without race categories.

Based on this chapter's findings, one main conclusion forms, and with important implications: the FBI Most Wanted program does not have a Muslim race, in other words, one racial category by which all or even most are identified; the program does not have a group that fits inside the FBI Most Wanted program's racial order as Muslims.[26] In other contexts, Muslims can be officially racially categorized as such—as Muslims (or North Africans) in the case of Algerians in France, or as natives in the case of colonial Algeria.[27] In the US context, there is inflection by Islam, or not-Islam, as in the case of the Negro (see chapter 2). Although Islam is attributed in some cases and extracted in other cases as part of shaping the color line, this does not necessarily mean that the Muslim has a spot on the color line in the United States. Islam is given a role in configuring the FBI's racial hierarchy, as something that some are supposed to have and others are not, but this, still, is not the same as racialization as Muslims. This finding does not mean that race is irrelevant to the analysis here, or to the FBI Most Wanted program, when it comes to Muslims. Rather, race is operating in a particular contextual way that requires taking seriously the wanted poster form on which the pattern of racelessness occurs.

The FBI wanted poster is a scientific racial form, as chapter 1 traces. The norm, or Quetelet's average man, is what explicitly organized the earlier forms of identification from which the FBI's wanted posters emerge. The entries under each category on wanted posters are meaningful based on their distance from the average man. These categories continue to be comparative and hierarchically organized; the average man continues to structure identification practices without being named as such when categories mark deviance from a predetermined norm and the question is how deviant. In this context, racelessness may indicate the extreme deviance of post-9/11 Muslim terrorists. What deviates the most from the average man is especially troubling for Quetelet. For example, he saw extremes in height, specifically "dwarfs" and "giants," which is to say those furthest away from the average man, as "preternatural" and "monstrous."[28] For the FBI Most Wanted program, the distance of Muslim terrorists from the norm is farther than all other deviants in the program. Muslim terrorists are off the charts in their deviance, while paradoxically marked as rivals. Rivalry implies relatively equal capacity, or at least competitive. And if competitive with man, who is raceless, then the enemy rival can perhaps also be raceless, where racelessness marks power (and racialization marks subordination).

Muslim terrorists, who function as a stand-in for Islam, are not considered a weak enemy in the war on terror, but as a formidable and terrifying one for those who wage this war.

This somewhat paradoxical positioning highlights the uneven and incomplete transition from a theocentric framework to a biocentric one. These are typically imagined as discrete frameworks, but as chapter 1 shows, there is much continuity between the former and the latter. In the move from a theocentric to biocentric mode of knowledge, the terms shift from grace to normality. There is indeed a "genealogical connection" between the forms of knowledge used to taxonomize "the West's abnormals," in scientific terms, and those "premodern monsters" that the West has tried so hard to defeat, as Jasbir Puar and Amit Rai argue.[29] The color line, by the time of the MWT list, continued to be organized by what David A. Hollinger calls the "ethno-racial pentagon" of white, Black, Asian, Latino, and Native American that Walter Mignolo further explains is "the re-articulation of the secular imaginary of the late eighteenth and nineteenth century, when racial classifications became 'scientific' instead of 'religious' (!)."[30] There is, on the one hand, the scientific Queteletian framework. It is geared toward state administration. As David Theo Goldberg argues, the failure to fit inside the contrasts guiding state racial classifications is to "fall outside the law," removable to spaces beyond borders, to prisons for example.[31] Raceless Muslims on the MWT list are thus what Sherene Razack calls "cast out."[32] Useful for the case of the raceless Muslims on the MWT list, Nasser Hussain argues that the prison at Guantánamo Bay is often imagined as outside law—such that its cruelties are due to the absence or suspension of law—but that this view is incorrect. Instead, it is better understood as a space of hyperlegality "in the interstices of multiple legal orders" that allow for the excesses of the famous prison there.[33] Behind the question of "what goes on at Guantánamo," he asks a "more abiding question: *What is Guantánamo?*"[34] He finds it worth asking this deceptively simple, chilling question because of how Guantánamo is a stand-in for a larger set of formations. He unsettles the idea that Guantánamo is exceptional, which is a concept used in much thinking on the war on terror.

A similarly structured question guides this book and, more specifically, this chapter. Underneath the racist violence against Muslims in the war on terror is the question of what race is such that the most wanted terrorist, in whose name the violence against other Muslims is rational, is then raceless. Also similar to but not fully mirroring Hussain's argument, applied to our case here, is the coming together of multiple frameworks in whose interstices certain cruelties are made possible. The biocentric clashes with the theocentric to make the paradoxical raceless position of Muslims on the MWT list. There is the religious-turned-secular mode of knowledge that reads Muslims as a theological premodern enemy representing a past that is not only incompatible with cherished values of liberalism but an existential threat to it. The older category of Muslims as a theological enemy does not translate to a clear scientific category as such. When it comes time to enter a race label on a form, the theological enemy must be accounted for in the scientific form somehow. But memories of Muslim powers prior to the 1492 moment—like Moors, the Persian Empire, and the earlier years of the Ottoman Empire—may inform this image. Eighteenth-century Barbary pirates, for example, posed a true material threat to the economic endeavors of early American settlers immediately following the American Revolution. Settlers feared being overpowered by Muslims, which included people who would appear to be all across the color line, much like those on the MWT list.[35] What remains of this history of Muslim power is the imprint of fear and rivalry, but not so much its material reality, as many Muslim-majority lands are colonized by Europe, and not the other way around, in modernity. All of this is contingent and historical, but the categories born of this history do not function that way when history is baptized as nature. Social science fixed the categories born of this history of religion, trade, conquest, and colonialism as natural, as Quetelet quite explicitly did in his project of sociological science that necessarily involves abstracting individuals' histories not only in order to focus on the group but to determine the properties of the populations, which assumes some degree of fixity of population.[36]

The history of Muslims as a powerful rival can be naturalized and translated into scientific race categories as racelessness, per R. A. Judy's analysis of Immanuel Kant's colorless human.[37] Also modeled on man, the assumption is that the Muslim is also the same kind of human as a rival colonizer who would do to Europe what Europeans (colorless humans) did to the rest of the world but with Islam (color added). To be human is to be colorless, and lesser humans, which is to say deviants, are colorless humans "with color added," per Judy, resulting (in the case of the MWT list) in a people who are both enemies and also unmarked. Perhaps it is useful for the enemy to be racially unmarked in the war on terror with its particular understandings of risk and danger, like the danger of an unmarked person with a shoe bomb who can evade airport security.[38] Perceptively, in his reading of American television programs about terrorists like *Sleeper Cell* and *24*, Leerom Medovoi notices that the slippage between the different referents of "Middle Eastern" (dangerous Muslim Arabs, nondangerous Sephardic Jews and Armenians, and those who "look" Middle Eastern) means that racial marking does not serve the function we typically put it to—identification—and could instead "paradoxically function as a disguise for the figure of the terrorist."³⁹ He raises the question, "What does it mean that the racism specific to the war on terror presupposes a potentially unmarked racial enemy who can camouflage himself or herself against the more conventional markers of color?" His answer is that such television shows "train their audiences into envisioning the field of race in stereo, tacking between the color and dogma axes to produce a racially diverse range of potential enemies."⁴⁰

On the invisible enemy of the war on terror but in the context of post-9/11 policing rather than representations, Jonathan Finn argues that the National Security Entry-Exit Registration System known as NSEERS or special registration "gave a visual face to a threat described as largely invisible and omnipresent. This not only enabled the public to participate in the surveillance of targeted populations but also served as a display of heightened state power."⁴¹ To Medovoi and Finn's conclusions on the utility of an invisible enemy, I add that racelessness on wanted posters in the war on terror is instructive of the productivity of the limits of race, both for official uses, like on wanted posters and, as chapter 4 explores, for those who seek to fight against the war on terror.

A final consideration in this discussion of factors that may come to bear on the FBI's racial logic is the state of diversity discourse and measurement by the twenty-first century. As sociologist Ellen Berrey explains, state integration measures "conceptualized race as countable minorities," a conceptualization that was formalized in 1977 by the US Office of Management of Budget, which is responsible for determining official race categories for state use.⁴² The complexion category that is also concentrated on the MWT list may allow the bureau to have it both ways: a visual cue related to color without the meanings of race that make reference to a (visible, or at least nameable) population of "countable minorities." Here, minorities are necessary for institutions to include to protect an image, making such minorities necessary, if irritating, to the institutions who need them. There is much literature on the discontents of this situation and its politics. But for our purposes here, what is important is the question of measurement: Who is included as a countable (deserving) minority? How are they defined in order to be countable (measurable)? And with whom do they contrast, on both counts? Perhaps this understanding of race is at play in the categorizations on wanted posters, too, such that those who represent Islam/terrorism (and here the false synonymity is important) are a foil as nondeserving and uncountable. If race comes to have an association with deserving subordinates, then perhaps the terrorist of 9/11 may be classified under a different rubric, that of colonialism, leading Salman Sayyid to remark that "what was distinctive about the attacks ... was precisely their unmistakable postcoloniality"; it is a postcoloniality that "the War on Terror is directed towards eradicating," in part through the "direct colonial rule over Iraq and Afghanistan."[43] In that context of direct rule, the terrorists of 9/11 have a particular place in that US gulag, "treated as uppity colonials."[44] As uppity colonials, there is the implication not only of subordination but of an attempt to equalize their footing that is an affront to colonial hubris.

At stake in the high-profile racelessness of the archetypal Muslim terrorist is the integrity and coherence of the now common argument that Muslims are racialized. The FBI is a major player in executing material violence against Muslims, between surveillance, infiltration, detention, the No Fly List, and other means of repression that are otherwise put forth as evidence that Muslims are racialized. However, the raceless Muslim terrorist suggests that the frame of racialization has not necessarily gotten us closer to understanding some of the nefarious, updated, and elaborate ways that material violence is enacted and interacts with representation. This frame of racialization that sees race everywhere does not allow us to perceive the defects in racial epistemology—that race is not actually the all-encompassing system that its creators believe it to be, intentionally and perhaps unexpectedly missing as it is in some unusual and significant cases like the Most Wanted Terrorist list. And as this book asks, are racialization frameworks perhaps even correcting that defect in service of racial epistemology, unintentionally facilitating the epistemological work of race making for new times with new pressures? Chapter 4 looks at this progressive race making in the context of Assata Shakur's addition to the MWT list alongside its raceless Muslims to further explore this question.

4

ASSATA, BLACK MADONNA

In his essay "Assata Shakur, Excluding the Nightmare after the Dream: The 'Terrorist' Label and the Criminalization of Revolutionary Black Movements in the USA," former Black Panther and Black Liberation Army member Dhoruba Bin Wahad offers an argument on how and why Shakur was added to the FBI Most Wanted Terrorist (MWT) list in 2013 while she lived as an asylee in Cuba. He makes a specific case for why she should remain free that distinguishes between law and all other realms. As far as the legal sphere is concerned, he says that Shakur and her legal advisors should make whatever arguments they need to maintain her freedom. For everyone else, however, Bin Wahad advises, specifically "supporters and those interested in justice and in an end to racist and political repression," her legal innocence is not to be the basis of why she should remain free. Instead, they must, "as a matter of principle, place her case, and the 'terrorist' designation placed on her by the FBI, in its proper context: as the continuation of a criminalization and demonization of the Black Liberation Movement."[1] He critiques how some of Shakur's supporters from the millennial generation of activists and advocates, as well as "progressive civil libertarians and Black cultural figures," challenge her terrorism designation in a way that fashions her into a "Black Madonna of abstract resistance."[2] In the rest of the essay, he argues that the Black liberation movement, its people, and its conditions of emergence are not safely tucked away in the past, and that Shakur's terrorism designation should be understood in this context rather than as a calamity befalling her alone that she must be rescued from by making her innocent. To rely on the innocence defense outside the legal sphere is to misunderstand or distort the movement and the conditions that gave rise to it, which he emphasizes are also the conditions in which we continue to live.

What arises in Bin Wahad's essay is a generative critique of contemporary liberal antiracist politics that frame Shakur as an innocent not only in legal terms but in other ways as well: in political, social, and ethical terms, and, more precisely for my interest here, through racial blackness. As this chapter demonstrates, claiming racial blackness or proximity to it makes a certain type of innocence claim possible in the context of the domestic war on terror. This sort of claim also becomes available to groups not racially categorized as Black. For example, as this chapter discusses, it appears in the "Muslim immigrant rights movement," which makes claims about its relation to racial blackness not only in order to seek legal redress but also as an entry point to coalition building for political advocacy and grassroots political organizing.[3] Relatedly, it appears in the intersectionality framework, which is used so often in these arenas and in relation to Shakur. Intersectionality is mentioned in Bin Wahad's disapproval of millennial activists who turn Shakur into a Black Madonna when he says they are seeking to "develop [their] politics of 'intersectional' oppression." A careful reading of his essay highlights how intersectionality is a version of the innocence defense, and it has been a widely used concept for the identity-based analyses that, I argue, fail to explain the significance of Shakur's positioning on this list because of their reliance on the epistemology of man. "Black Madonna" highlights this problem.[4]

The Black Madonna is an innocent in black, a heroine figure, an ideal of another color; it is a type built on a similar model as nineteenth-century man of science Adolphe Quetelet's average man or *l'homme moyen* (chapter 1). Quetelet believed each nation had its own average man, or superior human characterized by beauty and goodness. The Black Madonna is an intersectional version of this model, reproducing man's structure of thought and its categories, with the gendered theological significance of the Madonna.[5] One might maintain that intersectionality is a case of using or inverting man's categories for goals contrary to man's goals, and that such an approach has had its strategic uses especially in the context of law.[6] But this chapter draws on Bin Wahad's distinction between law and other realms with regard to the innocence defense to continue to think on some of the questions of this book: Has any possible benefit derived from such an approach outside the legal sphere been exhausted? Has this approach run its course now, two decades into the twenty-first century, on the heels of contestations around race ranging from holocausts to antidiscrimination laws of the previous century, to the implementation and pulling back of diversity initiatives, and the defunding of the very same humanities that allowed "Human Others" into the fold of the human as others nevertheless? To what extent are the uses of the same categories, for purposes other than what the categories are oriented toward, doomed from the start, condemned to remain faithful to their creators?

These questions have immediate relevance for developing an understanding of Shakur's criminalization and its significance. When identities accorded by the system of thought built around man become the unit of analysis, it becomes challenging to make sense of Shakur's addition to the MWT list, as the following headlines and quotes suggest. All are taken by a specific contrast between Assata Shakur and the rest of the MWT list (see chapter 3):

> How did Shakur become a woman considered so dangerous by the US government that her name is ranked alongside members of Hezbollah?[7]

> There is no question that Shakur was on the scene when the state trooper was murdered. But does she belong on a list that includes affiliates of international jihadist groups?[8]

> "It's incredibly frustrating that the first woman to be on the FBI's most wanted terrorist list, the same list as Osama bin Laden, would be a 65 year-old grandmother in Cuba," writer and filmmaker dream hampton told radio host Davey D.[9]

> Nine of the 10 people on the FBI's list of Most Wanted Terrorists are Islamic militants.... The 10th and last name stands out not only because it echoes a completely different historical struggle, but also because it belongs to the only woman on the list: JoAnne Chesimard, better known as Assata Shakur.[10]

These quotes suggest Assata Shakur is out of place or does not belong. The impasse they point to is due to making man's identity categories the unit of analysis. There are indeed important differences between Shakur and the rest of the list, but man's categories that define similarity and difference of struggle along racial lines do not capture them, nor do they promote explanation. On the MWT list, the highest-value targets are foreign-born Muslim men, for the most part, some of whom are Black, and the decades-long pursuit of one Black woman, who was Muslim herself in the 1970s (see chapter 2), is advanced in intensity by positioning her next to this group on the list, as this chapter shows. In official US racial categories, Shakur and most of the rest of the list are different from one another, but analysis relying on notions of fixed or even clearly demarcated identity groups does not help in this case anyway, as chapter 3 showed, because the race labels on the MWT list are especially unreliable, missing as they are for most of those whose photographs sit next to Shakur's. This alone suggests the need for analysis not relying on fixed categories. Rather than focusing analysis on arrangements and combinations of identity categories to understand the significance of Shakur's addition to the MWT list, analysis is opened up if the locus of critique shifts from the contents of the list to the existence of the list itself, as Bin Wahad's analysis would encourage. The MWT list frames *terrorists* as exceptional, as deviant, as atavistically violent in order to rationalize the tactics of the global war on terror—from extrajudicial killing to surveillance and deportations, military occupation, and drone warfare. The categories of analysis for the Black liberation movement are also anchored to their interests.

The Black liberation movement articulated their analysis of similarity and difference to their goal of liberation that shared a model not with man's epistemology but with international, Muslim-led, anti-imperialist struggles. So in the case of the MWT list and the issues it is connected to, the Black liberation movement's thought is especially instructive. The Black liberation movement's notions of difference and similarity are useful here not as an object of study but as reflecting a way of thinking to engage for analysis. Their thought offers a valuable counterweight to most analysis used to make sense of the war on terror that relies on man's epistemology and racial innocence.

Infinite Exclusion for Inclusion

Intersectionality is a key concept for analysis of mechanisms of legal redress. Legal scholar Kimberlé Crenshaw famously coined the term in her analysis of US antidiscrimination law, a site where her work is indispensable. Categories for gender and race, along which lines *woman* and *Black* were the bottommost subjects, could not be relied upon to make a case for discrimination against Black women. The limits of these legal categories in antidiscrimination law, as Crenshaw shows through analysis of legal cases, prevented Black women from securing legal remedy.[11] The impact of the concept of intersectionality beyond the realm of law has been profound.[12] Feminist theory is transformed by it, indebted to Crenshaw. The use of the concept in the study of Muslims in the war on terror has applied it outside the legal context, as we will see. The general analytical approach based on intersectionality identifies particular identities (e.g.,

Black) within relevant categories (e.g., race), then examines the experiences of those who occupy this position at the crossroads of the selected categories as factors of those identities in combination. As Crenshaw's initial elaboration of the concept of intersectionality in antidiscrimination law models, the next step of the analysis is to identify how the experiences of the selected group differ from the experiences of those who occupy other identity positions within the relevant categories. A problem with this method of analysis is that it "produces new subjects of inquiry that then infinitely multiply exclusion in order to promote inclusion," as Jasbir Puar writes on Rey Chow's question of whether the subject is even a viable place from which to produce politics.[13] If we consider that "concepts do not prescribe relations, nor do they exist prior to them; rather, relations of force, connection, resonance, and patterning give rise to concepts," then perhaps we take a different analytical approach to these categories outside the context of law: categories then function less as fixed attributes of subjects (as in law, per the epistemology of man), and instead as a matter of "events, actions, and encounters" that are not determining but contested (which can be understood as an invitation to contest them more deeply rather than as a throwaway or muddying observation, as often happens in the social sciences).[14]

The enumeration of infinite subject positions is a feature of the Muslim question, as Salman Sayyid articulates it. Much like the Jewish and Negro questions, the Muslim question "refers to a series of interrogations and speculations in which Islam and/or Muslims exist as a difficulty that needs to be addressed."[15] The Muslim question is itself a mode of inquiry.[16] One of its key tropes is "the problem of the Double Muslims and their difference from other Muslims."[17] Sayyid borrows from Richard Pryor's description of "Double Muslims" as one of several kinds of Black people in prison, including "the Mau Mau" and "Muslims." What distinguishes Double Muslims from the other kinds of people in Pryor's typology is that they "can't wait to get to Allah and want to take eight or nine" with them. They are that orientalist caricature of zeal, Sayyid observes, that is transformed into a "strangely liberating assertion of autonomy within the context of the American penal system."[18] Put in terms of Mahmood Mamdani's characterization of Bush's approach to the war on terror, Double Muslims are a case of Bad Muslims of the Good Muslim/Bad Muslim binary. My point here, however, is not simply to point out that there exist Muslims who behave, who serve US interests, and are thus good, in contrast to those who do not and are thus bad. The point is to identify the very fact of comparison of fixed types, or the enumeration of different subject positions, as a defining feature of the question of what to do with the problem that is Muslims. Making typologies of humans is a technique of analysis that fits well within this mode of inquiry.

Take, for example, the case of the label *Black Muslim* from the mid-twentieth century to the early twenty-first century. The term *Black Muslim* was once used to describe the Nation of Islam (NOI). C. Eric Lincoln coined the phrase in his 1961 book, *The Black Muslims in America*. The NOI was critical of the term as it became a way to dismiss the religious nature of the Nation and to characterize it as a solely political organization. They argued that it suggested their Islam was inauthentic or derivative, which was indeed the federal government's early characterization of the NOI.[19] Malcolm X and the NOI would argue that to be Black is to be Muslim, and so *Black Muslim* functions as both an insult and a redundancy.[20] *Black as Muslim* is a geographic and historic claim that flows from the reorientation that the mid-twentieth-century Muslim organizations sought to achieve: to understand themselves as having history and civilization prior to Western obliteration. Their identity is tied to an epistemological shift and is not based on man's history. They argued that the notions of history, civilization, and personhood supporting the racial order are fabrications relying on writing them out of civilization and humanity; and thus identities defined with reference to that history are fabrications as well. They did not do away with all language related to color and Western race, but redefined it in a way that disarticulated certain words from man's notions of history. For example, Malcolm X cites anticolonial movements in Asia as examples of "Black revolution" in his famous "Message to the Grassroots" speech along with such movements in Africa, which immediately suggests an understanding of *Black* that is not racial blackness.

Whereas *Black Muslim* was rejected by most of those whom it was used to describe in the mid-twentieth century, it is a term of self-identification for many in the late twentieth and early twenty-first centuries. Sunni and Shi'i Muslims of African descent, who rejected the term decades earlier due to its association with the NOI, came to adopt it in a different political context. In the context of the new and highly diverse demographics of Muslims after 1965 when the doors of immigration opened up to Asians, along with the rise of intersectional analysis and neoliberalism, the term became a valued self-identification to demarcate difference among Muslims. Why, now, is *Black Muslim* not understood as derogatory or as denying the religious commitments of Muslims of African descent, especially when intra-Muslim racism after 1965 involves questioning their piety and religious knowledge? Sylvia Chan-Malik's case for the term in 2018 points to "political insurgency," which "has always marked being at once Black and Muslim in the United States," and therefore, "it is critical to claim—not elide—this affiliation."[21] In this sort of analysis, intersectional in its structure, it is not necessary for a definition of Black or Muslim that differs from that of

US racial logic for a term to be transformative or powerful, unlike the basis of the NOI's rejection of the term decades earlier as a rejection of racial blackness as an identity.

Interestingly, the history of the resistance of groups like the NOI becomes a reason to accept the very phrasing they rejected. This suggests a change in the times, and, as we see in Bin Wahad's analysis of Shakur's designation, a change in political arguments. As Sayyid points out, Muslims are not immune to the excesses of the Muslim question; we use essentialist tropes to describe ourselves. This is because "the assertion of a Muslim identity occurs in a world in which there is no epistemological or political space for it."[22] But there is space for typologies, for what Sayyid calls the ontic perspective that enumerates Muslim types, for the creation of more and more types: not just along a good/bad binary, but with increased specificity and adjectives, in a move that, even when self-driven, may serve the purposes of taming and making legible on man's terms that "unruly aggregate" of Muslims.[23] This is where intersectional analysis, applied to understand Muslims, proceeds in step with the assumptions of the Muslim question, struggling to make an epistemological space for an assertion of Muslim identity on terms other than man's.

Other terms, such as those engaging Islamic theology as the basis of identity claims, for example, may have their own challenges as a potential site for alternative epistemologies informing ways of understanding ourselves politically when Islamic political theology is the stuff of radicalization theories according to self-styled experts on the subject. Thoroughly debunked, these theories of radicalization are nevertheless employed in counterterrorism efforts like "countering violent extremism." Does the repression of the global war on terror also involve the foreclosing of Islam as an archive from which alternative notions of humanity are possible, not only for Muslims but beyond, as an example of what Corey D. B. Walker calls "theological thinking," that have the ability to serve as a counterweight to the racism of man, much like the role of Islam in the lives and politics of those Black revolutionaries who explored Islam in the mid-twentieth century?[24]

Have concepts like intersectionality facilitated that foreclosure but with the appearance of providing an opening? The broad understanding of intersectionality as "analyses that foreground the mutually co-constitutive forces of race, class, sex, gender, and nation" has helped provide a place for analysis of Islamophobia in the liberal academy that is otherwise allergic to religion as ritual devotion but can accommodate it as the name for the racism faced by a distinct, racially subordinated identity group alongside others.[25] On this thinking of intersectionality and also racialization, distinction is important to establish—to be a distinct race with distinct forms of racism, with redress keyed to these distinctions, as the earlier discussion of the analytical structure of intersectional thinking shows. The phrase *Black Muslim* is one especially illustrative example of intersectionality: its structure of analysis and the limits of the questions it is possible to ask inside of intersectionality's terms when it comes to Muslims and Islamophobia in the United States. The questions are on distinction. For example: How do experiences of Black Muslims differ from those of Arab Muslims, South Asian Muslims, and so on?[26] One may further ask the same but about Black Arab Muslims, for example, who are not recognized in the aforementioned categories of analysis. New research in this area can only ask the same questions with new and different subjects along the lines of race, gender, sexuality, class, color, education level, and so on, and chart out differences between increasingly fine-tuned subject positions, "infinitely multiply[ing] exclusion in order to promote inclusion."[27]

The intersectional perspective that makes Black Muslim a valuable self-identity in the twenty-first century is also taken up as useful for what Hajar Yazdiha calls the Muslim immigrant rights movement. This movement has roots in the mid-1980s, consists of post-1965 Arab and South Asian immigrants and their second-generation children, and is led mostly by the wealthy among them. She argues that after decades of this movement shrinking away from Black politics while seeking the wages of whiteness through cultivating relationships with the conservatisms of the time, the 9/11 moment ruined their efforts. The strategy of the movement had to shift after 9/11. They shifted based on an understanding of themselves she calls "stigmatized but not like Black," and then a decade later to "racialized like Black," followed by the budding 2020s "also Black," which refers to the Muslim immigrant rights movement's recognition that there are Muslims in the United States who are raced as Black, and therefore, Muslims in the United States bear some relation to racial blackness because they are "also Black"; this recognition offers a pathway to belonging in the United States—to the degree and in the specific symbolic ways in which Black people belong in the United States. The "also Black" approach would come from "young, second-generation Muslims," who, "growing up alongside Black classmates," would be inducted into American history in schools and university campus politics.[28] As with Bin Wahad's critique of millennials, a marked generational difference is clear in how Muslim immigrants and their descendants think about who they are, as Neda Maghbouleh finds in the related case of Iranians. "As the American-born second generation [of Iranians] comes of age," for example, they are "eschewing the 'white' category altogether."[29] American universities are an important site for this self-fashioning. They teach and cultivate proper ways of embodying and performing identity, particularly hyphenated identities such as African-American, Asian-American, Iranian-American, Muslim-American, and so on.[30] Cultivation is precisely the task of universities, serving the function of forming global citizens for transnational capitalism.[31] Adolph Reed's charge that race as identity (and diversity on its basis) comes in to make class inequality more palatable finds strong evidence at the university.[32] This cultivation of properly embodied racial identity is contested. Students, faculty, staff, and university administration do not always agree on what it looks like, but that is part of the point. There is a possibility in these elite educational spaces of "societal critique as a mode of inclusion," as Yazdiha suggests, that this younger generation may be counting on when they take the "also Black" perspective.[33] The "also Black" perspective may be an example of the sort of calculus that "pleased their creators more than enlightened them," as Eqbal Ahmad put it.[34]

Although seemingly an improvement from earlier approaches of the Muslim immigrant rights movement that would rebuff the possibility of political alliance with Black people, both "like Black" and "also Black" are nevertheless conceptualizations of blackness as racial blackness.[35] It is worth asking the extent to which the stability of this conceptualization is responsible for the failures of Muslims in the United States to organize politically across difference. By seeking out racial blackness as a model, the movement is employing another iteration of race, but with racial blackness as its center or point of comparison rather than whiteness. This, too, is an inversion of Quetelet's average man: the margins of the bell curve become the locus of the new model human (much like Bin Wahad's Black Madonna), and the center of the bell curve is judged based on the degree to which it deviates from the new, once-marginal iteration of average man. Those in the margins move to the center; the model remains. This inversion of Quetelet's average man maintains the same overall logic in which there is a need for a central figure characterized by beauty and goodness, as he puts it, against whom all others are measured as deviant to some degree. Racial blackness is especially vulnerable to this inversion because it is the quintessential race category. This inversion is evident in other debates on racial blackness, for example, debates about who is the "new Black." For example, "Using a Critical Race Theory (CRT) analysis," legal scholar Adrien Wing argues that Arabs and Muslims "have been socially constructed as 'Black,' with the negative legal connotations historically attributed to that designation.... Racial profiling, which originated as a term synonymous with Blacks and police traffic stops, now equally applies to both Arabs and Muslims in many contexts."[36] Others like Khaled Beydoun, Saher Selod, and Erica R. Edwards argue against this idea that

"Muslims are the new Black," not because they believe that Arabs and Muslims avoid suffering and racial profiling but because of the place of racial blackness in a particular economy of knowledge.[37]

As Sylvia Wynter argues, it is not possible for blackness to be valorized in man's system of knowledge because it is a main referent for subordinated humanity; however, it is possible for blackness to be incorporated on man's terms in more sympathetic ways as a Human Other, perhaps as *the* Human Other, to whom something is owed, which can make that a symbolism that can be usurped for some benefit. After all, a central tension that makes Shakur's addition to the MWT list so effective as a spectacle is that her racial blackness is the very (official) definition of a race matter that can potentially itself make her innocent in the dominant "officially antiracist" terms that control "what counts as a race matter, an antiracist goal, or a truism about racial difference," thus making space for the argument that she does not belong on a terrorism list.[38] Race-based arguments open up certain possibilities and foreclose others. It is important to note, however, that to question the race-based arguments of the Muslim immigrant rights movement is not to automatically become untethered from the bloody realities of racist violence they face. Instead, a move away from accepting the terms of racial blackness opens up room for a more accurate understanding of that violence and the possibility of directing attention toward the conditions under which that violence takes place, which are shared in many respects because of the scope of capitalism, technological development, and other means that shrink the world.

THE ARGUMENT SEEKING TO establish that Muslims are a race or racialized intends to help make the case for redress for actual harms, and this argument can be seen in scholarship coming out of sociology, anthropology, legal studies, women's studies, American studies, and English.[39] As John Tehranian argues on the heavily interrelated case of "Middle Eastern Americans," they experience "relative invisibility and absence from civil rights dialogue" by making a "Faustian pact with whiteness" in which they "avoid discrimination at an individual level" while lessening "the ability of the community, as a whole, to systematically fight invidious discrimination and stereotyping in the long term."[40] Maghbouleh makes a similar observation in the case of "Iranian Americans" who "are not white enough to avoid racial discrimination but too white to have it legally redressed."[41] Where legal redress is connected to definition as a race, this amalgamated group, that goes by many names and acronyms—SWANA (South West Asian and North African), MASA (Muslim, Arab, and South Asian), AMSA

(Arab, Muslim, and South Asian), BAMEMSA (Black, Arab, Middle Eastern, Muslim, South Asian), Arabs and Muslims, Arab and South Asian Muslims, and so on—is unable to traverse what would appear to be an otherwise obviously useful path to redress. In this way, one might benefit from having a defined race. In the absence of an official race designated by the Office of Management and Budget at least until the 2030 US census that includes a new racial category called "Middle Eastern or North African," the argument that this amalgamated group is racialized has served other purposes.

For example, some scholarship on the war on terror makes clear that the project of establishing Muslims as a racialized group is not only about seeking legal redress but also for coalition building. Importantly, the space sought out for Muslims on the left in this argument is under the rubric of race, not religion, on the reasoning that classification as a religious group leads to a pathway for liberal inclusion, whereas classification as a race, or as racialized, allows for entry into radical antiracist political organizing. Junaid Rana explains this view: "In some ways Muslim racial becoming," which refers to a state of being in which Muslims are in a space that is neither here nor there, as always in the process of becoming a race but never making it so far as to be fully identified as such, "is about a kind of visibility in liberal political systems in which difference in multi-cultural structures is a veritable seat at the table of democratic inclusion, not as people of color but as people of faith. It is thus that the language of racism and hence antiracism is foreclosed in the possibility of organizing in terms of racial solidarity and broad-based multiracial alliance."[42] This argument for "race not religion" provides a way to smuggle Muslims into the concerns of the secular left given its stubborn aversion to religion while avoiding the association of religion-based politics with an undesirable liberalism (or a criminalized radicalism).[43] Along similar lines, racialization can function as a straightforward and easy concept to understand, exceeding the academy as it does. It may facilitate a kind of "strategic essentialism" per Gayatri Spivak.[44] In the world of advocacy and political organizing where citations do not follow every claim, the racialization invoked tends to match the definition offered by Michael Omi and Howard Winant that has been so useful for scholarly treatments of Muslims and race. It is a capacious definition in which racial meaning has to appear in some way in order for something or someone to be considered racialized; the bar is quite low and easily met.

We might briefly consider to what extent there is a difference between claiming a racial identity and arguing that one is racialized. Some would argue that the former is grounded in liberal multicultural identity politics, and the latter is merely a description of the obvious empirical reality of violence and discrimination. But attention to epistemology forces acknowledgement of the nonneutral terms of description that enable the problems we seek to address. Scientific race and the criminal identification practices reviewed in chapter 1 put forth description as well; the terms of description are tethered to state projects of controlling and managing its populations, and they are organized around the figure of a normal human. Further, as the earlier discussion of Muslim racialization research shows, the simple description of Muslims as racialized is a political claim, which means that its politics are to be considered. It is worth considering then whether making a case for Muslims as racialized is doing the work of race, whether the reliance on racial blackness is doing the work of sustaining racial blackness, and whether such work cannot be vindicated by the otherwise reasonable goal of redress. This is precisely the argument of Karen E. and Barbara J. Fields, who argue that belief in race is like belief in the geocentric model of the universe: it is either true, or it is not, no matter who holds this belief or what causes they put it toward. Although arguments can be made applying Fields and Fields's analysis to demonstrate Muslim racialization after 9/11, we may also ask if we are unwittingly colluding in the work of something like proving that the geocentric model is true because enough people believe it, in order to show that this falsehood has an impact.[45] As many of the thinkers I draw on in this book show, it is perfectly possible to show this impact without agreeing to operate inside the terms of race (see introduction).

What other paths may be possible if the work of providing proof of racialized identity is replaced by shattering the logic of race that creates the very conditions for which redress is sought? Is it possible that the former is not just a quicker and thus more desirable means of pursuing relief in the face of immediate threat, but rather that it is actively deepening the problem? In a context in which legible marginality means there is the possibility of redress, and in which certain ways of inhabiting marginal identities are given some direct attention by powerful institutions such as through university programming, it can be useful to assert proximity to racial blackness—that penultimate race. To readers steeped in the literature on the sociology of race, this line of argument may sound similar to the right-wing campaign against diversity policies and any sort of power gained by people of color, but my argument could not be more different. In other words, this is not to say that there is a privilege afforded to Black people in the United States that must be stripped bare for the sake of equality, per the conservative arguments; but it is to say that Black has become a sign, among many signs, under a neoliberal order that profits (socially, economically, and politically) off the production of marginality as desirable. If those of us against racism can face the fact of this development, we can deal with some of the contradictions under which we struggle and try to find a way out that does not just lead to a more attractive version of the same problem. The average man has a prominent place in the contradictions to be reckoned with. The Muslim immigrant rights movement's desire to symbolically move closer to racial blackness—without ceding the material benefits of proximity to racial whiteness—is the same logic of average man in that (1) its desires for whiteness and blackness accept the terms of man's racial ordering as legitimate ways of understanding oneself, and (2) its Islam is secularized by being pushed into the personal and private, made unable to inform an understanding of who one is, in any material, political context, aside from serving as the shared, inert feature of a group facing discrimination as Muslims.[46]

To shift away from racial blackness was, of course, the work of some of the major figures that shaped that important dimension of Islam in Black America. There is value in such a perspective, as this book has argued throughout, not only for a project of social change but, relatedly, as this chapter considers, for the practice of thought and explanation on terms that recognize the fictions that man's epistemology relies on to make its arguments about fact. Turning to a discussion of Assata Shakur's addition to the MWT list in 2013, I extend the critique in this section to the case of her terrorism designation to think further on racial blackness as innocence and the layers of fabrication needed to legitimize official designations of terrorism. Of course, many have argued that terrorism is poorly defined by the United States and other powerful and repressive states.[47] With this in mind, a reading of her posters does provide further evidence of the shaky foundation of any terror designation by the United States, but more specifically, it draws attention to the ways in which the wanted poster form and its average man help to make Shakur a symbol that can be used instrumentally for a range of political purposes.

Through the Most Wanted Program, 1980s–2021

Assata Shakur's journey through the Most Wanted program after her 1979 escape from prison is important for understanding the circumstances leading up to her addition to the Most Wanted Terrorist list in 2013. Despite the long attachment between terrorism and the political formations of which she was a part, as much research has documented, and despite the continual efforts of New Jersey state officials and police organizations to extradite her, the FBI did not add her to its MWT list immediately upon the list's availability in 2001.[48] In fact, after she surfaced in Cuba in 1984, published an autobiography, and lived a relatively public life there, she was not even actually represented on any FBI wanted list for the next two decades.⁴⁹ In between, from the mid-1980s until 2005, there was a silence in the FBI's archive of posters for her even as material pursuit continued.

This representational silence contrasts with the material pursuit of the federal government, the New Jersey state government, and collaborating police organizations. While Shakur lived as an asylee in Cuba in the late 1980s and '90s, and during a time when she was absent from the Most Wanted program, the US pursuit continued and proceeded in step with its efforts to oust Fidel Castro. The breakup of the Soviet Union, Cuba's struggling economy, and the passage of the March 1996 Helms-Burton Act all signaled US efforts to oust Castro. Castro's Cuba was a final stronghold in Latin America that was unique for its ability to operate independently of the CIA control that had toppled democratically established governments in Chile and El Salvador, among others. Castro's communist refuge was thus saturated with great significance in the Cold War. Some of the efforts to remove Castro invoked Assata Shakur. In March 1998, New Jersey congressman Robert Franks sponsored a congressional resolution calling on the Cuban government to extradite Shakur and other asylees. The Cuban government responded that their sovereignty meant that it was their right to grant asylum, particularly in the absence of an active extradition treaty, the existence of which was contested by the United States. The United States nevertheless added Shakur's return to their list of formal conditions for the normalization of diplomatic relations with Cuba. In addition to the federal government, the state of New Jersey and some of its police organizations, such as the State Troopers Fraternal Association of New Jersey and the New Jersey State Association of Chiefs of Police, have been persistent in demanding her return to the United States. The state of New Jersey has also circulated its own wanted poster of Shakur. Supporting the 1998 congressional resolution, New Jersey governor Christine Todd Whitman announced a $100,000 reward for Shakur's capture that was later raised to $150,000. Whitman wrote a letter to then president Bill Clinton on March 25, 1998, about "this brutal murderer [who] idylls in tropical splendor" and urged him "to make Joanne Chesimard's return to the custody of the State of New Jersey—and the extradition of all other fugitives Cuba harbors—a necessary first condition before any further steps towards a normalization with Cuba are taken."⁵⁰ The previous year, a New Jersey state police lieutenant wrote a letter to the pope asking him to pressure Cuba to extradite Shakur when he visited the island nation, to which Shakur penned an open letter to the pope in response. When the pope visited Cuba, Shakur allowed NBC's Ralph Penza to interview her for the network in a three-part series. The series, however, contrasted images of Shakur walking around Havana markets with footage of the mourning family of the police officer who died at the New Jersey Turnpike scene, making for a representation that fit what New Jersey police would later call a matter of Shakur "flaunting her freedom."[51]

During the summer of 2005, Republican New York congressional representative Pete King, chairman of the House Committee on Homeland Security, introduced an amendment to the Foreign Relations Authorization Act with Republican New York representative Vito Fossella to block normalization of relations with Cuba until Assata Shakur and William Morales of the Fuerzas Armadas de Liberación Nacional (FALN) were sent back to the United States.[52] The FBI Most Wanted program's Domestic Terrorism (DT) list was the basis of the July 20, 2005, amendment. Fossella explained, "And those two are not alone. The fact as we know it, while so many are oppressed under the communist regime, there are scores of people on the FBI terrorist watch list who live peacefully in Cuba." The amendment read, "(I) Dissemination of names of fugitives residing in cuba [sic].—Of the amounts authorized to be appropriated under subparagraph (A), an appropriate amount of such funds for each of the fiscal years 2006 and 2007 are authorized to be appropriated for the U.S. Interests Section, Havana, to disseminate the names of fugitives, such as Joanne Chesimard and William Morales, who are residing in Cuba, and any rewards for their capture."[53] Republican representative Robert Menendez of New Jersey spoke in strong support of the amendment. "This amendment simply requires the United States Interests Section in Havana to publicize the names of these fugitives and make sure Cubans are aware that there is a reward for helping them to bring these criminals to justice. The FBI is currently offering $1 million for Joanne Chesimard's capture. Mr. Chairman, $1 million is a very powerful incentive, but the incentive only works if people know about it."[54]

In short, state-level New Jersey and New York–area pressure for Shakur's return to the United States was more high-profile and relentless than the federal pressure until the post-9/11 years, but again, not immediately after 9/11. In the early years of the war on terror, she cannot be found in the FBI's public, celebrated archive of wanted posters. Starting in 2010 in honor of the sixtieth anniversary of its Most Wanted program, the FBI's website has maintained a list of the names and photographs of everyone who has ever been on the Ten Most Wanted list. On a page called "Ten Most Wanted History Pictures," each individual is numbered, from 1 to 506, as of 2022. This is the FBI's public archive of its Most Wanted program from which Shakur is absent. Black revolutionaries such as Jamil Al-Amin (H. Rap Brown), Angela Davis, and Twymon Myers are in this archive, numbered 308, 309, and 319, respectively. The FBI circulated wanted posters for Shakur in the 1970s and in later decades only in select regions, like Black neighborhoods in New York and New Jersey, but it appears they never deemed her high priority enough to either (1) place her on their Ten Most Wanted list, or (2) to preserve that record in their public archive.[55] Shakur is also absent from books on the FBI Most Wanted program, published in the early and mid-1990s and early 2000s, that display the names and descriptions of the Ten Most Wanted roster for those first forty or fifty years of the program. Shakur is further absent from the FBI's website for its first nine years until 2005.

This representational silence ends sharply in 2005, when the bureau added her to their Most Wanted program as a "featured fugitive" with a new poster calling her a "domestic terrorist" (figure 4.1) during a time when the bureau had a resurgence of interest in "domestic terrorism." In 2005, the FBI raised the reward from the state of New Jersey's $150,000 to $1 million, whereas her 1983 poster did not list a reward. The million-dollar reward listed on her 2005 poster was announced on an anniversary of the New Jersey Turnpike shootout, as her 2013 poster would be as well. The massive leap in reward money is rightly understood by her allies as intensifying the hunt. Importantly for this chapter, Assata Shakur's supporters challenged her terrorism designation. As Castro said in 2005: "They wanted to portray her as a terrorist, something that was an injustice, a brutality, an infamous lie."[56] The 2005 poster put her in danger. Once relatively safe in her home in Cuba, Shakur began moving about only secretly with the Cuban government's protection.[57] Hands Off Assata committees formed in several US cities. Essays came out: rapper Mos Def wrote an essay called "The Government's Terrorist Is Our Community's Heroine," and former Panther Kathleen Cleaver published "Why Has the FBI Placed a Million-Dollar Bounty on Assata Shakur?" in the *Independent*.[58] Both argued that the trial was unfair, that Shakur's fugitivity is in the tradition of escaped slaves and the criminalization of the Black liberation movement, and that it is Cuba's right to grant her asylum. The following year, in the fall of 2006, City College of New York students named a clubroom in the student center after Shakur and Morales. After pressure from a police association, the college administration backed off from their support of the students and removed the names from the clubroom entrance.[59] This was followed by a resolution from the New Jersey State Assembly supporting the removal of their names. Shakur's name and image came to be well represented on either side of the police barricade.

In 2006, the very same poster moved from Featured Fugitives to the program's newly created DT list. Although the word *terrorist* appeared on Shakur's poster while she was on a fugitive list in 2005, it is significant that she was

FIGURE 4.1. FBI wanted poster for Assata Shakur, 2005. Source: FBI.

moved to a crime-specific list (Domestic Terrorism) in 2006. Crime-specific lists tend to be smaller (see chapter 1). It is through these mundane categories and organizing features, like movement from one list to another, that the FBI can increase and decrease the attention and priority given to any wanted individual. The FBI uses these means in the twenty-first century to signal Shakur as an increasingly high priority terrorist, specifically, so her 2006 transition to a terrorism list suggests an escalation. On the DT list, she was next to Black and white antiwar activists and leftists until 2013, when she was moved to the higher-priority MWT list alongside about two dozen Muslim men whose officially racelessness is the subject of chapter 3. The composition of the DT list, compared to the MWT list, is also important for signaling priority. In 2006, two on the DT list are labeled "White (Hispanic)" and are wanted for their membership in a Puerto Rican independence group. Eight are "White" and wanted for "eco-terrorism," some as Earth Liberation Front / Animal Liberation Front (ELF/ALF) members, or antiwar resistance from the 1970s. Shakur is the only Black person on the DT list initially. More Black people are added later, some of them Muslim, like Ishmail Muslim Ali, but the list continues to have only people who are raced as "White," "Black," or "White (Hispanic)." Everyone else on the DT list is clearly of lower priority than she is, as only four of the total six to fourteen people on the list at any given time from 2006 to 2021 even have

TABLE 4.1. Assata Shakur's FBI Wanted Posters, 1972–2021

	Race	Clothing	"Terrorist"	List
1972*	Negro	N/A	No	N/A
1983	Black	Muslim or men's	No	N/A
2005	Black	African tribal	Yes	2005: Featured Fugitives 2006–13: Domestic Terrorism
2013	Black	African tribal	Yes	Most Wanted Terrorist
2019	Black	African tribal	Yes	Most Wanted Terrorist

*An identification order, not a wanted poster; see chapter 1 on the difference.

rewards for information leading to capture. Their rewards range from $50,000 to $250,000, in contrast to her $1 million reward.

Timothy Thomas Coombs is useful to briefly compare to Assata Shakur because both are accused of killing police and both have what the state considers radical politics, but on opposite ends of the political spectrum. He is one of those labeled white on the DT list, and he is the only right-wing political actor ever to be on the list over the period of this study from the list's beginnings in 2006 to 2021. He is a member of the right-wing Christian Identity Movement, and he is wanted for killing a police officer, like Shakur.[60] In the eyes of US law, these two people committed the same crime. However, Coombs's trajectory and Shakur's move in opposite directions in the FBI Most Wanted program. He is on the DT list for 2006 only, and then disappears from any FBI wanted list on their website until 2014, when he surfaces on the Additional Violent Crimes list—that is, not a terrorism list. Despite being wanted for killing a police officer, which is often a high-priority crime, Coombs seems to have shaken free not only of the Domestic Terrorism designation but of any kind of representation in the Most Wanted program at all for eight years. Meanwhile, Shakur stays on the DT list for seven more years before she is moved to the even higher-priority MWT list. Again, it is notable that she was not immediately added to the MWT list when it was made available in 2001, nor was she added to it in 2005 with the first new FBI poster for her since the 1980s. Despite the fact that the 2005 poster names her as a terrorist, the heading of her poster changes from "Wanted by the FBI" in 2005 to "Most Wanted Terrorists" in 2013, but the rest of the poster otherwise remains mostly the same (see table 4.1). The most dramatic representational change in 2013 is not on her poster itself (figure 4.2), but the backdrop, in the form of the other posters she appears next to (figure 4.3). The faces that surround her photograph on each of these lists—from Featured

FIGURE 4.2. FBI wanted poster for Assata Shakur, 2013. Source: FBI.

Fugitive, to Domestic Terrorism, to Most Wanted Terrorists—shift radically. As a most wanted terrorist, she is surrounded by many more Muslims, some in the leadership of Al-Qaeda, Egyptian Islamic Jihad, Tehrik-e-Taliban Pakistan, and more, who are wanted for providing material support for terrorist organizations, for conspiracy to murder a US national outside the United States, and other such charges.

Assata, the Symbol
Barbara Woodruff, an FBI special agent and spokeswoman, explains the decision to add Shakur to the MWT list in 2013: The FBI is "trying to bring the public's attention to the case," since "this case is 40 years old so there may be people who don't know anything about it."[61] By the time Assata Shakur was added to the MWT list in 2013, the Black Lives Matter movement was on the rise. The burgeoning movement had a special place for her due in part to its Black feminist commitments. It invoked her through slogans like "Assata Taught Me" and a chant quoting a letter she wrote from prison in 1973: "It is our duty to fight for

FIGURE 4.3. Photographs from the Most Wanted Terrorist list, 2013. Source: FBI.

our freedom. It is our duty to win. We must love each other and support each other. We have nothing to lose but our chains."[62] Taking notice of the timing of Shakur's addition to the MWT list in light of recent moments like Occupy Wall Street and Black Lives Matter, Angela Davis argued that the FBI was attempting to frighten a younger generation of activists who look up to her.[63] Indeed, the Shakur name represents different things to different generations. "To younger activists, it might represent the sagacity and defiance of Assata. To movement elders, it might represent Afeni or Mutulu."[64]

Woodruff's reference to those who did not witness the 1970s suggests a generational consideration. Woodruff continues to explain and pushes back against the view that the FBI are the ones who are being extreme with this move. "I don't think it's extreme to have her on this list.... Back in the '70s when the BLA were more active, they were looked at as part of an internal security investigation that *eventually would have morphed* into domestic security or domestic terrorism."[65] How is it possible for Woodruff to say that the BLA would have become terrorists, even though the bureau certainly considered them terrorists in the group's heyday? Perhaps this is an even more stilted version of what Lisa Stamp-

126 CHAPTER FOUR

nitzky observes is the already warped logic of preemption of the war on terror that plays with notions of time.[66] Under the logic of preemption, presumed terrorists are punished as terrorists for something they have not done but on the argument that they have not done it yet and eventually will, so they must be captured and stopped now. Woodruff's defense of the FBI's addition of Shakur to the MWT list in 2013, many decades after her conviction and prison escape, and with a younger generation in mind, suggests that the legacy of the Black liberation movement is at stake.

The legacy of the movement is precisely what Dhoruba Bin Wahad seeks to draw readers' attention to in his essay on Assata Shakur's terrorism designation. He argues that the FBI's purpose in adding her to this list is to criminalize Black resistance, specifically the Black liberation movement of the 1960s and '70s. However, this does not mean a symbolic criminalization of a closed chapter. He emphasizes that this criminalization is not in the past because (1) veterans of this movement are still political prisoners, and (2) the conditions that gave rise to the movement are still present. Thus it is a criminalization that is here and now. To misunderstand Shakur's terrorism designation and its context is to misunderstand the conditions in which we live. He critiques those who separate her from the movement and thus distort it and her, rendering her a symbol that is "disconnected as an activist, freedom fighter, and soldier of a legitimate anti-racist and anti-imperialist movement."[67] This making of Shakur into an icon comes at a particular time. She is made a Black Madonna during the Obama era—like Malcolm X and Martin Luther King Jr. during the Reagan–Bush era—and also a "decontextualized icon" from whom "nothing can be learned ... except timeless wisdom," which is "worse than useless for making sense of social life inside real history."[68]

Shakur's terrorism designation and posters shed light on the ways in which she has become a symbol for the right and left, for her enemies and her supporters, via the poster medium and its assumptions. The criminalization of resistance continues in the tradition of the early years of crime statistics recounted in chapter 1—the statistical modeling, measuring, and comparing to a hypervalued human.[69] The treatment of political dissent as crime (or as terrorism) recalls the anarchists targeted in those early years of crime statistics and anthropometry in which criminals were framed as problems not of politics but of individual deviance. Posters historically advertise deviance, going back to Alphonse Bertillon's development of mug shots and anthropometry to derive higher truths about the human based on bodily measurements and presentation. The medium of the FBI wanted poster as we know it is a racial form. It is racial not (only) for the (antiracist) political ideologies and causes it has been employed to squash; rather, the FBI wanted poster is racial in its particular sort of rational scientific epistemology establishing deviance and criminality in contrast to the presumed natural beauty and goodness of the average man.

Designed for one or a small handful of individuals, the atomizing medium of the wanted poster individualizes representationally and extracts people from their contexts, especially contexts like movements that are bigger than the individuals on any given poster, per Bin Wahad's critique. As Rachel Hall observed, the drama of these modes of display "derived from the filtering of the individual from the crowd" after the World War I era's growth of mass culture.[70] Although an older medium that can be traced back to the fourteenth century (in its prescientific rational form), the wanted poster form is consonant with the bureau's understanding of mid-twentieth-century Black politics. For the bureau, Black power was located in one or another messianic figure that could galvanize people and unify them, which also follows this criminological notion of individual power and culpability. This individual-focused logic allows for collective punishment. For example, the FBI and police beat down the doors of Black people's homes, destroying their possessions, battering and sexually harassing them in the name of finding just one wanted person.[71] Similarly, drones in the war on terror kill thousands, while sent in the name of targeting one or two people.

There is a making-exceptional of Assata Shakur as either an individual criminal or a singular heroine that shares a logic. In other words, the thought of her enemies and a set of her supporters are on the same model here: both assume and seek out a perfect subject. "People are always looking for heroes in the movement, especially in women," said Yaasmyn Fula, who worked with Afeni and Mutulu Shakur in the National Task Force for Cointelpro Litigation and Research.

> They're always looking for women to be superwomen, for Black women to be super warriors, and they were none of that. Afeni wasn't a superwoman. She just did superhuman things. It's the same with Assata. She wasn't a superwoman, but she did some superwoman damn things. That's what happens in the movement when it becomes hero worship and people are assigned these legendary characteristics. They're just regular people that are fighting because they believe so hard and so strongly in what they're fighting for.[72]

The hero framing distorts as much as the individual criminal frame, and a more accurate understanding considers what individual people were fighting for, where Fula redirects us, including the ways in which their fight does not lend itself to the innocence defense.

For supporters to make an argument for her innocence, Bin Wahad reasons, they have to argue that revolutionary violence, with its goal of self-determination, also did not happen and was merely an excuse for beefing up law enforcement. "What happened to Assata was but one part of a series of episodes during a systemic and coordinated campaign to crush a domestic revolutionary movement. A state of war existed between the state and that movement," he argues.[73] Criminalization, he shows, is collective and political, not individualized as scientific rational policing would see it. The innocence defense individualizes and also requires distortion of the movement. For the innocence defense, then, a possibly inconvenient reality enters here: the BLA did use violence against police, as other Black revolutionary movements did.[74] The innocence defense requires "dismiss[ing] the movement from which she emerged as a mere 'law enforcement fantasy' propounded to rationalize their illegal police actions and give them the cover of law."[75] In the liberal academy, revolutionary violence is fine theoretically, or as an artifact of the past, as long as it does not encroach on our present. This is an erasure of the movement in order to make it defensible, which is to say, closer to or on the model of the average man. Support for Shakur that requires her legal innocence may be guilty of accepting the terms of those who criminalize her—their narrative of the movement, and their conception of what counterterrorism is and what it means (see conclusion). The BLA's Coordinating Committee dismisses such terms in their special communique in 1980 on the occasion of Shakur's escape from prison: "In freeing Comrade-Sister Assata we have made it clear that such treatment and the 'criminal' guilt or innocence of a Black freedom fighter is irrelevant when measured by our people's history of struggle against racist u.s. domination."[76] Shakur's innocence, beyond the legal question of whether she killed that particular police officer, requires ignoring or distorting the scale and scope of violence of not only the movement but the conditions it was responding to. This distortion suggests a problem of thinking, cultivated by neoliberal diversity regimes and official antiracism. For example, literature by Black women, like Assata Shakur's autobiography, has been given the mission of diversity training.[77] Such developments make racial blackness innocent as compared to the political understanding of blackness, as a matter of consciousness, of the Black liberation movement. Again, my point is not to note the existence of good and bad types of blackness from the perspective of man, but to question the structure of knowledge producing such typologies in order to engage and understand them on different terms.

The analysis the Black liberation movement puts forth helps to create Black studies: a discipline that entered with an approach to thought that was promising as a counterweight to racial blackness. It is thus promising, too, for the Muslim immigrant rights movement and some others who have otherwise sought out racial blackness as a model. Rather than looking to racial blackness for a model, what if the original conception of Black studies, to which Islam is already connected, were a useful model for the Muslim immigrant rights movement?[78] Black studies in its original conception did not merely invert man's categories but challenged their full existence. The argument was that the very categories of man were fabrications that were to be parochialized, their assumed universality, neutrality, and truth pulled out from under them. Unevenly and incompletely, the movement for Black studies—the intellectual expression of the Black Aesthetics and Black Arts Movements—posed a substantive intellectual challenge to the epistemology of man.[79] Black studies' rejection of the presumed divinity of man is sometimes made explicit and is sometimes latent as an implication of work that has little interest in theology or that rejects such a category for thinking. Importantly, the role of religion in this Black studies pushback against the divinity of man is a matter of thought, and not mainly of (religious) identity. I am not arguing for the Muslim immigrant rights movement to throw its energies into developing more Critical Muslim studies or Muslim American studies units in an effort to borrow from Black studies as a model, but rather to model their attention to epistemology as linked to a project of social change. Such an approach would be rooted in an understanding of Islam as epistemological and relatedly an understanding of race that could identify the figure of man without identifying with that figure. The role of race would be as a thing rejected. Whereas political tactics like sit-ins and boycotts have been borrowed from Black movements, their rejection of man, which is to say their rejection of race, is part of the character of these movements. It is by moving against race that people like Elijah Muhammad and Malcolm X, whom Assata Shakur looked up to, made their engagement with Islam, rendering Islam especially powerful in the US context for the epistemological work of challenging race (chapter 2).

The question is whether we engage the logic of man to understand and move against the destruction it has wrought, which I argue enables it, or whether we engage other kinds of thought to build stronger explanations and alternatives. What could another epistemology bring about? What otherwise foreclosed options become available by a theoretical shift away from racial logic to account for racism and to challenge it? In what ways is this intervention happening now, but in modalities not understood as a challenge to racism because they are not trading in matters of fixed identity, that which is legible to Western epistemology?

CONCLUSION   *Race: Theirs and Ours*

In the months following the 2023 Al-Aqsa Flood, Israel killed and displaced even more Palestinians than in the Nakba that established the settler state seventy-five years earlier. The carpet-bombing and white phosphorus that Israel rained down on Palestinians made the previously densely populated Gaza into a "graveyard for children," as the United Nations chief reported. From starvation to mass graves at hospital sites uncovering Palestinians buried alive, the horrors unfolding are represented by Zionists as the activities of the true victims of the situation. They are victims of antisemitism—a type of racism. On this logic, Israel is an antiracist state and coming to its aid is antiracist. The genocide of Palestinians is then conducted with antiracism as its defense, if not itself as a series of antiracist acts. In this formulation, it is Palestinians who are racist. Antiracism for Palestinians on Israel's terms would be nothing short of death, denying their existence as a people, and full, willing concession of Palestinian land.

As the saying goes regarding friends and enemies: with antiracism like this, who needs racism? What is antiracism if genocide is one of its expressions? What does it mean that the moral righteousness accompanying the post–World War II consensus against racism—with the Jewish Holocaust as the defining moment of what *racism* is to mean—is shored up to legitimate genocide? Israel is not the first such state; as Mahmood Mamdani argues, it is the United States that invents the model that Israel builds on, a model in which ethnic cleansing is inherent.[1] The ideology of the older state of the United States, built on an idealized human representing the nation of the nation-state, echoes in the newer state of Israel. Benjamin Netanyahu's statement, "This is a struggle between the children of light and the children of darkness, between humanity and the law of the jungle," points to this model a bit too nakedly, perhaps, leading him to delete the social media post after pressure.[2] The Israeli defense minister's statement that Israel is "fighting against human animals" is similar.

This terrible moment, a moment that is both acute and longstanding, is a problem of categories used to conceptualize peoples, histories, land, rights, and violence. As this book has shown in its exploration of race, the problem of these categories is their structure and substance, not the fact of their existence, as categories are required for any kind of thinking. Eqbal Ahmad, a formidable critic of imperialism, including the knowledge apparatus supporting it, is useful here on the matter of categories of thought, particularly in his famous speech, "Terrorism: Theirs and Ours," delivered at the University of Colorado Boulder in October 1998. It was one of his last public talks in the United States and would go on to be printed and reprinted several times.

Eqbal Ahmad was born in Bihar, and the partition of India took him to Pakistan in 1948. Educated at Foreman Christian College in Lahore, at Occidental College, and eventually at Princeton, he joined the National Liberation Front in Algeria in his PhD years. Algerians were among the many colonized people alongside whom he was in struggle, and he helped to research the script for the famous film *The Battle of Algiers* (1966). He took a stand against the Vietnam War and the occupation of Palestine as a "relentless opponent of militarism, bureaucracy, ideological rigidity and what he called 'the pathology of power,'" as Edward Said wrote in Ahmad's obituary.[3] As one of the Harrisburg Seven, Ahmad was put on trial and eventually acquitted of charges including conspiracy to kidnap Henry Kissinger. Toward the end of his life, he sought to establish an alternative university in Pakistan. Steeped in revolutionary theory, Ahmad was deeply invested in the project of knowledge production, studied strategy, and discipline in pursuing goals. He emphasizes thought since "wrong premises do not usually produce right policies."[4] That is one of the main points across his work and in "Terrorism: Theirs and Ours."

There is much in Ahmad's speech that resonates with the critical post-9/11 reader. Some have looked to his speech as prophetic and eerily predictive of the post-9/11 global war on terror that he would not live to see. At the same time, there is much in his approach that may feel distant to readers who are critical of the post-9/11 war on terror; his thinking is simply different not only because it was not delivered in the post-9/11 context but also because his thinking avoided the traps of defensiveness, convenient falsehoods, and abstract moralism. For Ahmad, terrorism is to be condemned. In effect, he condemns all terrorism. This, too, differs from the position that those critical of the post-9/11 war on terror take when they react to the coercive post-9/11 condemnations of terrorism extracted from Muslims and others imagined as inherently terrorist. His goal is not to defensively condemn terrorism in order to get the state off his back. Nor does he try to define it in ways that lead to certain kinds of analyses. Instead, he sees terrorism as a tactic that should be "treated for what it is."[5] He uses a simple *Merriam-Webster's Collegiate Dictionary* definition of terrorism as illegal or extraconstitutional violence intended to coerce. He offers analysis of terrorism discourse, the material violence called terrorism, and its significance not in a vacuum defined only by an abstract morality but relative to broader politics and thought. In doing so, he offers a deep reading of how to move through analysis about a contentious topic for which many abandon basic logic and their capacity for complex thought, believing that condemnation of terrorism is a simple question that has a moral high ground claimable only by state officials, on their terms, rather than a question the rest of us may engage on other terms.

There is much to admire about Ahmad's speech, starting with the title's *theirs* and *ours*. They do not refer to actions called *terrorism* taken by either them or us (whomever that may be). In fact, *theirs* and *ours* do not rely on fixed groups of people called *them* and *us* at all. Instead, the title's *theirs* and *ours* refer to two different views of terrorism. *Theirs* is the official view, and *ours* is what he explicates over the course of the speech. *Ours* seeks explanation and analysis in order to establish the nature of the problem that is called *terrorism* and what is to be done about it. In contrast, *theirs* offers little by way of coherent analysis. What analysis *theirs* does offer is inconsistent and full of holes. This inconsistency in analysis is directly connected to the actions officials take. Officials go to war quickly and intensely against *terrorism*, without a consistent definition for what they are even fighting. This inconsistency gives them room to wage war as capriciously as they wish by condemning terrorism that does not serve their interests while applauding terrorism that does. As Ahmad explains, *ours* seeks explanation and analysis toward developing revolutionary goals and some discipline to carry them out. This requires clear and consistent thinking. The point is to "analyze and exploit the contradictions and vulnerabilities" of the oppressive force while not succumbing to their view that would repeat their repressive tactics or capitulate to their power.[6] *Theirs* and *ours* are not an inverse of the same, or two sides or poles on a spectrum; rather, they represent different terms of thought. It is this defining feature of "Terrorism: Theirs and Ours" that is especially useful for what might be called *race: theirs and ours*, for the task of summarizing the central tensions and debates in *No God but Man*. The distinction between *theirs* and *ours* captures this book's concern with the distortion of material reality and obliterating knowledge and peoples in service of useful falsehoods like the concept of race itself.

As Ahmad's *theirs* is the official view of terrorism, *race-theirs* is the official view of race. *Race-theirs* is the work of nineteenth-century man of science Adolphe Quetelet; Alphonse Bertillon, who adopts Quetelet's average man in policing; and the FBI, which uses Bertillon's organizational model (chapter 1). *Race-theirs* is man: an epistemology that overvalues one way of being human at the expense of all others, where the world is known or knowable through this distinction. And like Ahmad's *theirs*, *race-theirs* is built on falsehoods, on obliterating material history and peoples, which makes the social scientific concept of social construction rather feeble for capturing this reality. This emphasis on analysis and explanation, in the spirit of Ahmad, in the service of transformation, also drives the critique in *No God but Man*. Put in Ahmad's terms, it can be said that this book challenges *race-theirs* and looks to strengthen *race-ours*.

Race-ours seeks explanation and analysis to build a foundation for other ways of understanding, producing, and organizing knowledge; for other ways of understanding human difference; and for other ways of understanding the violence committed in its name. This is a foundation built on a commitment to good-faith attempts to perceive material reality rather than locating convenient falsehoods. It understands the task as the development of alternative terms of description, as Sylvia Wynter argues: a new science.[7] Since race is epistemological, structured by the subject-object relation, it is the very terms of description, not merely their deployment, that are the problem.[8] Description in racial terms captures X's distance or, more specifically, deviation from the hypervalued human. *Race-ours* is not a given but an ongoing project and effort building on earlier efforts.

Race-theirs and Ahmad's *theirs* have a lot in common when it comes to the distortion of reality. Ahmad points out that terrorism is widespread—tangible, material violence intended to coerce. But he says that *theirs* refuses to identify it everywhere that it actually exists and instead only does so selectively in ways that serve its interests. He condemns this selectiveness and the atrocity it allows. The problem is not just the fact of the inconsistency but the process, the knowledge-related process, by which that violence is made possible. *Race-theirs* operates similarly. It identifies racism and antiracism in ways that serve it (as in the case of Israel) or by defining some aggregates as races and not others depending on what serves it (see chapter 3 and the case of raceless Muslims on the FBI Most Wanted Terrorist list). This inconsistent classification practice, far from being reflective of material reality, allows the contradictory claims of *race-theirs* to be employed for whatever purpose is desired.

Intrepid inventors of the terrorism discourse so firmly attached to Palestinians, Zionists have worked hard to craft a narrative on the model of *theirs*, both *terrorism-theirs* and *race-theirs*. Israel is a shining example of *race-theirs*. Like much contemporary *race-theirs*, it is buttressed by antiracism, specifically the claim that it is a fortress providing protection from antisemitism. The claim that Israel is challenging racism is, of course, an absurdity that becomes clearer and clearer with each mutilated body pulled from the rubble. Some might respond to this situation by trying to reclaim antiracism away from Israel's understanding of it. However, it is worth raising the question: Would reclamation be an effort to claim something that is based on the falsehood of race anyway and thus not worth using as an analytical or political category to make the case for why mass killing, maiming, and dispossession must stop? The case of Israel indeed shows us how urgent it is that we distinguish and differentiate categories, but not between racism and antiracism; rather, between the structure of thought that legitimates Israel, using whatever words, and the structures of thought that condemn it. The structure of thought that legitimates it is the no-god-but-man epistemology that gives this book its title. That structure of thought is based on the establishment of a hypervalued type of human at its center called man, or the average man for Adolphe Quetelet, *Man2* for Sylvia Wynter, or the noble man for R. A. Judy. As Wynter says, that human is overrepresented and seen as the only and ultimate way of being human. As Quetelet says in so many words, the average man is a figure defined by beauty and goodness, and deviations from the average man are unnatural to varying degrees. Israel, too, establishes one type of human—European Jews—as a model human. Zionists define Jewishness in a way that creates a permanent victim, a hero figure, an innocent figure capable of receiving Western sympathy. On the model of Quetelet's figure characterized by beauty and goodness, that victimhood is fixed. Its victimhood is perpetual, regardless of a change in enemy, such that centuries of European *pogroms* against Jews differ little from the *utterances* of Palestinians occupied by Israel. The difference between representation and reality, or between a trope and a drone, as Mohammed El-Kurd puts it, is not a distinction worth making for *race-theirs*.[9] The case of Israel tragically shows that racism and antiracism are not so different from one another when they share a knowledge base and structures of thought that maintain a center and a periphery, as in Wallerstein's similar model.

This model of man, with different figures at the center and with different language, is replicated in analysis and explanation throughout much progressive, radical, and leftist thought, reminding us once again of the urgency of careful and critical analysis like Ahmad's. Marx, for instance, would favorably cite Quetelet in *Capital: Volume I* and use similar notions of the disappearance of errors, or those workers who deviate from the average worker, where each industry has its own average worker, just as each nation has its own average man, per Quetelet.[10] Marx's ultimate average worker is the western European male proletarian at the center of his thought. Another example of how man appears is in the familiar progressive call to "center" one or another political subject in academic analysis, in the representation of social movements, in protests, and in debates among activists. The organizational model of a particular type of human at the center and others at the margins is the exact model of Quetelet's average man on the bell curve. Contemporary theorizations of race and difference, like those using the concepts of racialization and intersectionality analyzed in chapter 4, also build their thought and political agendas on the foundation of man. This foundation is a problem not just for its political implications, but also because it is a case of what Ahmad calls wrong premises: using man's categories results in incoherence and weak explanatory power, as chapters 3 and 4 point out. My interpretation of the racelessness of Muslims on the FBI Most Wanted Terrorist list, in keeping the terms of *race-ours*, would forbid an analysis characterizing their racelessness as itself a case of racialization. The latter (1) does man's work of defining inside of his frameworks and (2) does not allow us to perceive the significance of racelessness in and of itself. Race theory is committed to ontology and a fixity that its critical versions also fall victim to at times; a way to protect against this is to revisit the false premises that make those ontologies possible. If there is any desire for other modes of organized human life, then race has to be condemned not merely on its surface, or in inconsistent ways as the official view does, but more deeply as Ahmad does with terrorism.

Another related example of the replication of man is visible in critical thinking on race in sociology, which often uses Quetelet's approach to knowledge. That approach involves determining the average man (white) and mapping the ways in which all others deviate from him to some degree (various nonwhites). In doing so, such work uses Quetelet's model while attempting to challenge the ravages of this model. The critique of racism sits atop the model and does not make its way to the epistemology of the model. Such critiques use the same epistemology as Quetelet to try to reach the opposite conclusion. All of this is not to say that thinkers in these areas are unaware of the structuring force of man. Many thinkers in the academy—and in movements ranging from Black cultural nationalist to abolitionist, feminist, and labor—have identified the risk of replicating what they seek to challenge.[11] They have argued that to continue to think inside the terms of these categories is to remain trapped by them, if unwillingly. The trap can appear attractive but must be struggled against, and the way to do that, as Ahmad reminds us, is by maintaining some fidelity to clear, consistent, and critical thought.

Throughout his writings, Ahmad holds revolutionaries to a high standard in their actions and in the integrity of their analysis. This characterized his thought and politics, and his relentless principle is emphasized by all who knew him and think with him. Ahmad's high standard for revolutionaries indicates a careful, thoughtful rejection of the dangerous idea that *ours* is a view that is correct simply because it is held by us (whomever that may be) and that, as such, whatever we may do, including the use of terrorism as a tactic, is right or justifiable because it was done by us. When a member of the audience listening to his speech suggests that the use of the tactic of terrorism by *us* is purified by its use toward revolutionary goals, Ahmad passionately explains that the listener has misunderstood him. In other words, Ahmad critiques the logic of *reclamation*.

There is much precedent for doing the same when it comes to race: for thinking outside the terms of race, as an analytical choice, and for rejecting it as something that cannot be reclaimed. For example, that is the work of the original conception of Black studies—tied to Third World and anticolonial understandings of blackness rather than a racial Queteletian understanding of blackness. It is also the work of many thinkers I build on in this book, as the introduction outlines. This precedent also lies in the choices Assata Shakur made in her trial for the killing of a police officer in the 1970s (chapter 2), when she engaged Islam as an alternative modality of blackness militating against the (racial) blackness of white creation. Other examples include Palestinians, in their most intense moments of suffering, crying out to God and reminding Israel (which again is on the theological model of man that has replaced God in the order of knowledge) that it is not God. Because man also involves the centering of an idealized human with regard to gendered and sexual order, capitalism and its class structure, theology, and really any number of infinite kinds of difference, moving against man, or *race-theirs*, can take many different languages. But what is important to identify is whether *race-theirs* really challenges the structure of thought itself, which is an idealized human at the center and all others deviant to some degree.

The temptation of reclamation is a great challenge to *race-ours*. Specifically, to try to reclaim race is to try to use the concept of race to fight racism, as is common in much contemporary antiracism. To retain race in self-proclaimed antiracism allows the fabrications of race to continue. Worse, they continue with the blessing and enthusiasm of those whose subjugation is rationalized by this fabrication of race. No reclaimed iteration of the race concept, and no change of central figure at the heart of it, can provide an alternative to the world that race enables, as Ahmad argues of terrorism. When these fabrications are allowed to continue, what ensues is a particular kind of antiracism that is both defanged and dangerous because of the transformative possibilities it forecloses and the legitimacy it lends to those foundational fabrications. Indeed, reclamation is the path to Israel.

Ahmad's *ours* and my version of *race-ours* are neither perfect nor pure. In fact, the claim to perfection is what they regard as damaging, because perfection is not possible and is instead a declaration of innocence, an innocence not really substantiated, an innocence that legitimates and enables action with impunity, a privilege afforded to false omnipotent-gods, victim-gods, and so on. The point instead is to continue in the tradition of those in these pages who understand that the urgent problem before us is not just the application of man's concepts but the very terms of description that constitute them. To think in this tradition is to understand that *ours* cannot operate within the terms of *theirs* and expect different results, and that the struggle for *ours* continues.

Notes

INTRODUCTION

1. Jeffreys-Jones, *The FBI*; Johnson and Weitzman, *The FBI and Religion*; Theoharis, *The FBI*; O'Reilly, *"Racial Matters"*; Gage, *G-Man*; Martin, *The Gospel of J. Edgar Hoover*.

2. See Cole, *Enemy Aliens*, for more on other sorts of lists, such as the FBI's Security Index (p. 102), and the custodial detention list circa World War II (p. 93).

3. The FBI Most Wanted program website, which is the central location for wanted posters dating from the 2000s, has hundreds of other posters that are not included in the analysis here. There are posters of missing persons, as well as posters for events featuring several unnamed individuals who are wanted in connection with the event but not charged with any crimes. To the extent that missing persons, specifically, need to be identified, the format of their posters is the same as the wanted posters.

4. In 2002, it was called Seeking Information—War on Terrorism; in 2012, it was called Seeking Terror Information; and from 2015 until 2020, it was called Seeking Information—Terrorism.

5. On Bosnia as an early and important battleground in the global war on terror, see Li, *The Universal Enemy*.

6. Hussain, "The Sound of Terror."

7. There is a valuable scholarly literature tracking cases in which groups fall out of whiteness or become white, but this is not a directly comparable case. See Brodkin Sacks, "How Did Jews Become White Folks?"; Gualtieri, *Between Arab and White*; Ignatiev, *How the Irish Became White*; Haney-Lopez, *White by Law*. In sociology specifically, see Maghbouleh, *The Limits of Whiteness*.

8. To be sure, finding an explanation is a challenge considering the secrecy of an entity like the FBI. The power of an explanation also depends on what is deemed acceptable as a source and how it is interpreted—the words of the FBI? The thought process of the person making these posters? The press releases of the bureau when announcing new additions to their lists? These sources of explanations have their limits as well, since the FBI is interested in maintaining a positive public image and is also not a neutral provider of information. Because this book's interest is in race theory, the nature of the explanation for

the missing race provided in this book concerns what race means such that there is racelessness in this case.

9. The FBI is an example of what Ann Morning describes as an institution that will "interpret, act upon, and transmit to the public scientists' concepts of race" (Morning, *The Nature of Race*, 192). My argument, however, is not that the FBI or the state as a whole put forth one coherent definition or conceptualization of race, as Morning and others have also pointed out (see Goldberg, *The Racial State*, 182–83), noting important differences in the definitions of race in the census as compared to the legal system, for example.

10. Further, the establishment in 2024 of a MENA (Middle Eastern and North African) category on the 2030 US Census, after years of Arab American advocacy for it, is a logical conclusion to the debates that pushed race to the forefront as a useful concept for post-9/11 organizing against Islamophobia.

11. Cainkar, "Fluid Terror Threat"; Silva, *Brown Threat*.

12. Denvir, "Revisiting *Racecraft* with Barbara and Karen Fields."

13. On the benefit of analyzing media forms rather than only media representations to understand race, see Towns, *On Black Media Philosophy*.

14. Cole, *Suspect Identities*.

15. Hoover, "Criminal Identification."

16. Hoover, "Criminal Identification."

17. Moten, "Of Human Flesh."

18. I use *man* interchangeably with *average man*, *noble man*, *Man2*, and other such versions unless I am giving a genealogy or more detailed discussion of one in particular, like the average man in chapter 1. See chapter 1 and the conclusion on the similarity between these versions of man.

19. Bhattacharya, "Somapolitics."

20. Bhattacharya, "Somapolitics," 136.

21. Wynter, "On How We Mistook the Map for the Territory."

22. Quetelet, *A Treatise on Man*, 74.

23. For a critique of these metaphors, see Hickman, "Globalization and the Gods."

24. Dussel, *The Theological Metaphors of Marx*, 166.

25. Assata Shakur Defense Committee, February 14 and 21, 1977, box 1, folder 15–16, Majority Report Research Files, Articles, Statement, Bulletins, Newspaper, Tamiment Library and Wagner Labor Archives, NYU; *Attica News*, p. 2, box 8, folder 5, Assata Clippings, Tamiment Library and Wagner Labor Archives, NYU.

26. Box 1, folder 15, Majority Report Research Files, Articles, Statement, Bulletins, Newspaper, Tamiment Library and Wagner Labor Archives, NYU.

27. Jackson, *Islam and the Blackamerican*.

28. Box 1, folder 15, Majority Report Research Files, Articles, Statement, Bulletins, Newspaper, Tamiment Library and Wagner Labor Archives, NYU.

29. Johnson, *African American Religions*, 299–300.

30. Robinson, *Black Marxism*, 82.

31. Robinson, *Black Marxism*, 82.

32. Robinson, *Black Marxism*, 67–68.

33. Robinson, *Black Marxism*, 67–68.

34. Judy, *DisForming the American Canon*.

35. There is a need for understanding "the *actual* interaction between Britons and Muslims," and not only representations of Muslims in English plays and literature, for Nabil Matar, whose work on the relations between Muslims and Britons in the Age of Discovery is relevant here (Matar, *Turks, Moors, and Englishmen*, 7). He notices a contrast between those multidimensional, actual interactions, and the one-dimensional English representations of Muslims. Piracy was one of several sites of actual encounter between Britons/settlers and Muslims. The other ways, during the English Renaissance and its Age of Discovery, that Britons had real encounters with Muslims, specifically Turks and Moors, were trade in English, Welsh, and Mediterranean ports, and ambassadors' and emissaries' visits to London; Britons helped transport Muslims to Hajj when the latter were threatened by Maltese pirates; and Britons could be found as fighters on Barbary pirate ships, as well as among those enslaved by Barbary pirates. "To numerous Britons, the Turks and Moors were men and women they had known, not in fantasy and fiction, but with whom they had worked and lived, sometimes hating them yet sometimes accepting or admiring them" (5–6). Evidence of actual interaction appears in prison depositions and captives' memoirs, among other sources. Actual interactions with Muslims in Britain, North Africa, and the Levantine region were characterized by "familiarity along with communication and cohabitation," but "in literature and theology, and thus in the emergent ideology of early modern Britain, the Muslim was depicted as occupying a place beneath the civilized European/Christian" (14). Notably, and similar to my argument about FBI representations of the Muslim in the war on terror, this was the "construction of an image that was independent of and contrary to empirical evidence," and understanding that gap between reality and representation is critical for understanding the work of the representation (14–15). An important example is in the representation of "Barbary pirates." The word *Barbary* originates in the Greek and Latin *barbarus*, referring to the foreign and uncivilized (see Ben Rejeb, "Barbary's 'Character' in European Letters"). Although the term had existed prior to the early modern period, it was not until that time that English and other European writers began to use the term for Muslims of the Ottoman Empire and North Africa, "paradoxically when [European writers] had access to extensive and reliable information about the advanced, not 'barbaric,' military and historical civilization of the Muslim Empire" (Matar, *Turks, Moors, and Englishmen*, 15). European hopes for conquering the Muslim were central to this characterization. It did not reflect a material reality of domination; it was aspirational, and the idea of barbarism helped this desire along. The idea of barbarism linked the Muslim with Indian "savages," which had become superimposed on one another in late seventeenth-century English thought and ideology (170). Materially, "in the Muslim world... the Muslims were religiously and militarily powerful, were widely influencing English culture, and were dictating their own terms of commercial and industrial exchange" (15–16), whereas Indigenous people in the Americas had been conquered. Despite these critical material differences between the Muslim and the Indian, this European reading of them together was transferred into colonial discourse by the eighteenth century (170). Europeans rationalized their domination of Indigenous people through the idea that they were barbaric;

but "Britons categorized the Muslims as barbaric even though they, the Britons, had not dominated them" (14–15). Thus, Britons produced "a representation of a representation" (15) based on a representation of Indigenous peoples of the Americas as Indians (a European construct, a distortion). The goal was to position Muslims in their worldview in a way that was convenient for their goals. The wish for domination of Muslims shaped European representations of the Muslim as though already conquered like the Indian. As Lotfi Ben Rejeb writes, "It is an extraordinary ideological feat in literature," as one site of representations of the Muslim, "for concreteness to be so abstracted and abstraction then presented as concreteness, fancy as reality" (Ben Rejeb, "Barbary's 'Character' in European Letters," 352–53).

36. Newton, *Revolutionary Suicide*, 178.

37. Along similar lines, Vincent Lloyd argues that Huey P. Newton presented a "black political theology as critique of idolatry" (Lloyd, *Religion of the Field Negro*, 196).

38. Newton, *Revolutionary Suicide*, 179.

39. Newton, *Revolutionary Suicide*, 179.

40. Some religious studies scholars emphasize continuity and the legitimacy that comes with a long genealogy of Islam, while others emphasize the creative agency of later generations in forming an Islam of their own. On this debate, see Adhami, "W. D. Muhammad's Hermeneutics"; Dorman, *The Princess and the Prophet*; Curtis, *Islam in Black America*. This debate is often concerned with the place of agency, but for me the case made by those with the long genealogy view is especially interesting for their argument against the religious dimension of race.

41. Fields and Fields, *Racecraft*, 17.

42. Quijano, "¡Qué tal raza!"

43. All take seriously that the fabrication of race has real effects, as they show how the world as we know it is organized racially; the contradiction between race as fabrication and race as having real effects is a limitation not of their arguments, but of the concept itself. On *mention* versus *use*, see Goldberg, *Racist Culture*, viii.

44. Shelby, *We Who Are Dark*.

45. Adolph Reed argues that "black power activism's sole critical category was race," so "radicals were generally unprepared to respond when the new, mainstream black political elite gained momentum in the late 1960s and began to consolidate a new kind of racially assertive but still accommodationist politics" (Reed, "The Allure of Malcolm X," 204). There is a difference, as Reed also notes, between what race meant for Black power compared what it means for this Black political elite. Black power's race analysis is tied to material politics, which Reed praises. To this I add that *race* may be the same word, but the difference in what it makes reference to for Black power versus the Black political elite is critical for my analysis. The religious dimensions of the materialist race concept that Black power used and their understandings of human difference may have potential to challenge the accommodationism that Reed rightly critiques.

46. Rana, "No Muslims Involved."

47. Rana and Rosas, "Managing Crisis," 225.

48. Appiah, "The Uncompleted Argument," 35.

49. Omi and Winant, *Racial Formation in the United States*, 108.

50. A representative example of one such definition of racial identity: "Racial identity is more than a mere performance of culture, more than the fact of skin color, and more than phenotype. It is also shared history, an ancestry, and community connection, a bricolage of internal and external practices, and subjectivation. It is dynamically co-created by the practices of gender, sexuality, and class." Choudhury, "Racecraft and Identity," 14.

1. *L'HOMME MOYEN* AND AMERICAN ANTHROPOMETRY

1. An 1893 meeting in Chicago resulted in the creation of the National Chiefs of Police Union. In 1902, it changed its name to the International Association of Chiefs of Police.

2. King, "Foreword," v.

3. Hoover, "Criminal Identification."

4. Sekula, "The Body and the Archive," 19; Sarton, "Preface to Volume XXIII," 14. See also Hacking, *The Taming of Chance*, on key differences between Comte and Quetelet. Quetelet took much of Comte's work, including the term *social physics*, and used it in ways Comte would strongly dislike. Comte was more interested in the historicist terrain of moral science, Hacking argues, while Quetelet explored the numerical terrain (39). Relatedly, Comte did not think of the normal (which for Quetelet would distill down to *average*) as a statistical idea while Quetelet did, being among those who would go on to make "normal" the "premier statistical idea of the late nineteenth century" (144–45). For more on Quetelet and sociology, see Beirne, "Adolphe Quetelet and the Origins of Positivist Criminology"; Beirne, *Inventing Criminology*; Lazarsfeld, "Notes on the History of Quantification."

5. Lazarsfeld, "Notes on the History of Quantification," 194.

6. Goldthorpe, *Pioneers of Sociological Science*, 1.

7. Quetelet, *A Treatise on Man*, 6.

8. Porter, *The Rise of Statistical Thinking*, 42.

9. Hankins, *Adolphe Quetelet as Statistician*.

10. Lazarsfeld, "Notes on the History of Quantification," 295.

11. Donnelly, *Adolphe Quetelet*.

12. Donnelly, *Adolphe Quetelet*.

13. Hacking, *The Taming of Chance*, 112.

14. Quetelet, *A Treatise on Man*, 96.

15. "While social physics has been acknowledged for its direct influence on Galton, Pearson, Lombroso and Durkheim and its indirect influence on Darwin, Comte and Maxwell, it has just as often been treated as an absurd overextension of a quantifying fetish. At its worst critics derided a philosophy of crude materialism and determinism. At best, more sympathetic readings saw *l'homme moyen* as an unfortunate diversion on the road to the more mature social sciences of the late nineteenth-century." Donnelly, *Adolphe Quetelet*, 135.

16. Moten, "Of Human Flesh," 260.

17. My use of Quetelet in this book is not as a hero or antihero figure himself, or as singularly responsible for the trajectory leading to wanted posters, but as having a specific contribution whose argument I am focusing on. However, the institutional aspects are

important, and Libby Schweber's book is useful for this while taking a similar approach. Her approach, she argues, differs from that of Latour, who says to follow the scientists to identify the heterogeneous sets of entities and alliances involved in establishing scientific fact and theory. Whereas he uses individual trajectories to document scientific claims, she uses individual trajectories to explore institutional contexts in which scientists promoted their projects, seeking recognition. She notes that Latour's approach could be taken as support for a heroic story of a great individual. Instead, these men of science may be used as "heuristic devices to sketch out the contours of the world in which they worked ... to identify the social and epistemological logics informing the French and British practice of national population statistics." Schweber, *Disciplining Statistics*, 10.

18. Johnson and Weitzman, *The FBI and Religion*, 15.

19. An example of how the logic of the average man guided FBI ways was that Hoover demanded that FBI agents maintain a particular weight. If he deemed them overweight or underweight, they would need to make adjustments accordingly to fit into the range Hoover determined. Gage, *G-Man*.

20. Ginzburg, "Clues," 113.

21. In one argument Quetelet makes for the use of the average man for the state, he studies the distributions of heights of "100,000 French conscripts [which] shows a close agreement between the actual distribution: a congestion below the required height and a scarcity just above it indicate that some 2000 have escaped service by reducing their height two or three centimeters. Thus he finds not only confirmation but a practical use of the conception that there is a type-man from which all men are but variations." Hankins, *Adolphe Quetelet as Statistician*, 65–66.

22. See Krüger, Daston, Heidelberger, *The Probabilistic Revolution, Volume 1*; Kruger, Gigerenzer, and Morgan, *The Probabilistic Revolution, Volume 2*. On political arithmetic versus descriptive "styles of reasoning" and how Quetelet developed a third form of statistical reasoning, see Schweber, *Disciplining Statistics*.

23. Hacking, *The Taming of Chance*, 3.

24. Gordon, "Race, Theodicy, and the Normative Emancipatory Challenges."

25. Long, "The Humanities and 'Other' Humans," 324.

26. Long, "The Humanities and 'Other' Humans," 324.

27. Long, "The Humanities and 'Other' Humans," 327.

28. Quetelet is sensitive to "the charge of materialism" and mentions it several times in *A Treatise on Man*. "Certainly, the knowledge of the wonderful laws which regulate the system of the world, gives us a much nobler idea of the power of the Divinity, than that of the world which sublime superstition wished to impose upon us." Quetelet, *A Treatise on Man*, 9.

29. Gordon, "Race, Theodicy, and the Normative Emancipatory Challenges," 727.

30. Gordon, "Race, Theodicy, and the Normative Emancipatory Challenges," 727.

31. Gordon, "Race, Theodicy, and the Normative Emancipatory Challenges," 727.

32. Quetelet, *A Treatise on Man*, 7.

33. Porter, *The Rise of Statistical Thinking*, 51.

34. Hankins, *Adolphe Quetelet as Statistician*, 56–57.

35. Goldthorpe, *Pioneers of Sociological Science*, 30.

36. Quetelet put collected data like height and weight on the normal curve, and the result gave the average height/weight of the groups studied, and Quetelet called such a result a quality of the average man. He argued that if the qualities of the average man are to be determined at all, it must be by such a process, based on the measurements of the whole population or a large group. However, this was not the process for data for which Quetelet relied on rates, John H. Goldthorpe points out. These rates were taken as "*indicators of a propensity*: that is, of a propensity to commit suicide or a crime or to enter into marriage—*that was not itself measured*" (Goldthorpe, *Pioneers of Sociological Science*, 28, emphasis in original). Quetelet was unable to show which individual propensities were expressed in behavior and under which conditions. For Goldthorpe, Quetelet's inability to measure propensities is partially due to Quetelet being ahead of his time; data on attitudes did not yet exist. In the absence of such data, we can read Quetelet's concern with propensities as an assumption in his work. Along similar lines, on where Quetelet's abilities stop but his desires nevertheless extend, Hankins comments that in Quetelet's work "the actual distribution, however, is not made. Moreover . . . his curve actually represents the comparative probability of committing crime at each age. It does not represent the distribution about the average propensity or probability." Hankins, *Adolphe Quetelet as Statistician*, 76.

37. Porter, *The Rise of Statistical Thinking*, 44.

38. See Donnelly, *Adolphe Quetelet*, on this point and on competing understandings between sociologists and philosophers on the meaning of Quetelet's work and specifically his average man. Goldthorpe discusses what he regards as Durkheim's misreading of Quetelet (Goldthorpe, *Pioneers of Sociological Science*, 36–37).

39. Quetelet, *A Treatise on Man*, 8.

40. In short, for Quetelet, morality was to be measured by the quantity of moral acts. See Hacking, *The Taming of Chance*, 107; and Donnelly, *Adolphe Quetelet*, 130–33.

41. Gilroy, *Against Race*, 14. A debate that is close enough to the subject of this book but not my direct site of intervention is the debate on race and the question of anti-essentialism. See the work of Kwame Anthony Appiah and the debate between Gordon, Newfield, and Michaels: Gordon and Newfield, "White Philosophy"; Michaels, "Race into Culture." Some, like Michaels, point out the inconsistencies of the anti-essentialist position, arguing that it is racial like the essentialism it critiques. I agree that much of what seeks to challenge racism ends up reproducing the same. However, some of what I see as challenging race, like the notions of blackness and difference animating mass conversion to Islam in mid-twentieth-century Black America, would be considered wholly essentialist by some thinkers in this debate. The theological critique of man at the heart of race is part of what makes such notions of difference promising, I argue, as they challenge the role of the secular in race-making, which is otherwise not a major consideration in the debate on race, essentialism, and anti-essentialism. Disagreements notwithstanding, critics of anti-essentialism pose a valuable challenge to the primacy of identity that is useful for the questions asked in this book.

42. Davis, *Enforcing Normalcy* (also a useful source on the influence of Quetelet with regard to disability).

43. My argument is not that all types of secularism are untenable, as Sherman A. Jackson makes a compelling case for the Islamic secular, but rather that this statistical version has a

specific move of replacing God with man. When I refer to the secular in this book, I am referring to Western secularism specific to the statistical genealogy traced in this chapter.

44. Quetelet, *A Treatise on Man*, 8.
45. Quetelet, *A Treatise on Man*, 108, emphasis in original. *Beautiful* and *good* are adjectives that follow *average man* in several of Quetelet's descriptions. See p. 100 also.
46. Porter, *The Rise of Statistical Thinking*, 52.
47. Quetelet, *A Treatise on Man*, x.
48. Quetelet, *A Treatise on Man*, x.
49. Ian Hacking is extraordinarily doubtful that Quetelet's method can even be regarded as systematic. See Hacking, *The Taming of Chance*.
50. Porter, *The Rise of Statistical Thinking*, 46.
51. Quetelet, *A Treatise on Man*, 96.
52. Quetelet, *A Treatise on Man*, 8.
53. Porter, *The Rise of Statistical Thinking*, 47.
54. Judy, "Kant and the Negro."
55. Lloyd and Thomas, *Culture and the State*, 13.
56. Lloyd and Thomas, *Culture and the State*, 13.
57. Lloyd and Thomas, *Culture and the State*, 13.
58. Quetelet, *A Treatise on Man*, 99. He repeats that each nation has its own average man several times (9, 74, 99). For more on race for Quetelet, see 88–90, and the translator's appendix with Quetelet's consultation, 122–23.
59. Hacking, *The Taming of Chance*, 107.
60. Quetelet, *A Treatise on Man*, 74.
61. Quetelet, *A Treatise on Man*, 108.
62. Quetelet, *A Treatise on Man*, 5.
63. Quetelet, *A Treatise on Man*, 5.
64. Quetelet, *A Treatise on Man*, 98.
65. Quetelet, *A Treatise on Man*, 98.
66. Quetelet, *A Treatise on Man*, 8, 7.
67. Schweber, *Disciplining Statistics*, 21.
68. For Paul Lazarsfeld, in contrast to my point here, it is possible to think about the average man independently of Quetelet's theory of measurement: "Debates about Quetelet's work usually focus on his idea of an 'average man' or his shifting pseudo-psychological comments on his data. A careful reading would show, however, that his underlying theory of measurement, partly brilliant and partly a confused foreshadowing of later developments, gives clues to much of his work" (Lazarsfeld, "Notes on the History of Quantification," 300). Theodore Porter disagrees with Lazarsfeld. Porter further remarks that it is not clear that Quetelet's contribution to measurement in sociology was significant; perhaps instead his contribution was simply that the average man was a useful tool (Porter, *The Rise of Statistical Thinking*, 53). In my view, the concept of the average man and the attending approach to measurement (not necessarily the specific procedures of measurement) are interrelated and carry assumptions of humanity.
69. Lécuyer, "Probability in Vital and Social Statistics." As Lécuyer shows, the father and brother of Alphonse Bertillon also engaged Quetelet's work, but rather critically. For

example, his father, Louis-Adolphe Bertillon, criticized Quetelet's process of combining average physical characteristics and his extension of that interest in averages to the moral and intellectual. This would suggest, Bertillon argued, that Quetelet's notion of the ideal in the form of the average man is a valuing of mediocrity and not actually perfection (Lécuyer, "Probability in Vital and Social Statistics," 330).

70. For a helpful account of Guillard and the elder Bertillon's thought and its relationship to Quetelet, see Schweber, *Disciplining Statistics*. From this, Alphonse Bertillon's father's work on race and averages is worth a brief discussion as it shows how race is built into the distinction of types of averages. This is useful for understanding the relationship between the real and observed average of Quetelet and how he also fabricated it. It was both at the same time. The measurements are done to reveal what is hidden under the invented figure. More specifically on the elder Bertillon, "borrowing from Quetelet, Bertillon called on statisticians to distinguish between natural, physiological averages and arithmetic averages. The first were taken from a homogeneous or natural population, such that the average value and the probable value were one and the same. Thus, with heights taken from a racially uniform population, the average height will also be the most common or likely height. Arithmetic averages, by contrast, were averages calculated on the basis of a heterogeneous population. An arithmetic average had no actual referent and did not correspond to the probable or most common value. In Bertillon's terms, it was artificial" (Schweber, *Disciplining Statistics*, 55). This artificiality challenged Quetelet's project and Guillard's. Bertillon's position in 1853 challenges the conventional perspective in the history of statistics regarding the nineteenth-century statistics obsessed with averages. At this time, anthropologists were divided between two perspectives: that humans developed from a single race, and the polygenist perspective in which humans have multiple origins. Bertillon took the latter, and he measured skulls to prove it. "These data provided the one and only time when Bertillon attempted to apply Quetelet's claim that normal statistical distributions can be taken as evidence of an underlying homogeneous population (a claim contained in Quetelet's concept of 'the average man')" (62). Bertillon's way of proving polygenism—to determine whether two skeletons came from the same race or two different ones—was by studying the "averages and the distribution of observations around the mean. Bertillon began his exposition by drawing on Quetelet's example of the circumference of the chests of Scottish conscripts, and how they were distributed. As Quetelet had demonstrated, the observed measures were symmetrically distributed about the mean such that (in Bertillon's terms) the arithmetic average corresponded with the physiological mean. Among Scottish military recruits, the average circumference was also the most likely (frequent). Moreover, Bertillon explained, once the underlying distribution was known, it was possible to calculate the likelihood that a single new observation would occur in the population. Quetelet used this demonstration to establish the existence of an 'average man,' or underlying human type; Bertillon applied it to the concerns of anthropologists and argued that it provided a tool to distinguish between racially pure and mixed populations. Following his reasoning of 1853, Bertillon argued that the presence of a normal distribution confirmed that the underlying population corresponded to a distinct race" (62). To show this, Bertillon compared heights of conscripts from two places in France, Finistere and Doubs.

In Finistere, distribution followed a bell-shaped curve, which indicated the presence of a single race, whereas Doubs had a distribution of heights as a double hump, suggesting the presence of a crossed or mixed population, one short, one tall. "In 1863 Bertillon accepted that anthropometric data could be used to discern the existence of racial groups" (63).

71. Rhodes, *Alphonse Bertillon*.
72. Rhodes, *Alphonse Bertillon*, 17.
73. Kaluszynski, "Republican Identity," 125.
74. Rhodes, *Alphonse Bertillon*, 52.
75. On how *bertillonage* was a response to recidivism, see Cole, *Suspect Identities*; Kaluszynski, "Republican Identity."
76. Donnelly, *Adolphe Quetelet*.
77. Blanchard, "French Colonial Police."
78. Prakash, *Empire on the Seine*.
79. Kaluszynski, "Republican Identity," 124.
80. Sekula, "The Body and the Archive," 34; Marx et al., *Paris Commune 150*.
81. Ginzburg, "Clues," 119.
82. Bertillon, "The Bertillon System of Identification," 331.
83. Bhattacharya, "Somapolitics," 130.
84. Ginzburg, "Clues," 120.
85. Rhodes, *Alphonse Bertillon*.
86. Piazza, "Alphonse Bertillon and the Identification of Persons."
87. Piazza, "Alphonse Bertillon and the Identification of Persons."
88. Hoover, "Criminal Identification," 206.
89. Hoover, "Criminal Identification," 205.
90. Hoover, "Criminal Identification," 205.
91. Finn, *Capturing the Criminal Image*.
92. Armstrong, *Fiction in the Age of Photography*, 16.
93. Bertillon, "The Bertillon System of Identification," 333.
94. Bertillon, "The Bertillon System of Identification."
95. Sekula, "The Body and the Archive," 29, 16.
96. Rhodes, *Alphonse Bertillon*, 97.
97. Rhodes, *Alphonse Bertillon*, 97.
98. Armstrong, *Fiction in the Age of Photography*, 22.
99. Armstrong, *Fiction in the Age of Photography*, 21.
100. Armstrong, *Fiction in the Age of Photography*, 21.
101. Bhattacharya, "Somapolitics," 148.
102. Lombroso, *Criminal Man*.
103. Bertillon, "The Bertillon System of Identification," 334.
104. Bertillon, *Ethnographie moderne*, 62–63.
105. In his article describing his system of identification, Bertillon writes, "since police identification uses the same material as ethnologic description, the new science founded by Camper, Morton, Broca, and Virchow should serve us as a guide in our task." Virchow applied Quetelet's statistical work to delineating race types, so this suggests another way

in which Bertillon's work had racial implications. Bertillon, "The Bertillon System of Identification," 334.

106. Cole, *Suspect Identities*, 51.

107. From 1925 to 1945, the Paris Prefecture of Police housed a North African brigade that focused on colonized North Africans living as French citizens. For more, see Prakash, *Empire on the Seine*. See also About, "Identités indigènes et police coloniale."

108. Cole, *Suspect Identities*, 52.

109. Hacking, *The Taming of Chance*, 108.

110. Hacking, *The Taming of Chance*, 182.

111. Cole, *Suspect Identities*.

112. Cole, *Suspect Identities*, 148.

113. Cole, *Suspect Identities*, 148.

114. Hoover, "Criminal Identification," 206.

115. Fingerprinting as a practice has a longer and disparate history, but the work of Johannes E. Purkinje in the 1820s is considered the first systematic classification of fingerprints. The practice was further advanced in the colonies. The colonies were a mine of all sorts of data, as well as methods. British colonial administrative officer William Herschel began the widespread use of fingerprints in 1858 in Bengal for colonial purposes after appropriating the practice of inking the fingertips from Bengalis, who were already doing it but toward a different goal, as Galton reported in *Nature*. See Ginzburg, "Clues."

116. Hoover, "Criminal Identification."

117. On the move from anthropometry to fingerprinting, see Cole, *Suspect Identities*, chapter 6. Cole argues that it was "a gradual process that had more to do with competing models of science and the social construction of race in America than with a single decisive case" (146).

118. Hoover, "Criminal Identification," 208.

119. Fox, "Unique unto Itself." On how the progressive era was the founding moment for race statistics, see Muhammad, *The Condemnation of Blackness*, 7.

120. Beverly Gage details this system for organizing FBI files, which was different from the organization of Bertillon cards described earlier. They were similar systems in that they involved index-size cards representing something larger—a criminal to be located, or a set of records—and the goal was to find the card as quickly as possible: Gage, *G-Man*, 69.

121. Gage, *G-Man*, 113.

122. Muhammad, *The Condemnation of Blackness*, 7.

123. On the enthusiastic reception of *bertillonage* in the United States, see Dilworth, *Identification Wanted*.

124. Dilworth, *Identification Wanted*, 141; Gage, *G-Man*, 114.

125. Fox, "Unique unto Itself," 475.

126. Hoover, "Address of Hon. J. Edgar Hoover," 164–65. Also see Fox, "Unique unto Itself," 475; Powers, *Secrecy and Power*, 155–58.

127. Hoover, "Address of Hon. J. Edgar Hoover," 163.

128. Dilworth, *Identification Wanted*, 131; Fox, "Unique unto Itself," 477.

129. Dilworth, *Identification Wanted*, 88.

130. Dilworth, *Identification Wanted*, 54.
131. Kidd, "The Right to Take Fingerprints," 117.
132. Dilworth, *Identification Wanted*, 178.
133. Dilworth, *Identification Wanted*, 172.
134. Greening, "The Fingerprint Campaign," 219.
135. Beverly Gage connects the "bureaucratic triumph" of Hoover's 1930s crime statistics to the crime debate of the 1960s. Although the latter was "increasingly framed in terms of race, civil rights, and a growing 'urban crisis,' to Hoover it also looked like what had happened in the 1930s, when the FBI had made its reputation as a crime-fighting force." Crime statistics helped Hoover influence discourse on crime. Gage, *G-Man*, 628.
136. Dilworth, *Identification Wanted*, 172.
137. Gage, *G-Man*, 277.
138. "All Aliens to Be Fingerprinted."
139. Hall, *Wanted*. Hall's book also offers a genealogy of wanted posters, with special attention to the FBI, but it is primarily concerned with visual culture, and I am more interested in the scientific, statistical roots.
140. Hall, *Wanted*, 147.
141. Sekula, "The Body and the Archive," 55–56.
142. Jerry Clark and Ed Palattella argue along similar lines that the creation of the Most Wanted program "brought together two approaches that had proven beneficial for the FBI for years. The most-wanted program melded the staid system of the identification orders (IOs), invented in 1919, while the FBI was still called the Bureau of Investigation; and the public enemies list that generated so much publicity for the FBI during the gangster era, even as J. Edgar Hoover said the FBI never officially identified John Dillinger or anyone else as the top public enemy in the United States." Clark and Palattella, *On the Lam*, 71.
143. Fox, "Unique unto Itself," 475.
144. Hall, *Wanted*, 102.
145. Hall, *Wanted*, 102.
146. Blanchard, "French Colonial Police."
147. Goldberg, *Racial Subjects*, 31.
148. Hoover, *Fugitives Wanted by Police*. In 1935, the publication name was changed to *Law Enforcement Bulletin*, and it continues under this name. An antecedent to this bulletin in England was "route forms"—the form included a description and photograph of the arrested person. The form was "routed" to select police offices for the purposes of tracing rather than proving identity. These are a form of the wanted poster but routed internally to police rather than distributed to the public. Joseph, "Anthropometry," 165.
149. Groebner, "Describing the Person," 25–26.
150. Groebner, "Describing the Person," 26.
151. Former FBI agent Mike German, personal communication, April 18, 2022.
152. FBI, "Ten Most Wanted Fugitives FAQ."
153. The FBI is not the only agency in the United States or internationally to have a Most Wanted program. Local and state police; the Bureau of Alcohol, Tobacco, Fire-

arms, and Explosives; the Drug Enforcement Administration; the Secret Service; the Air Force Office of Special Investigations; and the Naval Criminal Investigations Service all have such lists. There are also newer iterations like BOLOS (Be on the Lookout), run by a private Canadian foundation. As Clark and Palattella note, "The U.S. Marshals Service, like the FBI, also reached into the past to create one of its signature efforts: the Fifteen Most Wanted fugitive program and its list. In 1982, top officials of the agency were exploring ways to publicize high-profile fugitive cases. They decided to [distribute] posters that marshals and their deputies used to their advantage in the Old West. The director of the US Marshals Service, William Hall, developed the Fifteen Most Wanted fugitive program along with Howard Safir, the service's associate director of operations, and its inspector, Robert Leschorn. They came up with the idea in July 1982, three years after the land-mark memorandum of understanding between the U.S. Marshals Service and the FBI delineated their responsibilities for capturing fugitives—the marshals adopted less of an investigative role than the FBI and took on finding fugitives who had already broken the law: escaped federal prisoners, federal bail jumpers, witnesses who failed to appear in court, federal offenders who had violated probation and parole. The U.S. Marshals Service launched the Fifteen Most Wanted fugitive program in 1983." Clark and Palattella, *On the Lam*, 84.

154. Prior to the creation of the Most Wanted program, the FBI used to distribute photographs with descriptions of fugitives through its *Law Enforcement Bulletin* in the earliest decades of the journal in the 1930s. A Santa Barbara, California, police chief in 1939 called it "a 'want' file" from "F.B.I. 'wanted' bulletins"; such a file takes "little space, is easy to keep filed by clipping each want and filing it by classification. A search of this file is routine in the system, as well as the search of other outside wants." Hoelscher, "Should a Small City Have Its Own Fingerprint File?," 213. The FBI Most Wanted program is different in function, form, and audience from the *Law Enforcement Bulletin*.

155. Debord, *The Society of the Spectacle*.

156. In 1983, the FBI estimated that they spent $20,000 to $30,000 to publicize each fugitive added to the Ten Most Wanted list. This amount covered 900 news releases, 500 spot announcements for radio and television stations, 1,500 posters, and 1,000 photographs and placards for the forty thousand police departments in the country. Sabljak and Greenberg, *Most Wanted*, 5.

157. Gaylin, "What's an FBI Poster Doing in a Nice Journal Like That?," 1.

158. FBI, "The FBI Website at 20."

159. Miles, "An Empirical Analysis of the FBI's Ten Most Wanted"; Sabljak and Greenberg, *Most Wanted*; Swierczynski, *The Encyclopedia of the FBI's Ten Most Wanted List*.

160. FBI, "FBI's Ten Most Wanted Fugitives 60th Anniversary," 3.

161. Theoharis, *The FBI and American Democracy*.

162. Swierczynski, *The Encyclopedia of the FBI's Ten Most Wanted List*; Sabljak and Greenberg, *Most Wanted*; Miles, "An Empirical Analysis of the FBI's Ten Most Wanted."

163. Waddell, "The FBI's Most-Wanted Cybercriminals."

164. Walker, "Assata Shakur."

165. See Miles, "An Empirical Analysis of the FBI's Ten Most Wanted."

166. Ahmed, *On Being Included*, 97.

167. See Miles, "An Empirical Analysis of the FBI's Ten Most Wanted."

168. Kumar, *Islamophobia and the Politics of Empire*.

169. Sabljak and Greenberg, *Most Wanted*.

170. Chard, *Nixon's War at Home*.

171. Miles, "An Empirical Analysis of the FBI's Ten Most Wanted"; FBI, "Ten Most Wanted Fugitives FAQ." By 1990, over 400 fugitives had been added to the Ten Most Wanted over the course of the program's forty-year history until that point, and of these, 398 had been apprehended. Tips were involved in at least 122 of these apprehensions, and, as noted earlier, the rates of apprehension are not stable across the life of the Most Wanted program.

172. Jamil Al-Amin (H. Rap Brown), chairman of the Student Nonviolent Coordinating Committee, was added in 1970. Angela Davis was a well-known university professor and prominent in the Communist Party–USA in these years when she was among the Ten Most Wanted.

173. On listing, see Young, *List Cultures*.

174. Miles, "An Empirical Analysis of the FBI's Ten Most Wanted"; Sabljak and Greenberg, *Most Wanted*; Swierczynski, *The Encyclopedia of the FBI's Ten Most Wanted List*; Clark and Palattella, *On the Lam*.

175. Theoharis, *The FBI*.

176. James, "Assata Shakur and Black Female Agency"; Umoja, "The Black Liberation Army and the Radical Legacy"; Latner, "'Assata Shakur Is Welcome Here.'"

177. Respectively: Clark and Palattella, *On the Lam*; Hall, *Wanted*; Miles, "An Empirical Analysis of the FBI's Ten Most Wanted."

178. On the link between modern quantitative statistics and social science more broadly, see Porter, *The Rise of Statistical Thinking*.

179. Ginzburg, "Clues," 105.

180. See Davis, *Enforcing Normalcy* and *The End of Normal*, on the legacy of Quetelet's norm.

181. On the French categories, in which North African and Muslim were synonymous for French police, see Prakash, *Empire on the Seine*.

182. Melamed, *Represent and Destroy*; Morning, *The Nature of Race*. Biological notions of race persist in educational institutions well into the twenty-first century as explanations for apparent inequality and difference.

183. On discrimination in FBI ranks and the experiences of Black FBI employees, see the interview-based research in Martin, *The Gospel of J. Edgar Hoover*.

184. Gerstein, "The FBI Looks Like Trump's America." For further discussion, see German, *Disrupt, Discredit, and Divide*, 12.

185. Shakur, *Assata*, 234.

186. Schrader, "Wanted."

187. Quetelet, *A Treatise on Man*, 7.

2. ASSATA, THE MUSLIM

1. See Taylor, *The Promise of Patriarchy*; Chan-Malik, *Being Muslim*; Gibson and Karim, *Women of the Nation*. And on the term *Black Islam* as a big-tent term for the various sects and strands of Islam practiced by the African diaspora in the United States, see Khabeer, *Muslim Cool*.

2. Washington, *All Power to the People*, 57; Bukhari, *The War Before*, 64–78.

3. Holley, *An Amerikan Family*, 32.

4. Holley, *An Amerikan Family*, 32.

5. There is debate on the extent to which Shakur is ordinary, singular, or unique in any way in the story of the Panthers and BLA, as published works across the popular/scholarly spectrum and the political spectrum note her larger-than-life status as a symbol for many things (see chapter 4). For example, BLA attorney Robert Boyle is quoted as saying, "Assata was never this massively important figure the police portrayed her as. She was important, but the police made up this mythic image of a super black woman, with the afro and the machine gun. She was never that" (Burrough, *Days of Rage*, 239). Joy James writes on her symbolism as a female revolutionary: "Assata Shakur is extraordinary... unique not only because she has survived in exile as a political figure despite the U.S. government's bounty—'dead or alive'—on her head but also because she may prove to be 'beyond commoditization' in a time in which political leadership seems to be bought and sold in the marketplace of political trade, compromise, and corruption. Above all, Assata Shakur is singular because she is a recognizable female revolutionary, one not bound to a male persona" (James, "Assata Shakur and Black Female Agency," 93). And yet, "For some, how frightening must be the prospect that *any* ordinary colored girl, within the appropriate context, could grow up to become a revolutionary" (97).

6. For more on the BPP and its founding, including its relation to the Black Panthers of Lowndes County, Alabama, see Bloom and Martin, *Black against Empire*; Jeffries, *Bloody Lowndes*; Jones, *The Black Panther Party Reconsidered*.

7. Holley, *An Amerikan Family*, 151.

8. According to Frank Donner, the source for these numbers, the situation was worse for Panthers in New York due to the infiltration work of BOSS (Bureau of Special Services) that allowed local police to exercise greater control than they had in other cities. This police control was leveraged not as much through the "almost obligatory raid and shootout" as through "the lethal instrument" of "a mass trial." The Panther 21 trial was "overflowing with melodrama: BOSS infiltrators, FBI agents, double agents, wiretaps, wireless transmitters, over $1 million in bail, interrogations and confessions, pistols, rifles, dynamite, bombs, reams of 'guerrilla literature,' feature length movies, terrorist plots to kill police and bomb women and children, heroic agents who escaped with their lives by inches, and last-minute arrests that saved the city from widescale death and destruction." Donner, *Protectors of Privilege*, 180–81.

9. The BLA was a clandestine, underground formation of mostly former Black Panther members on the East Coast. Zayd Shakur described the BLA as "small urban guerrilla units, waging armed struggle against the agents of death—the united states government, operating throughout Babylon" (Shakur and members of the Black Liberation Army, "Spring Came Early This Year," 14). The BLA understood the police as an occupying

force and Black people as a colonized nation subject to this occupying force. On this understanding, the BLA targeting police was not a matter of crime but rather a matter of war, as some would later argue in court. On the matter of prison as warfare, see Burton, *Tip of the Spear*. Between 1971 and 1973, the US government attributed twenty police officers' deaths to the BLA, writes attorney Evelyn Williams, who served as a lawyer for several BLA members including her niece, Assata Shakur; Williams puts this number in context: in that same two-year period, police killed nearly a thousand Black people (Williams, *Inadmissible Evidence*, 74). See also Umoja, "The Black Liberation Army and the Radical Legacy," for a list of several of what the BLA called "revolutionary executions" for which the BLA claimed responsibility or for which the state suspected BLA involvement. Akinyele O. Umoja's work on the history of the BLA offers a useful discussion of the different positions on the question of the BLA's origin: some argue that the BLA was an outgrowth of the Black Panther Party; some Panthers such as Dhoruba Bin Wahad, Sundiata Acoli, and Jalil Muntaqim argue that the BLA formed as a result of state repression and the FBI exploiting existing differences inside the BPP; and although not necessarily in conflict with the second view, some such as Geronimo Ji Jaga and Assata Shakur emphasize that the movement concept of a clandestine, armed wing predates the BLA. In her opening statement to the Brooklyn Supreme Court on January 7, 1976, Shakur says that the BLA is not an organization but an idea, a movement, that emerged from the conditions in which Black people lived. On the final perspective, Umoja notes armed rebellions of enslaved Africans, the 1919 African Blood Brotherhood, the 1950s–1960s Deacons for Defense and Justice, and the Revolutionary Action Movement of the 1960s.

10. See chapter 1 on the identification order: an FBI document that brings together the anthropometric approach of police clerk Alphonse Bertillon and the fingerprinting innovations of eugenicist Francis Galton.

11. *Assata Bulletin*, January 1977, box 1, folder 15–16, Majority Report Research Files, Articles, Statement, Bulletins, Newspaper, Tamiment Library, NYU.

12. "Since [Shakur] was seriously wounded in the right shoulder during the shoot-out, we tried to prove that she could not have been holding a weapon when she herself was shot. Our expert, pathologist Dr. David Spain, testified that the bullet could not have entered Assata's shoulder the way it did if she was holding a gun. According to Spain, Assata was shot while sitting in a noncombative position in the car and did not participate in the shoot-out." Kunstler and Isenberg, *My Life as a Radical Lawyer*, 276–77.

13. "Shakur Wins Court Decision."

14. "Friends of Assata Shakur and Sundiata Acoli Bulletin," box 1, folder 16, Printed Ephemera Collection on Organizations 1973–74, Tamiment Library, NYU.

15. As the classic volume *Black Power: The Politics of Liberation in America* argues, "Those who have the right to define are the masters of the situation." Carmichael and Hamilton, *Black Power*, 36. That power to define is central to the project of Black Power that Carmichael and Hamilton argued was a form of political modernization (44). To this end, "The extent to which black Americans can and do 'trace their roots' to Africa, to that extent will they be able to be more effective on the political scene" (45). This reclamation of history, culture, and asserting self-definition can be seen in the "growing

resentment of the word 'Negro,' for example, because this term is the invention of our oppressor; it is *his* image of us that he describes" (37).

16. FBI, "The Muslim Cult of Islam," 18.

17. Johnson, *African American Religions*, 379.

18. McCrary, *Sincerely Held*, 141.

19. Diouf, *Servants of Allah*, 48. Michael A. Gomez estimates that tens of thousands were Muslim; Allan Austin puts it at thirty thousand to forty thousand between 1711 and 1808. Gomez, *Black Crescent*, 143; Austin, *African Muslims in Antebellum America*, 22.

20. Gomez, *Black Crescent*, 13. Gomez argues that the sense of superiority that some enslaved African Muslims felt over enslaved African non-Muslims was due to the former being slaveholders themselves, and African Muslims' relative power based on the establishment of Muslim theocracies, as well as their descent from prominent clerical and educated families in West Africa. See Gomez, *Black Crescent*, 97, 177–84. On African Muslims and the abolition of slavery, see Ware, *The Walking Qur'an*.

21. Wynter, "On How We Mistook the Map for the Territory," 126.

22. Wynter, "On How We Mistook the Map for the Territory," 126.

23. Sources who were close to her say she was not a Muslim in a religious sense. They immediately add that they cannot know what was in her heart then or how she feels now. As pious Muslims, they are concerned with whether she believes; it is an extension of their concern and care for her. Nevertheless, several aspects of this issue—the question of whether Assata Shakur's engagement with Islam was purely strategic or from the heart—are worth a brief response here. Specifically, her letters from prison to Nuh Washington in which she expressed interest in Islam were written before she attempted to exercise her religious freedom in the courtroom. For a similar discussion about timing in the case of MOVE and religious freedom, see McCrary, *Sincerely Held*, 228–29n78. Finally, as Maryam Kashani points out, Muslims "harbor noncommittal and contradictory feelings" about Islam, among other things, "but that doesn't make [it] any less constitutive of everyday life and relations" (Kashani, *Medina by the Bay*, 12). Along similar lines, then, Shakur's religious freedom case had its impacts no matter the particular feelings and intentions motivating it.

24. Spencer Dew's book on the religious groups descended from Noble Drew Ali's Moorish Science Temple highlights the place of law in their rejection of US racial categories. They differentiate between the US legal system and true law or God's law, where the former can be worked with to be in alignment with the latter. Dew, *The Aliites*.

25. Failinger, "Islam in the Mind of American Courts."

26. Williams, *Inadmissible Evidence*, 124.

27. On prisoners' struggles for the right to practice Islam in prison, see Felber, *Those Who Know Don't Say*; Moore, *Al-Mughtaribun*; Gardell, *In the Name of Elijah Muhammad*. See also Berger, *Captive Nation*. The issue of attending Friday prayer is weaponized by prison authorities who, in the case of Imam Jamil Al-Amin, did not allow him to participate in Friday prayer after his 2000 arrest and solitary confinement. Thelwell, "Foreword," xxxvi–xxxvii.

28. Acoli, "An Updated History of the New Afrikan Prison Struggle," 143.

29. Moore, *Al-Mughtaribun*.

30. Gordon, *The Spirit of the Law*.
31. Felber, *Those Who Know Don't Say*, 55.
32. Gordon, *The Spirit of the Law*.
33. Acoli, "An Updated History of the New Afrikan Prison Struggle," 150.
34. Acoli, "An Updated History of the New Afrikan Prison Struggle," 150.
35. "Chesimard Defense Team Grows."
36. "Chesimard Will Take Stand."
37. Looking at the post-9/11 context, Sahar Aziz discusses the limited success of Muslim plaintiffs' challenges to national security practices based on the First, Fourth, Fifth, or Fourteenth Amendment. The basis of the courts' dismissal of these claims would be that the plaintiff could not prove that the government intended to discriminate on the basis of religion. Aziz, *The Racial Muslim*.
38. "Lawyers' Group Aiding Mrs. Chesimard."
39. Hinds, "A Decade in Defense of Human Rights." By the late 1970s, with the death of Elijah Muhammad, Sunni Islam had gained more strength inside prisons.
40. Kavanaugh, "Chesimard Ruling Expected This Week."
41. Kavanaugh, "Chesimard Trial Postponed." On the moving of trials to ensure white juries in line with the "reasonable man standard," see David Theo Goldberg's discussion of the O. J. Simpson trial. Goldberg, *The Racial State*, 150–51.
42. Hays and McIntyre, "Joanne Loses 2 Rounds on Trial Transfer."
43. For a summary of which courts the issue traveled through, see State of New Jersey v. Chesimard, Joanne D. 555 F.2d 63, 77–1104.
44. Williams, *Inadmissible Evidence*, 157.
45. Kavanaugh, "Chesimard Ruling Expected This Week."
46. Kavanaugh, "Chesimard Ruling Expected This Week."
47. Evans, MOVE. On MOVE and religion, see also McCrary, *Sincerely Held*; Gordon, *The Spirit of the Law*.
48. Kavanaugh, "Chesimard Jury Selection to Resume."
49. Kavanaugh, "Chesimard Ruling Expected This Week."
50. Kavanaugh, "Chesimard Jury Selection to Resume."
51. Kavanaugh, "Chesimard Jury Selection to Resume."
52. Kavanaugh, "Chesimard Jury Selection to Resume."
53. Kavanaugh, "Chesimard Ruling Expected This Week."
54. McCrary, *Sincerely Held*, 234.
55. A phrase from Hugo Grotius in the seventeenth century, *etsi Deus non daretur*, is identified by Charles Taylor as a key logic in the mode of secularism taken up in the United States. Taylor, "Modes of Secularism," 33–34.
56. On law, Islam, and prisoners' rights, see Felber, *Those Who Know Don't Say*; Moore, *Al-Mughtaribun*; Gordon, *The Spirit of the Law*.
57. Holley, *An Amerikan Family*, 175.
58. *Assata Bulletin*, March 2, 1977, box 1, folder 15, Majority Report Research Files, Articles, Statement, Bulletins, Newspaper, Tamiment Library, NYU.
59. *Assata Bulletin*, March 2, 1977.
60. Sullivan, "Chesimard Defense Loses on Shift."

61. See McCloud, *African American Islam*.
62. Holden v. Board of Education of City of Elizabeth, 216 A.2d 387 (N.J. 1966).
63. Williams, *Inadmissible Evidence*, 163.
64. Williams, *Inadmissible Evidence*, 163.
65. Goldberg, *The Racial State*, 148.
66. Andrews et al., "Gunman Frees 4 after 5-Hr. Siege."
67. "Chesimard Judge Says Jury Unaware of Moslem Siege."
68. "Chesimard Judge Says Jury Unaware of Moslem Siege."
69. On how the FBI and other state agencies responded to Shakur's escape, see Rosenau, *Tonight We Bombed the U.S. Capital*; Castellucci, *The Big Dance*.
70. Umoja, "Black Liberation Army," 114; Holley, *An Amerikan Family*, 195.
71. Umoja, "The Black Liberation Army and the Radical Legacy"; Holley, *An Amerikan Family*, 195.
72. Umoja, "The Black Liberation Army and the Radical Legacy." On the RNA, see Onaci, *Free the Land*.
73. Umoja, "Repression Breeds Resistance."
74. Blumenthal, "FBI Wiretaps"; Saunders and Singleton, "FBI Just Missed Brink's Suspect."
75. Subseries B. Cases pleaded or initiated, 1960–1995 (#10.10–13.13), Papers of Florynce Kennedy, 1915–2004 (inclusive), 1947–1993 (bulk), MC 555; Vt-133, MP-56, Schlesinger Library on the History of Women in America, Radcliffe Institute for Advanced Study, Cambridge, MA. Kennedy was briefly on Shakur's legal team. See also Randolph, *Florynce "Flo" Kennedy*.
76. Sullivan, "Courthouse Is Picketed as Chesimard Trial Starts."
77. Williams, *Inadmissible Evidence*, 102.
78. On the contemporary racial politics of hijabs and wraps vis-à-vis Islam, see Khabeer, *Muslim Cool*.
79. The FBI has been relatively late to diversity and inclusion policies. In the early 1970s, less than 1 percent of agents were Black and there were no women agents. By 1988, the few Black, Latino, and women agents in the bureau were filing class action lawsuits for discrimination. And in 1992, agents were 87.4 percent white and 88.7 percent male. Theoharis, *The FBI*, 197.
80. The New Jersey State Police's 1980 poster still calls her "Negro," and their 1985 poster calls her "Black." The New Jersey State Police could then be similar to the FBI in their switch or slightly behind: the FBI's 1980 posters say "black."
81. Spillers, "Mama's Baby, Papa's Maybe," 67.
82. For further description of these conditions, see Shakur, *Assata*; Shakur, "Women in Prison"; Williams, *Inadmissible Evidence*; Hinds, "A Decade in Defense of Human Rights."
83. "Joanne Claims Bias in Jail."
84. Spillers, "Mama's Baby, Papa's Maybe," 68.
85. Some reports say she was the first woman in a men's jail in the area, some say the second. She was the second woman to be at Middlesex County Jail and first held in solitary confinement, Hinds notes (Cooke, "Chesimard Move Challenged"). And earlier,

newspapers report Shakur was the only woman in Middlesex County Jail while lawyers were working to transfer her to the county workhouse. Kavanaugh, "Chesimard Lawyers Lose Round." See also Hinds, *Illusions of Justice*, 255–56. Patrice Douglass also argues that Assata Shakur was ungendered in being sent to Middlesex County Jail: Douglass, "Assata Is Here," 94.

86. Hinds, "A Decade in Defense of Human Rights," 15.
87. Wahad, "Assata Shakur," 120. And see chapter 9 of O'Reilly, *"Racial Matters."*
88. Browne, *Dark Matters*.
89. Others have also argued that part of the mid-twentieth-century association between Islam and blackness is established in a national security context: Johnson, *African American Religions*; Curtis, "The Black Muslim Scare of the Twentieth Century."
90. Reitan, "Cuba, the Black Panther Party and the US Black Movement."
91. Latner, "'Assata Shakur Is Welcome Here,'" 470. Much of the remaining biographical information on Shakur's life in Cuba, unless cited otherwise, is also from the work of Latner, including *Cuban Revolution in America*.
92. Latner, "'Assata Shakur Is Welcome Here.'"
93. For example, an interview with Shakur in *Souls* was published by Manning Marable and the Columbia University African-American Studies delegation to Cuba in 1997: Marable, "Assata Shakur."
94. For research on Assata Shakur, see Dhoruba Bin Wahad on her terrorism designation, Joy James on her gendering, Teishan Latner on her relation to Cuba, Evelyn A. Williams on her trials, and Akinyele Umoja on what her escape meant in and for the history of the BLA. Wahad, "Assata Shakur"; Wahad, Abu-Jamal, and Shakur, *Still Black, Still Strong*; James, "Assata Shakur and Black Female Agency"; Latner, *Cuban Revolution in America*; Umoja, "The Black Liberation Army and the Radical Legacy"; James, "Sorrow." See also Dillon, *Fugitive Life*; Lindsey, "Negro Women May Be Dangerous." There is brief mention of her New Jersey 12 Most Wanted poster in Rodriguez, *Forced Passages*.

Her Islam is either absent in most of these works or mentioned briefly, as in the case of Latner. Her attorneys William Kunstler, Evelyn Williams, and Lennox Hinds all mention her Islam in their respective writings, which are autobiographical with the exception of Hinds, *Illusions of Justice*; see Kunstler and Isenberg, *My Life as a Radical Lawyer*; Williams, *Inadmissible Evidence*. Accounts of these events by former police, FBI, intelligence, journalists, and others drawing on materials privileging the state's narrative of Shakur are more likely to mention her Islam: see Castellucci, *The Big Dance*. Altogether, this pattern in which sorts of texts mention her being Muslim and which do not, may attest to the significance of Islam in her story in the legal sphere, specifically, as well as in the media.

95. Analyses of Shakur's autobiography include: Hames-Garcia, *Fugitive Thought*, chapter 3; Perkins and Phelps, *Autobiography as Activism*.
96. Shakur, *Assata*, 92.
97. James, "Framing the Panther," 155.
98. Shakur, *Assata*, 92.
99. Bukhari, *The War Before*, 65.
100. Bukhari, *The War Before*, 73.
101. Bukhari, *The War Before*, 74.

102. Bukhari, *The War Before*, 75.

103. Bukhari, *The War Before*, 75.

104. Bukhari, *The War Before*, 76. For similar accounts from Muslim political prisoners in Egypt and at US black sites, see Quisay and Qureshi, *When Only God Can See*.

105. Bukhari, *The War Before*, 76.

106. Bukhari, *The War Before*, 77. Shakur's eulogy: Shakur, "Message of Condolences"; and Joy James's analysis of the eulogy: James, "Assata Shakur and Black Female Agency," 112–13.

107. Jackson, *Islam and the Blackamerican*. This term was coined by Rudolf Otto, developed by Charles H. Long for the case of Black people in the New World, and engaged by Sherman A. Jackson for the case of Black American Muslims.

108. Long, "The Gift of Speech," 410.

109. Qur'an 3:173.

110. Another example worth noting is the case of Black Salafi Muslims in Philadelphia. "Broadly conceived, what Philadelphia's Salafis do not talk about is race or politics," and the community goes a step further and "explicitly denounces those Muslims that do engage race and politics." They have constructed "a radical alternative lifestyle that pays no heed to the existing racial and secular order." In so doing, they reflect an epistemology that goes beyond a refusal of the terms of racism. They engage alternative terms altogether. Blecher and Dubler, "Overlooking Race and Secularism."

111. Aminah McCloud makes a somewhat similar point when she draws on C. Eric Lincoln to argue against the idea that "African American Islam is only or 'at bottom' a nationalistic movement." McCloud, *African American Islam*, 51.

112. For Wynter, Islam is a competing alternative monotheistic force, and it is worth asking to what extent and on which bases this characterization matches up with the Western understandings being critiqued, or if this characterization is made possible if the definition of the Negro for the West is taken on its own terms as actually bearing no relation to Islam as an indigenized religion for those who would be called Negroes.

113. Al-Amin, *Revolution by the Book*, 140.

114. Al-Amin, *Revolution by the Book*, 140.

115. Al-Amin, *Revolution by the Book*, 141–42.

116. Mahmood, *Politics of Piety*.

117. Jackson, "Black Orientalism," 35.

118. The inverse also applies. For example, through hip-hop and other cultural means, blackness moves through Muslim spaces to shape what it means to be a Muslim in general. See Khabeer, *Muslim Cool*; Daulatzai, *Black Star, Crescent Moon*.

119. To this point, for psychologist William E. Cross, joining the Muslims was the third stage of what he called the Negro-to-Black conversion experience. Cross, "The Negro-to-Black Conversion Experience," 273.

120. Johnson and Weitzman, *The FBI and Religion*.

121. Felber, *Those Who Know Don't Say*.

122. Assata Clippings, box 8, folder 5, Tamiment Library, NYU.

123. One major moment of resistance described in both Shakur's and Williams's autobiographies is in their recounting of FBI agents attempting to take photographs of Shakur in

court. On December 11, 1974, a judge ordered her "to submit to the photographing of her person by Agents of the Federal Bureau of Investigation for the purpose of comparison of such photographs during the armed robbery of the Bankers Trust Company" (Williams, *Inadmissible Evidence*, 131–32). The judge had issued an earlier order for such a photograph to be taken. Shakur was ill and recovering after having recently given birth, so she remained in her cell. Williams reports that the judge was outraged at Shakur's refusal to appear in court. He ordered that US marshals accompany her, "employing such force as is reasonably necessary to accomplish her transportation and appearance for said photographing" (132). Shakur wrote, "I have decided to refuse" to allow such a photograph to be taken: "As far as i am concerned, the reasons are obvious. You put anybody in a monkey suit and they're gonna end up looking like a monkey. Besides, someone had told me about some trick the FBI uses. They take a photo of you in the same angle as the bank photo and superimpose a transparency of the bank photo over it. If you are unfortunate enough to have two eyes, a nose, and lips, in more or less the same place, you end up looking like the bank robber, no matter what you really look like" (Shakur, *Assata*, 161). For a similar account of the FBI superimposing other images onto photographs of people for the purposes of discrediting and incriminating, see Cunningham, *There's Something Happening Here*, 1–2. She notes that she "permitted them to take all the photographs of [her] they wanted" when she was arraigned. Both Shakur and Williams resist the violence that followed, when FBI agents strangled and wrestled Assata Shakur in order to make her photographable. Shakur does so by contorting her face and Williams by narrating these events for the record. The near-totalizing control of imprisonment notwithstanding, Shakur's approach to the courtroom involved her ability to refuse, which the courts even recognized at times. Her ability to allow or not allow suggests that she is not simply acted upon—as property, as a commodity—but that she acts, speaks, and shapes the episode.

124. Shakur to Nuh Washington, July 2, 1973, AF 043, box 2, folder 002, Black Panther Party Archives of Frankye Adams-Johnson, Jackson State University Archives and Records Division, Jackson, Mississippi.

125. Shakur to Washington, July 2, 1973. For research on Muslim women, agency, and submission, see Taylor, *The Promise of Patriarchy*; Mahmood, *Politics of Piety*; Karim, *American Muslim Women*; Chan-Malik, *Being Muslim*.

126. Shakur to Washington, July 2, 1973.

127. Jones, *Is God a White Racist?*; Cone, *Black Theology and Black Power*.

128. Assata Shakur, "What Is Left?," box 1, folder 15, Majority Report Research Files, Articles, Statement, Bulletins, Newspaper, Tamiment Library, NYU.

3. THE RULE OF RACELESSNESS

1. White House, "The List of Most Wanted Terrorists."

2. In the seven years prior to 9/11, it has given out over $8 million to individuals who have come forward with information. The State Department cites the capture of Ramzi Yousef, who allegedly planned to blow up a dozen commercial airliners and participated in the 1993 World Trade Center bombing, as a success of the Rewards for Justice program prior to the creation of the MWT list. The program distributed wanted materials such as

posters, matchbooks, flyers, and newspaper ads about Yousef, and an informant came forward less than two years later. White House, "The List of Most Wanted Terrorists."

3. Gibson, "U.S. Casts Anti-terror Net."

4. "'Most Wanted Terrorists' List Released."

5. On continuities in counterterrorism in the immediate aftermath of 9/11, see Young, "Ground Zero"; as well as Cole, *Enemy Aliens*.

6. Bin Laden's November 2001 poster on the MWT list reads "The Rewards For Justice Program, United States Department of State, is offering a reward of up to $5 million for information leading directly to the apprehension or conviction of Usama Bin Laden. An additional $2 million is being offered through a program developed and funded by the Airline Pilots Association and the Air Transport Association." But his poster a month later on the Ten Most Wanted fugitives list, in contrast, mentions a reward five times that amount: $25 million from the Rewards for Justice program, along with the $2 million from the airline and pilots associations.

7. Fan-fiction versions of Osama bin Laden's wanted poster are available on eBay. These appear as though they are official FBI wanted posters. They list his race as Arab.

8. First, it must be made clear that this pattern can hardly be attributed to an oversight by an individual FBI agent or two who neglected to write something under "Race" while making wanted posters. If it is an oversight, it has been made repeatedly for twenty years, which has given it significance. Further, as chapter 1 shows, one of the central purposes of the posters is advertising, so even if just a handful of agents are responsible for what goes on posters, they complete this task with the American public in mind and, at times, international viewers, as some posters are distributed across the world and in languages other than English (see chapter 1 and Miles, "An Empirical Analysis of the FBI's Ten Most Wanted"). No matter what the idiosyncratic race perceptions of the FBI agents making posters, their work is distributed widely and thus has significance beyond the individual viewpoints of some agents.

9. Puar and Rai, "Monster, Terrorist, Fag," 123.

10. Selod and Embrick, "Racialization and Muslims"; Naber, "Arab Americans and U.S. Racial Formations"; Garner and Selod, "The Racialization of Muslims"; Cainkar, *Homeland Insecurity*; Cainkar and Selod, "Review of Race Scholarship"; Rana, *Terrifying Muslims*; Love, *Islamophobia and Racism in America*.

11. In the sociology of race, colorblindness or colorblind racism is one such framework. Research on colorblindness is one of few areas of study in the sociology of race that does take the absence of race as something to think about as an object of study. See Bonilla-Silva, *Racism Without Racists*. Colorblind ideology sought to explain away inequality as a matter of inherent difference, thus exculpating racist systems. Claims to colorblindness also rhetorically protect the claimant against the charge that they are racist. However, the claim that the raceless Muslims on the MWT list is a case of colorblindness would be a weak argument for several reasons related to the mismatch between this case and the theory of colorblind racism on most counts. First, the FBI has shown little to no sign that they fear being considered racist against Muslims, especially within the first month after 9/11 when the MWT list and its pattern of racelessness was established, so there is not much reason to believe that the bureau would omit the race category in order to avoid

the charge of racism. Second, colorblind ideology is heavily articulated to Black politics in the domestic sphere, but in the case at hand racelessness is applied to Muslims, who at this point are largely imagined as a non-Black group and with relation to global politics. While there are some on the MWT list who would easily be identified as Black, as the chapter later shows, racial blackness is not a shared feature of the raceless. Instead, identifiability as a Muslim and an association with terrorism are the two features that characterize the raceless. The colorblind ideology that seeks to preserve racism is contextually sutured to the civil rights movement and law, even as colorblind ideology can travel elsewhere. To the extent that Bonilla-Silva's theory of colorblind racism is an argument about a broad racial ideology after the mid-twentieth century, it is necessary but not sufficient for a robust analysis of the "missing race."

My questions of conceiving of human difference outside of race are not themselves an example of the colorblindness Bonilla-Silva and other sociologists of race critique; this is because my analysis does not have the same goals as state colorblindness, but more importantly, my analysis rejects the structure of thought that allows colorblind ideology.

12. Only posters of those with names who were accused of crimes were collected; missing persons posters, for example, were omitted, as well as those featuring multiple nameless individuals on one poster sought in connection with an event.

13. An unusual case worth mentioning is that of Fawzi Mustapha Assi on the Monthly Fugitives list in 2000. He has the race "white (Arabic)"—the only occurrence of this race category in the program. His poster says he is wanted for providing material support to "Hizballah." He is outside the scope here since his posters are from 2000, and the MWT list was not yet in existence.

14. For example, some, like Bhadreshkumar Chetanbhai Patel, are missing a race category while "looking Muslim," and on a nonterrorism list. Patel is in the Most Wanted program for killing his wife. His poster lists his nationality as Indian, his place of birth as Kantrodi Ta Viramgam, Gujarat, India, and his occupation as "Employee of donut shop." There is much literature on (non-Muslim) South Asians, and others who "look Muslim" according to post-9/11 notions of brownness and foreignness, being perceived as Muslim threats to national security. Based on this literature, we might expect that Patel's case is one of many across nonterrorism lists that fits within the terms of the rule of racelessness described so far for Muslims on the MWT list. However, Patel is one of a small handful of exceptions that do not threaten the sturdiness of the rule of racelessness, which, again, is reserved for Muslim terrorists, specifically. See Maira, "Citizenship, Dissent, Empire"; Volpp, "The Citizen and the Terrorist."

15. Sinnar, "Separate and Unequal."

16. All numbers in this section reflect only wanted posters of suspected criminals with names. For example, posters with "unknown suspect" in place of the name are not included. However, the fact that the same format of the wanted poster is used for noncriminals—missing persons, for example—shows how wanted posters suggest a broader way of knowing that exceeds the sphere of crime and policing, as this book argues.

17. Tehranian, "Selective Racialization"; Gualtieri, *Between Arab and White*; Naber, "Arab Americans and U.S. Racial Formations"; Thangaraj, "Playing through Differences"; Bakalian and Bozorgmehr, *Backlash 9/11*; Cainkar, "Fluid Terror Threat."

18. Schmitt, "Adam Gadahn Was Propagandist."
19. Botelho, "Adam Gadahn."
20. Burke, "Adam Gadahn."
21. Khatchadourian, "Azzam the American."
22. Rana, *Terrifying Muslims*, 18.
23. Rana, *Terrifying Muslims*, 57–63.
24. Analyzing the lives and worldviews of Muslims captured or sought in the global war on terror is beyond the scope of this book. On this and naming conventions, see Li, *The Universal Enemy*.
25. Another example is discussed in an earlier article on a snapshot of FBI wanted posters from 2017 in which I compare two Kuwaiti-born men on the Most Wanted Terrorist list. See Husain, "Deracialization, Dissent, and Terrorism."
26. There is a distinction between these two for much of the scholarship in the racialization of Muslims. Cyra Akila Choudhury, for example, argues that this is a matter of degree and a failure of such scholarship to stand behind the stronger claim that Muslims are a race. Choudhury, "Racecraft and Identity."
27. For example, Amit Prakash shows how French police documents used the words *Muslim* and *North African* synonymously. These specific categories did not travel as such across the ocean, but the method of identification did, accommodating the particular colonial categories in the places in which it was put to work. Prakash, *Empire on the Seine*.
28. Quetelet, *A Treatise on Man*, x.
29. Puar and Rai, "Monster, Terrorist, Fag," 124.
30. Hollinger, *Postethnic America*; Mignolo, "Islamophobia/Hispanophobia," 27.
31. Goldberg, *The Racial State*, 151–52.
32. Razack, *Casting Out*.
33. Hussain, "Beyond Norm and Exception," 738.
34. Hussain, "Beyond Norm and Exception," 736.
35. On Barbary pirates and terrorism, see Husain, "Terrorism and Violence in North America." On Barbary pirates' threat to American settlers' commercial endeavors to the point that one-sixth of the nation's budget in 1796 went to freeing captured sailors: Rojas, "'Insults Unpunished.'" On early Americans' fear of being enslaved in a perceived war between "Christian knights" and "Islamic pirates," see Kidd, *American Christians and Islam*; Baepler, "The Barbary Captivity Narrative"; Matar, *Turks, Moors, and Englishmen*; Allison, *The Crescent Obscured*.
36. Goldthorpe, *Pioneers of Sociological Science*, 1.
37. Judy, "Kant and the Negro."
38. Medovoi, "Dogma-Line Racism," 47.
39. Medovoi, "Dogma-Line Racism," 50.
40. Medovoi, "Dogma-Line Racism," 50.
41. Finn, *Capturing the Criminal Image*, xxii.
42. Berrey, *The Enigma of Diversity*, 29.
43. Sayyid, *Recalling the Caliphate*, 53.
44. Sayyid, *Recalling the Caliphate*, 53.

4. ASSATA, BLACK MADONNA

1. Bin Wahad, "Assata Shakur, Excluding the Nightmare," 121.
2. Bin Wahad, "Assata Shakur, Excluding the Nightmare," 121.
3. Yazdiha, *The Struggle for the People's King*.
4. Bin Wahad, "Assata Shakur, Excluding the Nightmare," 121.
5. The Madonna is a specific Christian image of purity and transcendent divinity. This image runs counter to Shakur's own notions of womanhood and the divine; she questioned understandings of womanhood and divinity that she understood as being on the model of man. Assata Shakur discusses her views on revolutionary women in her autobiography and other writings. In a letter from prison discussed in chapter 2, she speaks on how revolutionary women should be, and how she does not relate to "gods, you know, like from out of the sky and stuff like that because only the things that i can see, hear, touch, and conceive of seem real to me." Shakur to Nuh Washington, July 2, 1973, AF 043, box 2, folder 002, the Black Panther Party Archives of Frankye Adams-Johnson, Jackson State University Archives and Records Division, Jackson, Mississippi.
6. One such strategic use was in the Haitian Revolution. It is one major example that argued that they, too, fall under the category of man and should then have the liberty accorded to man. This argument accompanied a powerful, world-altering revolution.
7. Adewunmi, "Assata Shakur."
8. Thompson, "Assata Shakur Was Convicted of Murder."
9. Smith, "Assata Shakur Is Not a Terrorist."
10. Walker, "Assata Shakur."
11. Crenshaw, "Demarginalizing the Intersection of Race and Sex."
12. It is not possible to offer a comprehensive review of the vast literature on intersectionality and its critics in this chapter; for example, the Combahee River Collective and Black feminists' "triple jeopardy" are not covered here. My goal is instead to review some central arguments just enough to consider the particular variety of intersectionality that appears in the literature on Muslims and the war on terror.
13. Puar, "'I Would Rather Be a Cyborg Than a Goddess,'" 55.
14. Puar, "'I Would Rather Be a Cyborg Than a Goddess,'" 57, 58.
15. Sayyid, *Recalling the Caliphate*, 3.
16. Sayyid, *Recalling the Caliphate*, 3.
17. Sayyid, *Recalling the Caliphate*, 3.
18. Sayyid, *Recalling the Caliphate*, 5.
19. Johnson and Weitzman, *The FBI and Religion*.
20. For further discussion see Felber, *Those Who Know Don't Say*, 11.
21. Chan-Malik, *Being Muslim*, 37.
22. Sayyid, *Recalling the Caliphate*, 8.
23. Kashani, *Medina by the Bay*.
24. Walker, "The Infinite Rehearsals of the Critique of Religion." More specifically: "As a critical practice, theological thinking is not systematic and does not aspire to a rigid systematicity. Instead, it operates as a radical epistemic project that ruptures the dominant *epistème* undergirding the *theologico-political logic* of the Western world and disrupts any self-recuperative, egoistic, and triumphalist politics, even a politics of the multitude"

(200). I also see Sherman A. Jackson's "Islamic secular" similarly, as a way in which Islam is useful beyond Muslims for thinking about alternative models for understanding difference. Jackson, "The Islamic Secular."

25. Puar, "'I Would Rather Be a Cyborg Than a Goddess,'" 49.
26. Cainkar and Selod, "Review of Race Scholarship," 173.
27. Puar, "'I Would Rather Be a Cyborg Than a Goddess,'" 55.
28. Yazdiha, *The Struggle for the People's King*, 148.
29. Maghbouleh, *The Limits of Whiteness*, 171.
30. Melamed, *Represent and Destroy*.
31. Lloyd and Thomas, *Culture and the State*.
32. See, as a representative example of Reed's argument on this, *Class Notes*.
33. Yazdiha, *The Struggle for the People's King*, 153.
34. Ahmad, "PLO and ANC," 76.
35. See also Husain, "Official Antiracism and the Limits of 'Islamophobia.'"
36. Wing, "Civil Rights in the Post 911 World," 718. Then there is the idea that African American Muslims in the war on terror are "Black twice" (a construction that suggests that Muslim *is* Black). See Mauleón, "Black Twice."
37. Beydoun, "Antebellum Islam"; Selod, *Forever Suspect*; Edwards, *The Other Side of Terror*.
38. Melamed, *Represent and Destroy*, 11.
39. Cainkar and Selod, "Review of Race Scholarship," 169.
40. Tehranian, "Selective Racialization," 1201.
41. Maghbouleh, *The Limits of Whiteness*, 30. Her discussion of anthropometry and Iranians further illustrates my point about average man: that the categories can change any which way, any group is fair game, but what is at the root of it is the average man norm. By the mid-1930s, American physical anthropologists like Henry Field, head curator of Chicago Field Museum, "regularly collected 'anthropometrics' on groups from the Middle East. This was part of a larger geopolitical project in the interwar period, formalized by President Franklin Roosevelt. One of the intentions of this project was to use anthropological science to move away from American isolationism toward US-led internationalism.... For the explicit purposes of 'racial classification,' Field offered a taxonomic schema of Iranian facial and body types, including charts, graphs, and hundreds of anthropometrical (or proto-mug shot) photographs" (64).
42. Rana, "The Racial Infrastructure," 122.
43. Also on the limits of the secular left along these lines: Daulatzai and Rana, "Writing the Muslim Left."
44. Spivak, "Can the Subaltern Speak?"
45. For an example of uses of Fields and Fields that differ from my application of their work to similar subjects, see Choudhury, "Racecraft and Identity." One could use Fields and Fields's analysis as Choudhury does to say that because Muslims face racism (cause), they are therefore a race (effect), thus drawing on Fields and Fields's careful attention to cause and effect; also the work of Kumar, who is using Fields and Fields to argue that "terrorcraft" is the racialization of Arabs and Muslims as terrorists, which clearly draws on Fields and Fields's concept of racecraft. Kumar, "Terrorcraft."

46. Where seeking racial whiteness was incentivized for early immigrants from Syria, India, and Yemen, for example, owing to citizenship policies limiting naturalization to free white persons, racial blackness holds useful symbolic, representational cachet in twenty-first-century neoliberalism. But there are other political possibilities beyond racial blackness and whiteness.

47. Stampnitzky, *Disciplining Terror*; Erlenbusch-Anderson, *Genealogies of Terrorism*; Meier, "The Idea of Terror."

48. A number of works have demonstrated how terrorism discourse and counterterrorism have their roots in the politics and upheavals of the 1970s: Umoja, "Repression Breeds Resistance"; James, *Imprisoned Intellectuals*; James, "Framing the Panther"; Chard, *Nixon's War at Home*; Rosenau, *Tonight We Bombed the U.S. Capital*; Mamdani, *Good Muslim, Bad Muslim*; Kundnani, *The Muslims Are Coming!*

49. Aside from the arguments in this chapter based on materials from the FBI Most Wanted program, the biographical information on Shakur's life over these years is drawn primarily from Teishan A. Latner's work on the Cuban chapter of her life: Latner, *Cuban Revolution in America*; Latner, "'Assata Shakur Is Welcome Here.'" Additional sources, though journalistic and favoring police accounts, include Burrough, *Days of Rage*; Castellucci, *The Big Dance*. Shakur's own writings and interviews at assatashakur.org/ were also used here.

50. Christine Todd Whitman, "Letter to the President," March 25, 1998, Clinton Presidential Records, William J. Clinton Presidential Library, Little Rock, Arkansas.

51. Thompson, "Assata Shakur Was Convicted of Murder."

52. Meek, "Pols Seek 2 on Lam in Cuba."

53. Congressional Record (House), July 20, 2005, p. H6144, https://www.congress.gov/congressional-record/2005/07/20/house-section/article/H6117-3.

54. Congressional Record (House), July 20, 2005, H6145.

55. On the FBI's main list, the Ten Most Wanted, there would typically be ten posters (give or take a few, since the FBI sometimes had a sixteen-person-long Ten Most Wanted list) along with some posters of wanted individuals that never made it to the Ten Most Wanted but were nevertheless of interest. Assata Shakur would be among the latter in the 1970s and '80s.

56. Walker, "Assata Shakur."

57. Latner, "Assata Shakur."

58. Mos Def, "Assata Shakur"; Cleaver, "Why Has the FBI Placed a Million-Dollar Bounty?"

59. Arenson, "CUNY Chief Orders Names Stripped."

60. On the Christian Identity Movement, see Belew, *Bring the War Home*.

61. Adewunmi, "Assata Shakur."

62. Shakur, "To My People."

63. Davis and Hinds, "Angela Davis and Assata Shakur's Lawyer."

64. Holley, *An Amerikan Family*, 270.

65. Adewunmi, "Assata Shakur," emphasis added.

66. Stampnitzky, *Disciplining Terror*.

67. Bin Wahad, "Assata Shakur, Excluding the Nightmare," 121.

68. Reed, "The Allure of Malcolm X and the Changing Character of Black Politics," 202.

69. Fahad Ahmad and Jeffrey Monaghan show how the probabilistic thinking of traditional criminal law and criminology, per chapter 1 of this book, are adjusted to accommodate "possibilistic logics" such that the burden of proof for granting a terrorism peace bond in Canada—a type of restraining order based on the fear of a future terrorist attack—is moved from demonstrating that an individual will engage in terrorism to demonstrating that an individual may do so. Ahmad and Monaghan, "From Probabilities to Possibilities."

70. Hall, *Wanted*, 21.

71. On the example of federal agents raiding an apartment complex in Harlem in 1980 looking for Assata Shakur: Umoja, "Repression Breeds Resistance," 149.

72. Holley, *An Amerikan Family*, 175.

73. Bin Wahad, "Assata Shakur, Excluding the Nightmare," 122.

74. Umoja, "The Black Liberation Army and the Radical Legacy."

75. Bin Wahad, "Assata Shakur, Excluding the Nightmare," 121.

76. "Assata Is Free!," 12.

77. As Erica R. Edwards argues, "Black literature, especially by Black women writers, bore the mission of diversity training as it passed through post-1968 classrooms." Examples include the works of Alice Randall, Danielle Evans, and Gloria Naylor. Assata Shakur's autobiography, too, continues to be on university syllabi since its 1987 publication. It is easily reread today as a story of individual struggle, safely in the past, when interpreted through diversity frames. Edwards, *The Other Side of Terror*, 29.

78. Judy's *DisForming the Canon* is important to consider here. He argues against the view that enslaved Africans wrote themselves into being and that slave narratives are to be read as such. He takes seriously that many of these narratives were in Arabic, and their authors Muslim. The place of (Arabic) slave narratives in the establishment of African American literary studies' foundational concerns raises questions about how to understand the place of Islam with relation to African American studies while establishing that such a place certainly exists.

79. Wynter, "On How We Mistook the Map for the Territory."

CONCLUSION

1. Mamdani, *Neither Settler Nor Native*.

2. This statement also appeared in Netanyahu's remarks at the opening of the Knesset, October 16, 2023, https://www.gov.il/en/pages/excerpt-from-pm-netanyahu-s-remarks-at-the-opening-of-the-knesset-s-winter-assembly-16-oct-2023.

3. Said, "Obituary of Eqbal Ahmad."

4. Ahmad, "Revolutionary Warfare," 14.

5. Ahmad, "Terrorism."

6. Ahmad, "PLO and ANC," 78.

7. Alagraa, "What Will Be the Cure?"

8. Quijano, "Coloniality and Modernity/Rationality."

9. El-Kurd, "Jewish Settlers Stole My House."

10. Davis insightfully points out the appearance of Queteletian thought in Marx's labor theory of value, appearing in how Marx thought about the worker, as well as "average social labor." Davis, *Enforcing Normalcy*, 28.

11. Kelley, Amariglio, and Wilson, "'Solidarity Is Not a Market Exchange'"; Gilmore, "Abolition Geography"; Wynter, "On How We Mistook the Map for the Territory." Also, in another example worth mentioning, Nation of Islam founder Elijah Muhammad reversed the racial hierarchy, while maintaining its form, after which his son Warith Deen Muhammad reinterpreted the black-white race politics of his father toward what the latter called "a universal language" through complex hermeneutical maneuvers and understandings of the contextual situatedness of truth such that various contradictions in NOI theology could be true in their time and place but not for all times and all places, including a few decades after Elijah Muhammad's death. Indeed, in the ways that Black Muslim movements and organizations have understood themselves, race was seriously implicated. Adhami, "W. D. Muhammad's Hermeneutics," 6.

Bibliography

About, Ilsen. "Identités indigènes et police coloniale: L'introduction de l'anthropométrie judiciaire en Algérie, 1890–1910." In *Aux origines de la police scientifique*, edited by Pierre PIazza, 280–301. Paris: Karthala, 2011.
Acoli, Sundiata. "An Updated History of the New Afrikan Prison Struggle (Abridged)." In *Imprisoned Intellectuals: America's Political Prisoners Write on Life, Liberation, and Rebellion*, edited by Joy James, 138–64. Lanham, MD: Rowman and Littlefield, 2003.
Adewunmi, Bim. "Assata Shakur: From Civil Rights Activist to FBI's Most-Wanted." *Guardian*, July 13, 2014.
Adhami, Zaid. "W. D. Muhammad's Hermeneutics of the Second Resurrection." In *Oxford Handbook of African American Islam*, edited by Aminah B. McCloud. New York: Oxford University Press, 2014.
Ahmad, Eqbal. "PLO and ANC: Painful Contrasts." In *The Selected Writings of Eqbal Ahmad*, edited by Carollee Bengelsdorg, Margaret Cerullo, and Yogesh Chandrani, 76–80. New York: Columbia University Press, 2006.
Ahmad, Eqbal. "Revolutionary Warfare: How to Tell When the Rebels Have Won." In *The Selected Writings of Eqbal Ahmad*, edited by Carollee Bengelsdorg, Margaret Cerullo, and Yogesh Chandrani, 13–23. New York: Columbia University Press, 2006.
Ahmad, Eqbal. "Terrorism: Theirs and Ours." Lecture, University of Colorado Boulder, October 12, 1998.
Ahmad, Eqbal. *Terrorism: Theirs and Ours*. Foreword and interview by David Barsamian. New York: Seven Stories Press, 2001.
Ahmad, Fahad, and Jeffrey Monaghan. "From Probabilities to Possibilities: Terrorism Peace Bonds, Pre-emptive Security, and Modulations of Criminal Law." *Crime, Law and Social Change* 74 (2020): 341–59.
Ahmed, Sara. *On Being Included: Racism and Diversity in Institutional Life*. Durham, NC: Duke University Press, 2012.
Alagraa, Bedour. "What Will Be the Cure? A Conversation with Sylvia Wynter." *offshoot*, January 7, 2021.

Al-Amin, Imam Jamil. *Revolution by the Book: The Rap Is Live*. Writers' Inc. International, 1994.
"All Aliens to Be Fingerprinted." *Detective*, June 1940.
Allison, Robert J. *The Crescent Obscured: The United States and the Muslim World, 1776–1815*. New York: Oxford University Press, 1995.
Andrews, Mark, Brian Kates, Patrick Doyle, and Robert Crane. "Gunman Frees 4 after 5-Hr. Siege." *Daily News*, March 26, 1977.
Appiah, Anthony. "The Uncompleted Argument: Du Bois and the Illusion of Race." *Critical Inquiry* 12, no. 1 (1985): 21–37.
Arenson, Karen W. "CUNY Chief Orders Names Stripped from Student Center." *New York Times*, December 13, 2006.
Armstrong, Nancy. *Fiction in the Age of Photography: The Legacy of British Realism*. Cambridge, MA: Harvard University Press, 1999.
"Assata Is Free!" *Breakthrough: Political Journal of Prairie Fire Organizing Committee* 4, no. 1 (1980): 12–13.
Austin, Allan D. *African Muslims in Antebellum America: Transatlantic Stories and Spiritual Struggles*. New York: Routledge, 1997.
Aziz, Sahar F. *The Racial Muslim: When Racism Quashes Religious Freedom*. Berkeley: University of California Press, 2022.
Baepler, Paul. "The Barbary Captivity Narrative in American Culture." *Early American Literature* 39, no. 2 (2004): 217–47.
Bakalian, Anny, and Mehdi Bozorgmehr. *Backlash 9/11: Middle Eastern and Muslim Americans Respond*. Berkeley: University of California Press, 2009.
Beirne, Piers. "Adolphe Quetelet and the Origins of Positivist Criminology." *American Journal of Sociology* 92, no. 5 (1987): 1140–69.
Beirne, Piers. *Inventing Criminology: Essays on the Rise of "Homo Criminalis."* Albany: State University of New York Press, 1993.
Belew, Kathleen. *Bring the War Home: The White Power Movement and Paramilitary America*. Cambridge, MA: Harvard University Press, 2018.
Ben Rejeb, Lotfi. "Barbary's 'Character' in European Letters, 1514–1830: An Ideological Prelude to Colonization." *Dialectical Anthropology* 6 (1982): 345–55.
Berger, Dan. *Captive Nation: Black Prison Organizing in the Civil Rights Era*. Chapel Hill: University of North Carolina Press, 2014.
Berrey, Ellen. *The Enigma of Diversity: The Language of Race and the Limits of Racial Justice*. Chicago: University of Chicago Press, 2015.
Bertillon, Alphonse. "The Bertillon System of Identification." *Forum* 11 (March 1891): 330–41.
Bertillon, Alphonse. *Ethnographie moderne: Les races sauvages*. Edited by G. Masson. Paris, 1883.
Beydoun, Khaled A. "Antebellum Islam." *Howard Law Journal* 58, no. 1 (2015): 141–93.
Bhattacharya, Baidik. "Somapolitics: A Biohermeneutic Paradigm in the Era of Empire." *boundary 2* 45, no. 4 (2018): 127–59.
Bin Wahad, Dhoruba. "Assata Shakur, Excluding the Nightmare after the Dream: The 'Terrorist' Label and the Criminalization of Revolutionary Black Movements in the

USA." In *Look for Me in the Whirlwind: From the Panther 21 to 21st-Century Revolutions*, edited by déqui kioni-sadiki and Matt Meyer, 103–23. Oakland, CA: PM Press, 2017.

Bin Wahad, Dhoruba, Mumia Abu-Jamal, and Assata Shakur. *Still Black, Still Strong: Survivors of the War against Black Revolutionaries*. Edited by Jim Fletcher, Tanaquil Jones, and Sylvère Lotringer. Los Angeles: Semiotext(e), 1993.

Blanchard, Emmanuel. "French Colonial Police." In *Encyclopedia of Criminology and Criminal Justice*, vol. 8, edited by G. Bruinsma and D. Weisburd, 1836–46. New York: Springer, 2014.

Blecher, Joel, and Joshua Dubler. "Overlooking Race and Secularism in Muslim Philadelphia." In *Race and Secularism in America*, edited by Jonathon S. Kahn and Vincent W. Lloyd, 122–50. New York: Columbia University Press, 2016.

Bloom, Joshua, and Waldo E. Martin. *Black against Empire: The History and the Politics of the Black Panther Party*. Berkeley: University of California Press, 2016.

Blumenthal, Ralph. "FBI Wiretaps: An Ear on the Brink's Case." *New York Times*, August 9, 1982.

Bonilla-Silva, Eduardo. *Racism without Racists: Color-Blind Racism and the Persistence of Racial Inequality in America*. Lanham, MD: Rowman and Littlefield, 2014.

Botelho, Greg. "Adam Gadahn, American Mouthpiece for Al Qaeda, Killed." CNN, April 23, 2015.

Brodkin Sacks, Karen. "How Did Jews Become White Folks?" In *Race*, edited by Steven Gregory and Roger Sanjek, 78–102. New Brunswick, NJ: Rutgers University Press, 1994.

Browne, Simone. *Dark Matters: On the Surveillance of Blackness*. Durham, NC: Duke University Press, 2015.

Bukhari, Safiya. *The War Before: The True Life Story of Becoming a Black Panther, Keeping the Faith in Prison and Fighting for Those Left Behind*. Edited by Laura Whitehorn. New York: Feminist Press, 2010.

Burke, Jason. "Adam Gadahn: California Death Metal Fan Who Rose Quickly in Al-Qaida's Ranks." *Guardian*, April 23, 2015.

Burrough, Bryan. *Days of Rage*. New York: Penguin, 2015.

Burton, Orisanmi. *Tip of the Spear: Black Radicalism, Prison Repression, and the Long Attica Revolt*. Berkeley: University of California Press, 2023.

Cainkar, Louise. "Fluid Terror Threat: A Genealogy of the Racialization of Arab, Muslim, and South Asian Americans." *Amerasia Journal* 44, no. 1 (2018): 27–59.

Cainkar, Louise. *Homeland Insecurity: The Arab American and Muslim American Experience after 9/11*. New York: Russell Sage, 2009.

Cainkar, Louise, and Saher Selod. "Review of Race Scholarship and the War on Terror." *Sociology of Race and Ethnicity* 4, no. 2 (2018): 165–77.

Carmichael, Stokely, and Charles V. Hamilton. *Black Power: The Politics of Liberation in America*. New York: Vintage, 1967.

Castellucci, John. *The Big Dance: The Untold Story of Kathy Boudin and the Terrorist Family That Committed the Brink's Robbery Murders*. New York: Dodd, Mead, 1986.

Chan-Malik, Sylvia. *Being Muslim: A Cultural History of Women of Color in American Islam*. New York: New York University Press, 2018.

Chard, Daniel S. *Nixon's War at Home: The FBI, Leftist Guerrillas, and the Origins of Counterterrorism*. Chapel Hill: University of North Carolina Press, 2021.
"Chesimard Defense Team Grows." *Home News*, February 24, 1976.
"Chesimard Judge Says Jury Unaware of Moslem Siege." *Home News*, March 11, 1977.
"Chesimard Will Take Stand." *Home News*, April 14, 1976.
Choudhury, Cyra Akila. "Racecraft and Identity in the Emergence of Islam as a Race." *University of Cincinnati Law Review* 91, no. 1 (2022): 1–81.
Clark, Jerry, and Ed Palattella. *On the Lam: A History of Hunting Fugitives in America*. Lanham, MD: Rowman and Littlefield, 2019.
Cleaver, Kathleen. "Why Has the FBI Placed a Million-Dollar Bounty on Assata Shakur?" *Independent*, July 20, 2005.
Cole, David. *Enemy Aliens: Double Standards and Constitutional Freedoms in the War on Terror*. New York: New Press, 2003.
Cole, Simon A. *Suspect Identities: A History of Fingerprinting and Criminal Identification*. Cambridge, MA: Harvard University Press, 2001.
Cone, James H. *Black Theology and Black Power*. Ossining, NY: Orbis, 1997.
Cooke, Annemarie. "Chesimard Move Challenged: 'Hasn't Seen Sun for a Year.'" *Home News*, January 14, 1977.
Crenshaw, Kimberlé. "Demarginalizing the Intersection of Race and Sex: A Black Feminist Critique of Antidiscrimination Doctrine, Feminist Theory, and Antiracist Politics." In *Feminism and Politics*, edited by Anne Phillips, 314–43. Oxford: Oxford University Press, 1998.
Cross, William E. "The Negro-to-Black Conversion Experience." In *The Death of White Sociology: Essays on Race and Culture*, edited by Joyce A. Ladner, 267–86. Baltimore, MD: Black Classic Press, 1973.
Cunningham, David. *There's Something Happening Here: The New Left, the Klan, and FBI Counterintelligence*. Berkeley: University of California Press, 2004.
Curtis, Edward E. "The Black Muslim Scare of the Twentieth Century: The History of State Islamophobia and Its Post-9/11 Variations." In *Islamophobia in America: The Anatomy of Intolerance*, edited by Carl Ernst, 75–106. New York: Palgrave Macmillan, 2013.
Curtis, Edward E., IV. *Islam in Black America: Identity, Liberation, and Difference in African-American Islamic Thought*. Albany: State University of New York Press, 2002.
Daulatzai, Sohail. *Black Star, Crescent Moon: The Muslim International and Black Freedom beyond America*. Minneapolis: University of Minnesota Press, 2012.
Daulatzai, Sohail, and Junaid Rana. "Writing the Muslim Left: An Introduction to Throwing Stones." In *With Stones in Our Hands: Writings on Muslims, Racism, and Empire*, edited by Sohail Daulatzai and Junaid Rana, ix–xxiii. Minneapolis: University of Minnesota Press, 2018.
Davis, Angela, and Lennox Hinds. "Angela Davis and Assata Shakur's Lawyer Denounce FBI's Adding of Exiled Activist to Terrorists List." *Democracy Now!*, May 3, 2013.
Davis, Lennard J. *The End of Normal: Identity in a Biocultural Era*. Ann Arbor: University of Michigan Press, 2013.
Davis, Lennard J. *Enforcing Normalcy: Disability, Deafness, and the Body*. New York: Verso, 1995.

Debord, Guy. *The Society of the Spectacle*. Berkeley, CA: Bureau of Public Secrets, 2014.

Denvir, Daniel. "Revisiting *Racecraft* with Barbara and Karen Fields." *The Dig*, December 13, 2017. https://thedigradio.com/podcast/revisiting-racecraft-with-barbara-and-karen-fields/.

Dew, Spencer. *The Aliites: Race and Law in the Religions of Noble Drew Ali*. Chicago: University of Chicago Press, 2019.

Dillon, Stephen. *Fugitive Life: The Queer Politics of the Prison State*. Durham, NC: Duke University Press, 2018.

Dilworth, Donald C., ed. *Identification Wanted: Development of the American Criminal Identification System 1893–1943*. Gaithersburg, MD: International Association of Chiefs of Police, 1977.

Diouf, Sylviane A. *Servants of Allah: African Muslims Enslaved in the Americas*. New York: New York University Press, 1998.

Donnelly, Kevin. *Adolphe Quetelet, Social Physics and the Average Men of Science, 1796–1874*. London: Pickering and Chatto, 2015.

Donner, Frank J. *Protectors of Privilege: Red Squads and Police Repression in Urban America*. Berkeley: University of California Press, 1990.

Dorman, Jacob S. *The Princess and the Prophet: The Secret History of Magic, Race, and Moorish Muslims in America*. Boston: Beacon Press, 2020.

Douglass, Patrice D. "Assata Is Here: (Dis)Locating Gender in Black Studies." *Souls* 22, no. 1 (2020): 89–103.

Du Bois, W. E. B. "Jefferson Davis as a Representative of Civilization." June 1890. W. E. B. Du Bois Papers (MS 312), Special Collections and University Archives, University of Massachusetts Amherst Libraries. https://credo.library.umass.edu/view/full/mums312-b196-i029.

Edwards, Erica R. *The Other Side of Terror: Black Women and the Culture of US Empire*. New York: New York University Press, 2021.

El-Kurd, Mohammed. "Jewish Settlers Stole My House. It's Not My Fault They're Jewish." *Mondoweiss*, September 26, 2023.

Ellison, Ralph. "An American Dilemma: A Review." In *The Death of White Sociology: Essays on Race and Culture*, edited by Joyce A. Ladner, 81–95. Baltimore, MD: Black Classic Press, 1973.

Erlenbusch-Anderson, Verena. *Genealogies of Terrorism: Revolution, State Violence, Empire*. New York: Columbia University Press, 2018.

Evans, Richard Kent. *MOVE: An American Religion*. New York: Oxford University Press, 2020.

Failinger, Marie A. "Islam in the Mind of American Courts: 1960 to 2001." *Southern California Review of Law and Social Justice* 28, no. 1 (2019): 21–105.

FBI. "FBI's Ten Most Wanted Fugitives 60th Anniversary, 1950–2010." *Federal Documents* 38 (2010). https://digitalcommons.law.ggu.edu/federal_documents/38.

FBI. "The FBI Website at 20: Two Decades of Fighting Crime and Terrorism." Federal Bureau of Investigation, June 30, 2015. https://www.fbi.gov/news/stories/the-fbi-website-at-20-2.

FBI. "The Muslim Cult of Islam." In *Nation of Islam*, part I. Washington, DC: US Department of Justice, Federal Bureau of Investigation, 1955.

FBI. "Ten Most Wanted Fugitives FAQ." Federal Bureau of Investigation. https://www.fbi.gov/wanted/topten/ten-most-wanted-fugitives-faq.

Felber, Garrett. *Those Who Know Don't Say: The Nation of Islam, the Black Freedom Movement, and the Carceral State*. Chapel Hill: University of North Carolina Press, 2020.

Fields, Karen E., and Barbara J. Fields. *Racecraft: The Soul of Inequality in American Life*. New York: Verso, 2022.

Finn, Jonathan. *Capturing the Criminal Image: From Mug Shot to Surveillance Society*. Minneapolis: University of Minnesota Press, 2009.

Fox, John F. "Unique unto Itself: The Records of the Federal Bureau of Investigation 1908 to 1945." *Journal of Government Information* 30, no. 4 (2004): 470–81.

Gage, Beverly. *G-Man: J. Edgar Hoover and the Making of the American Century*. New York: Viking, 2023.

Gardell, Mattias. *In the Name of Elijah Muhammad: Louis Farrakhan and the Nation of Islam*. Durham, NC: Duke University Press, 1996.

Garner, Steven, and Saher Selod. "The Racialization of Muslims: Empirical Studies of Islamophobia." *Critical Sociology* 41, no. 1 (July 7, 2015): 9–19.

Gaylin, Willard. "What's an FBI Poster Doing in a Nice Journal Like That?" *Hastings Report* 2, no. 2 (1972): 1–2.

German, Mike. *Disrupt, Discredit, and Divide: How the New FBI Damages Democracy*. New York: New Press, 2019.

Gerstein, Josh. "The FBI Looks Like Trump's America." *Politico*, November 4, 2016. https://www.politico.com/story/2016/11/fbi-donald-trump-base-230755.

Gibson, Dawn-Marie, and Jamillah Karim. *Women of the Nation: Between Black Protest and Sunni Islam*. New York: New York University Press, 2014.

Gibson, Gail. "U.S. Casts Anti-terror Net." *Baltimore Sun*, October 11, 2001.

Gilmore, Ruth Wilson. "Abolition Geography and the Problem of Innocence." In *Futures of Black Radicalism*, edited by Gaye Theresa Johnson and Alex Lubin, 225–40. New York: Verso, 2017.

Gilroy, Paul. *Against Race*. Cambridge, MA: Belknap Press of Harvard University Press, 2000.

Ginzburg, Carlo. "Clues: Roots of an Evidential Paradigm." In *Myths, Emblems, Clues*, edited and translated by John Tedeschi and Anne Tedeschi, 96–105. London: Hutchinson Radius, 1986.

Goldberg, David Theo. *The Racial State*. New York: Blackwell, 2002.

Goldberg, David Theo. *Racial Subjects: Writing on Race in America*. New York: Routledge, 1997.

Goldberg, David Theo. *Racist Culture: Philosophy and the Politics of Meaning*. London: Blackwell, 1993.

Goldthorpe, John H. *Pioneers of Sociological Science: Statistical Foundations and the Theory of Action*. Cambridge: Cambridge University Press, 2021.

Gomez, Michael A. *Black Crescent: African Muslims in the Americas*. New York: Cambridge University Press, 2005.

Gordon, Avery, and Christopher Newfield. "White Philosophy." In *Identities*, edited by Kwame Anthony Appiah and Henry Louis Gates Jr., 380–400. Chicago: University of Chicago Press, 1995.

Gordon, Lewis R. "Race, Theodicy, and the Normative Emancipatory Challenges of Blackness." *South Atlantic Quarterly* 112, no. 4 (2013): 725–36.

Gordon, Sarah Barringer. *The Spirit of the Law: Religious Voices and the Constitution in Modern America*. Cambridge, MA: Belknap Press of Harvard University Press, 2010.

Greening, J. A. "The Fingerprint Campaign in Berkeley, California (Proceedings of the IACP, 1936)." In *Identification Wanted: Development of the American Criminal Identification System 1893–1943*, edited by Donald C. Dilworth, 218–21. Gaithersburg, MD: International Association of Chiefs of Police, 1977.

Groebner, Valentin. "Describing the Person, Reading the Signs in Late Medieval and Renaissance Europe: Identity Papers, Vested Figures, and the Limits of Identification, 1400–1600." In *Documenting Individual Identity: The Development of State Practices in the Modern World*, edited by Jane Caplan and John Torpey, 15–27. Princeton, NJ: Princeton University Press, 2001.

Gualtieri, Sarah. *Between Arab and White: Race and Ethnicity in the Early Syrian American Diaspora*. Berkeley: University of California Press, 2009.

Hacking, Ian. *The Taming of Chance*. Cambridge: Cambridge University Press, 1990.

Hall, Rachel. *Wanted: The Outlaw in American Visual Culture*. Charlottesville: University of Virginia Press, 2009.

Hallaq, Wael. *Restating Orientalism: A Critique of Modern Knowledge*. New York: Columbia University Press, 2018.

Hames-Garcia, Michael. *Fugitive Thought: Prison Movements, Race, and the Meaning of Justice*. Minneapolis: University of Minnesota Press, 2004.

Haney-Lopez, Ian. *White by Law: The Legal Construction of Race*. New York: New York University Press, 2006.

Hankins, Frank H. *Adolphe Quetelet as Statistician*. New York: AMS Press, 1908.

Hays, Daniel, and Joy McIntyre. "Joanne Loses 2 Rounds on Trial Transfer." *Daily News*, January 21, 1977.

Hickman, Jared. "Globalization and the Gods, or the Political Theology of 'Race.'" *Early American Literature* 45, no. 1 (2010): 145–82.

Hinds, Lennox S. "A Decade in Defense of Human Rights, 1968–1978." New York: National Conference of Black Lawyers, 1978.

Hinds, Lennox S. *Illusions of Justice: Human Rights Violations in the United States*. Iowa City: University of Iowa Press, 1978.

Hoelscher, Fred. "Should a Small City Have Its Own Fingerprint File? (Proceedings of IACP, 1939)." In *Identification Wanted: Development of the American Criminal Identification System 1893–1943*, edited by Donald C. Dilworth, 212–14. Gaithersburg, MD: International Association of Chiefs of Police, 1977.

Holden v. Board of Education of City of Elizabeth, 216 A.2d 387 (N.J. 1966).

Holley, Santi Elijah. *An Amerikan Family: The Shakurs and the Nation They Created*. New York: Mariner, 2023.

Hollinger, David A. *Postethnic America: Beyond Multiculturalism*. New York: Basic Books, 1995.
Hoover, J. Edgar. "Address of Hon. J. Edgar Hoover, Director of the Bureau of Investigation, Department of Justice, Washington, D.C." In *Identification Wanted: Development of the American Criminal Identification System 1893–1943*, edited by Donald C. Dilworth, 163–69. Gaithersburg, MD: International Association of Chiefs of Police, 1977.
Hoover, J. Edgar. "Criminal Identification." *Annals of the American Academy of Political and Social Science* 146 (November 1929): 205–13.
Hoover, John Edgar. "Fugitives Wanted by Police." *Fugitives Wanted by Police* 1, no. 1 (1932).
Husain, Atiya. "Deracialization, Dissent, and Terrorism in the FBI's Most Wanted Program." *Sociology of Race and Ethnicity* 7, no. 2 (2020): 208–25.
Husain, Atiya. "Official Antiracism and the Limits of 'Islamophobia.'" *Social Identities* 27, no. 6 (2020): 611–25.
Husain, Atiya. "Terrorism and Violence in North America." In *Oxford Research Encyclopedias*, 2023. https://doi.org/10.1093/acrefore/9780199340378.013.870.
Hussain, Nasser. "Beyond Norm and Exception: Guantánamo." *Critical Inquiry* 33, no. 4 (2007): 734–53.
Hussain, Nasser. "The Sound of Terror: Phenomenology of a Drone Strike." *Boston Review*, October 14, 2013.
Ignatiev, Noel. *How the Irish Became White*. New York: Routledge, 1995.
Jackson, Sherman A. "Black Orientalism: Its Genesis, Aims, and Significance for American Islam." In *Black Routes to Islam*, edited by Manning Marable and Hishaam D. Aidi. New York: Palgrave Macmillan, 2009.
Jackson, Sherman A. *The Islamic Secular*. New York: Oxford University Press, 2024.
James, Joy. "Assata Shakur and Black Female Agency." In *Seeking the Beloved Community: A Feminist Race Reader*, 93–116. Albany: State University of New York Press, 2013.
James, Joy. "Framing the Panther: Assata Shakur and Black Female Agency." In *Want to Start a Revolution? Radical Women in the Black Freedom Struggle*, edited by Dayo F. Gore, Jeanne Theoharis, and Komozi Woodard, 138–60. New York: New York University Press, 2009.
James, Joy, ed. *Imprisoned Intellectuals: America's Political Prisoners Write on Life, Liberation, and Rebellion*. Lanham, MD: Rowman and Littlefield, 2003.
James, Joy. "Sorrow: The Good Soldier and the Good Woman." In *Warfare in the American Homeland: Policing and Prison in a Penal Democracy*, 58–73. Durham, NC: Duke University Press, 2007.
Jeffreys-Jones, Rhodri. *The FBI: A History*. New Haven, CT: Yale University Press, 2008.
Jeffries, Hasan Kwame. *Bloody Lowndes: Civil Rights and Black Power in Alabama's Black Belt*. New York: New York University Press, 2010.
Jhally, Sut, Jeremy Smith, and Sanjay Talrej. "Edward Said: On 'Orientalism.'" Northampton, MA: Media Education Foundation, 1998.
"Joanne Claims Bias in Jail." *Courier-News*, April 9, 1976.
Johnson, Sylvester A. *African American Religions, 1500–2000: Colonialism, Democracy, and Freedom*. Cambridge: Cambridge University Press, 2015.

Johnson, Sylvester A., and Steven Weitzman, eds. *The FBI and Religion: Faith and National Security before and after 9/11*. Berkeley: University of California Press, 2017.

Jones, Charles E., ed. *The Black Panther Party Reconsidered*. Baltimore, MD: Black Classic Press, 1998.

Jones, William R. *Is God a White Racist? A Preamble to Black Theology*. Boston: Beacon Press, 1997.

Joseph, Anne M. "Anthropometry, the Police Expert, and the Deptford Murders: The Contested Introduction of Fingerprinting for the Identification of Criminals in Late Victorian and Edwardian Britain." In *Documenting Individual Identity: The Development of State Practices in the Modern World*, edited by Jane Caplan and John Torpey, 164–83. Princeton, NJ: Princeton University Press, 2001.

Judy, Ronald A. T. *DisForming the American Canon: African-Arabic Slave Narratives and the Vernacular*. Minneapolis: University of Minnesota Press, 1993.

Judy, Ronald. "Kant and the Negro." *Surfaces* 1, no. 8 (1991): 1-81.

Kaluszynski, Martine. "Republican Identity: Bertillonage as Government Technique." In *Documenting Individual Identity: The Development of State Practices in the Modern World*, edited by Jane Caplan and John Torpey, 123–38. Princeton, NJ: Princeton University Press, 2001.

Karim, Jamillah. *American Muslim Women: Negotiating Race, Class, and Gender within the Ummah*. New York: New York University Press, 2008.

Kashani, Maryam. *Medina by the Bay*. Durham, NC: Duke University Press, 2023.

Kavanaugh, Reginald. "Chesimard Jury Selection to Resume." *Home News*, January 21, 1977.

Kavanaugh, Reginald. "Chesimard Lawyers Lose Round." *Home News*, September 28, 1976.

Kavanaugh, Reginald. "Chesimard Ruling Expected This Week." *Home News*, January 26, 1977.

Kavanaugh, Reginald. "Chesimard Trial Postponed: Further Delays Possible." *Home News*, April 24, 1976.

Kelley, Robin D. G., Jack Amariglio, and Lucas Wilson. "'Solidarity Is Not a Market Exchange': An RM Interview with Robin D. G. Kelley, Part 1." *Rethinking Marxism* 30, no. 4 (2018): 568–98.

Khabeer, Su'ad Abdul. *Muslim Cool: Race, Religion, and Hip Hop in the United States*. New York: New York University Press, 2016.

Khatchadourian, Raffi. "Azzam the American." *New Yorker*, January 14, 2007.

Kidd, A. M. "The Right to Take Fingerprints, Measurements and Photographs (in *The Detective*, March 1920)." In *Identification Wanted: Development of the American Criminal Identification System 1893–1943*, edited by Donald C. Dilworth, 112–17. Gaithersburg, MD: International Association of Chiefs of Police, 1977.

Kidd, Thomas S. *American Christians and Islam: Evangelical Culture and Muslims from the Colonial Period to the Age of Terrorism*. Princeton, NJ: Princeton University Press, 2009.

King, Glen D. "Foreword." In *Identification Wanted: Development of the American Criminal Identification System 1893–1943*, edited by Donald C. Dilworth, v. Gaithersburg, MD: International Association of Chiefs of Police, 1977.

Krüger, Lorenz, Lorraine J. Daston, and Michael Heidelberger, eds. *The Probabilistic Revolution, Volume 1: Ideas in History*. Cambridge, MA: MIT Press, 1987.

Krüger, Lorenz, Gerd Gigerenzer, and Mary S. Morgan, eds. *The Probabilistic Revolution, Volume 2: Ideas in the Sciences*. Cambridge, MA: MIT Press, 1990.

Kumar, Deepa. *Islamophobia and the Politics of Empire*. Chicago: Haymarket, 2012.

Kumar, Deepa. "Terrorcraft: Empire and the Making of the Racialised Terrorist Threat." *Race and Class* 67, no. 2 (2020): 34–60.

Kundnani, Arun. *The Muslims Are Coming! Islamophobia, Extremism, and the Domestic War on Terror*. Brooklyn: Verso, 2015.

Kunstler, William M., and Sheila Isenberg. *My Life as a Radical Lawyer*. New York: Birch Lane Press, 1994.

Latner, Teishan A. "'Assata Shakur Is Welcome Here': Havana, Black Freedom Struggle, and U.S.-Cuba Relations." *Souls* 19, no. 4 (2018): 455–77.

Latner, Teishan A. "Assata Shakur: The Political Life of Political Exile." In *Black Power Afterlives: The Enduring Significance of the Black Panther Party*. Chicago: Haymarket, 2020.

Latner, Teishan A. *Cuban Revolution in America: Havana and the Making of a United States Left, 1968–1992*. Chapel Hill: University of North Carolina Press, 2018.

"Lawyers' Group Aiding Mrs. Chesimard." *Home News*, March 5, 1976.

Lazarsfeld, Paul F. "Notes on the History of Quantification in Sociology—Trends, Sources and Problems." *Isis* 52, no. 2 (1961): 277–333.

Lécuyer, Bernard-Pierre. "Probability in Vital and Social Statistics: Quetelet, Farr and the Bertillons." In *The Probabilistic Revolution, Volume 1: Ideas in History*, edited by Lorenz Krüger, Lorraine J. Daston, and Michael Heidelberger, 317–36. Cambridge, MA: MIT Press, 1987.

Li, Darryl. *The Universal Enemy: Jihad, Empire, and the Challenge of Solidarity*. Stanford, CA: Stanford University Press, 2020.

Lincoln, C. Eric. *The Black Muslims in America*. Grand Rapids, MI: Wm. B. Eerdmans, 1961.

Lindsey, Treva B. "Negro Women May Be Dangerous: Black Women's Insurgent Activism in the Movement for Black Lives." *Souls* 19, no. 3 (2017): 315–27.

Lloyd, David, and Paul Thomas. *Culture and the State*. New York: Routledge, 1998.

Lloyd, Vincent W. *Religion of the Field Negro: On Black Secularism and Black Theology*. New York: Fordham University Press, 2018.

Lombroso, Cesare. *Criminal Man*. Translated and with a new introduction by Mary Gibson and Nicole Hahn Rafter. Durham, NC: Duke University Press, 2006. First published 1876.

Long, Charles H. "The Gift of Speech and the Travail of Language." In *Ellipsis . . . The Collected Writings of Charles H. Long*, 403–11. New York: Bloomsbury, 2018.

Long, Charles H. "The Humanities and 'Other' Humans." *In Ellipsis . . . The Collected Writings of Charles H. Long*, 321–28. New York: Bloomsbury, 2018.

Love, Erik. *Islamophobia and Racism in America*. New York: New York University Press, 2017.

Maghbouleh, Neda. *The Limits of Whiteness: Iranian Americans and the Everyday Politics of Race.* Stanford, CA: Stanford University Press, 2017.

Mahmood, Saba. *Politics of Piety: The Islamic Revival and the Feminist Subject.* Princeton, NJ: Princeton University Press, 2004.

Maira, Sunaina. "Citizenship, Dissent, Empire: South Asian Muslim Immigrant Youth." In *Being and Belonging: Muslims in the United States Since 9/11*, edited by Katherine Pratt Ewing, 15–46. New York: Russell Sage Foundation, 2008.

Mamdani, Mahmood. *Good Muslim, Bad Muslim: America, the Cold War, and the Roots of Terror.* New York: Doubleday, 2004.

Mamdani, Mahmood. *Neither Settler nor Native: The Making and Unmaking of Permanent Minorities.* Cambridge, MA: Belknap Press of Harvard University Press, 2020.

Marable, Manning. "Assata Shakur: 'The Continuity of Struggle.'" *Souls* 1, no. 2 (1999): 93–100.

Martin, Lerone A. *The Gospel of J. Edgar Hoover.* Princeton, NJ: Princeton University Press, 2023.

Marx, Karl, V. I. Lenin, Bertolt Brecht, and Tings Chak. *Paris Commune 150.* New Delhi: LeftWord, 2021.

Matar, Nabil. *Turks, Moors, and Englishmen in the Age of Discovery.* New York: Columbia University Press, 1999.

Mauleón, Emmanuel. "Black Twice: Policing Black Muslim Identities." *UCLA Law Review* 65, no. 1326 (2018): 1326–91.

Mos Def. "Assata Shakur: The Government's Terrorist Is Our Community's Heroine." *All HipHop*, May 18, 2005. https://allhiphop.com/2005/05/17/assata-shakur-the-governments-terrorist-is-our-communitys-heroine/.

McCloud, Aminah Beverly. *African American Islam.* New York: Routledge, 1995.

McCrary, Charles. *Sincerely Held: American Secularism and Its Believers.* Chicago: University of Chicago Press, 2022.

Medovoi, Leerom. "Dogma-Line Racism." *Social Text* 31, no. 1 (2013): 43–62.

Meek, James Gordon. "Pols Seek 2 on Lam in Cuba." *Daily News*, August 5, 2006.

Meier, Anna. "The Idea of Terror: Institutional Reproduction in Government Responses to Political Violence." *International Studies Quarterly* 64 (2020): 499–509.

Melamed, Jodi. *Represent and Destroy: Rationalizing Violence in the New Racial Capitalism.* Minneapolis: University of Minnesota Press, 2011.

Michaels, Walter Benn. "Race into Culture: A Critical Genealogy of Cultural Identity." In *Identities*, edited by Kwame Anthony Appiah and Henry Louis Gates Jr., 32–62. Chicago: University of Chicago Press, 1995.

Mignolo, Walter D. "Islamophobia/Hispanophobia: The (Re)Configuration of the Racial Imperial/Colonial Matrix." *Human Architecture: Journal of the Sociology of Self-Knowledge* 5, no. 1 (2006): 13–28.

Miles, Thomas J. "An Empirical Analysis of the FBI's Ten Most Wanted." *Journal of Empirical Legal Studies* 5, no. 2 (2008): 275–308.

Moore, Kathleen M. *Al-Mughtaribun: American Law and the Transformation of Muslim Life in the United States.* Albany: State University of New York Press, 1995.

Morning, Ann. *The Nature of Race: How Scientists Think and Teach about Human Difference*. Berkeley: University of California Press, 2011.

"'Most Wanted Terrorists' List Released." CNN, October 10, 2001.

Moten, Fred. "Of Human Flesh: An Interview with R. A. Judy." *boundary 2* 47, no. 2 (2020): 227–62.

Muhammad, Khalil Gibran. *The Condemnation of Blackness: Race, Crime, and the Making of Modern Urban America*. Cambridge, MA: Harvard University Press, 2010.

Naber, Nadine. "Arab Americans and U.S. Racial Formations." In *Race and Arab Americans before and after 9/11: From Invisible Citizens to Visible Subjects*, edited by Amaney Jamal and Nadine Naber, 1–45. Syracuse, NY: Syracuse University Press, 2008.

Newton, Huey P. *Revolutionary Suicide*. New York: Penguin, 1973.

Omi, Michael, and Howard Winant. *Racial Formation in the United States*. New York: Routledge, 2014.

Onaci, Edward. *Free the Land: The Republic of New Afrika and the Pursuit of a Black Nation-State*. Chapel Hill: University of North Carolina Press, 2020.

O'Reilly, Kenneth. *"Racial Matters": The FBI's Secret File on Black America, 1960–1972*. New York: Free Press, 1989.

Perkins, Margo V., and Carmen L. Phelps. *Autobiography as Activism: Three Black Women of the Sixties*. Jackson: University Press of Mississippi, 2000.

Piazza, Pierre. "Alphonse Bertillon and the Identification of Persons (1880–1914)." *Criminocorpus*, August 26, 2016.

Porter, Theodore M. *The Rise of Statistical Thinking: 1820–1900*. Princeton, NJ: Princeton University Press, 2020.

Powers, Richard Gid. *Secrecy and Power: The Life of J. Edgar Hoover*. New York: Free Press, 1987.

Prakash, Amit. *Empire on the Seine: The Policing of North Africans in Paris, 1925–1975*. New York: Oxford University Press, 2022.

Puar, Jasbir K. "'I Would Rather Be a Cyborg Than a Goddess.'" *PhiloSOPHIA* 2, no. 1 (2012): 49–66.

Puar, Jasbir K., and Amit S. Rai. "Monster, Terrorist, Fag: The War on Terrorism and the Production of Docile Patriots." *Social Text* 20, no. 3 (2002): 117–48.

Quetelet, M. A. *A Treatise on Man*. New York: Burt Franklin, 1842.

Quijano, Aníbal. "Coloniality and Modernity/Rationality." *Cultural Studies* 21, no. 2–3 (2007): 168–78.

Quijano, Anibal. "¡Qué tal raza!" *America Latina en movimiento* 320, no. 29 (1999): 1–8.

Quisay, Walaa, and Asim Qureshi. *When Only God Can See: The Faith of Muslim Political Prisoners*. London: Pluto Press, 2024.

Rana, Junaid. "No Muslims Involved." In *Flashpoints for Asian American Studies*, edited by Cathy J. Schlund-Vials and Viet Thanh Nguyen. New York: Fordham University Press, 2017.

Rana, Junaid. "The Racial Infrastructure of the Terror-Industrial Complex." *Social Text* 34, no. 4, 129 (2016): 111–38.

Rana, Junaid. *Terrifying Muslims: Race and Labor in the South Asian Diaspora*. Durham, NC: Duke University Press, 2011.

Rana, Junaid, and Gilberto Rosas. "Managing Crisis: Post-9/11 Policing and Empire." *Cultural Dynamics* 18, no. 3 (2006): 219–34.

Randolph, Sherie. *Florynce "Flo" Kennedy: The Life of a Black Feminist Radical*. Chapel Hill: University of North Carolina Press, 2015.

Razack, Sherene. *Casting Out: Race and the Eviction of Muslims from Western Law and Politics*. Toronto: University of Toronto Press, 2008.

Reed, Adolph, Jr. *Class Notes: Posing as Politics and Other Thoughts on the American Scene*. New York: New Press, 2001.

Reed, Adolph, Jr. "The Allure of Malcolm X and the Changing Character of Black Politics." In *Stirrings in the Jug: Black Politics in the Post-Segregation Era*, 197–224. Minneapolis: University of Minnesota Press, 1999.

Reitan, Ruth. "Cuba, the Black Panther Party and the US Black Movement in the 1960s: Issues of Security." *New Political Science* 21, no. 2 (1999): 217–30.

Rhodes, Henry. *Alphonse Bertillon: Father of Scientific Detection*. New York: Abelard-Schuman, 1956.

Robinson, Cedric J. *Black Marxism: The Making of the Black Radical Tradition*. Chapel Hill: University of North Carolina Press, 1983.

Rodriguez, Dylan. *Forced Passages: Imprisoned Radical Intellectuals and the U.S. Prison Regime*. Minneapolis: University of Minnesota Press, 2005.

Rojas, Martha Elena. "'Insults Unpunished': Barbary Captives, American Slaves, and the Negotiation of Liberty." *Early American Studies* 1, no. 2 (2003): 159–86.

Rosenau, William. *Tonight We Bombed the U.S. Capital: The Explosive Story of M19, America's First Female Terrorist Group*. New York: Atria, 2019.

Sabljak, Mark, and Martin H. Greenberg. *Most Wanted: A History of the FBI's Ten Most Wanted List*. New York: Bonanza, 1990.

Said, Edward W. "Obituary of Eqbal Ahmad." *Guardian*, May 14, 1999.

Said, Edward W. *Orientalism*. 1979. Reprint, New York: Knopf, 2014.

Sarton, George. "Preface to Volume XXIII of Isis (Quetelet)." *Isis* 23, no. 1 (1935): 6–24.

Saunders, D. J., and Don Singleton. "FBI Just Missed Brink's Suspect." *Daily News*, August 13, 1982.

Sayyid, Salman. *Recalling the Caliphate: Decolonization and World Order*. London: Hurst, 2014.

Schmitt, Eric. "Adam Gadahn Was Propagandist for Al Qaeda Who Sold Terror in English." *New York Times*, April 23, 2015.

Schrader, Stuart. "Wanted: An End to Police Terror." *Viewpoint Magazine*, June 9, 2020. https://viewpointmag.com/2020/06/09/wanted-an-end-to-police-terror/.

Schweber, Libby. *Disciplining Statistics: Demography and Vital Statistics in France and England, 1830–1885*. Durham, NC: Duke University Press, 2006.

Sekula, Allan. "The Body and the Archive." *October* 39 (winter 1986): 3–64.

Selod, Saher. *Forever Suspect: Racialized Surveillance of Muslim Americans in the War on Terror*. New Brunswick, NJ: Rutgers University Press, 2018.

Selod, Saher, and David G. Embrick. "Racialization and Muslims: Situating the Muslim Experience in Race Scholarship." *Sociology Compass* 7, no. 8 (2013): 644–55.

Shakur, Assata. *Assata: An Autobiography*. Chicago: Lawrence Hill, 2001.

Shakur, Assata. "Message of Condolences on the Transition of Our Revolutionary Sista, Comrade and Friend, Safiya Bukhari." It's About Time, August 29, 2003. http://www.itsabouttimebpp.com/Memorials/Safiya_Bukhari.html.

Shakur, Assata. "To My People." Assatashakur.org, July 4, 1973. http://www.assatashakur.org/mypeople.htm.

Shakur, Assata. "Women in Prison: How We Are." *Black Scholar* 9, no. 7 (1978): 8–15.

"Shakur Wins Court Decision." *Black Panther*, February 19, 1977.

Shakur, Zayd Malik, and members of the Black Liberation Army. "Spring Came Early This Year." In *Break de Chains*, 10–16. New York: Community Press, 1973.

Shelby, Tommie. *We Who Are Dark: The Philosophical Foundations of Black Solidarity*. Cambridge, MA: Harvard University Press, 2007.

Silva, Kumarini. *Brown Threat: Identification in the Security State*. Minneapolis: University of Minnesota Press, 2016.

Sinnar, Shirin. "Separate and Unequal: The Law of 'Domestic' and 'International' Terrorism." *Michigan Law Review* 117, no. 7 (2019): 1333–1404.

Smith, Mychal Denzel. "Assata Shakur Is Not a Terrorist." *Nation*, May 7, 2013.

Spillers, Hortense J. "Mama's Baby, Papa's Maybe: An American Grammar Book." *Diacritics* 17, no. 2 (2006): 64–81.

Spivak, Gayatri Chakravorty. "Can the Subaltern Speak?" In *Marxism and the Interpretation of Culture*, edited by Cary Nelson and Lawrence Grossberg. Urbana: University of Illinois Press, 1988.

Stampnitzky, Lisa. *Disciplining Terror: How Experts Invented "Terrorism."* Cambridge: Cambridge University Press, 2013.

Sullivan, Joseph F. "Chesimard Defense Loses on Shift." *New York Times*, January 21, 1977.

Sullivan, Joseph F. "Courthouse Is Picketed as Chesimard Trial Starts." *New York Times*, January 18, 1977.

Swierczynski, Duane. *The Encyclopedia of the FBI's Ten Most Wanted List: Over Fifty Years of Convicts, Robbers, Terrorists, and Other Rogues*. New York: Skyhorse, 2014.

Taylor, Charles. "Modes of Secularism." In *Secularism and Its Critics*, edited by Rajeev Bhargava, 31–53. New York: Oxford University Press, 1999.

Taylor, Ula Yvette. *The Promise of Patriarchy*. Chapel Hill: University of North Carolina Press, 2017.

Tehranian, John. "Selective Racialization: Middle-Eastern American Identity and the Faustian Pact with Whiteness." *Connecticut Law Review* 40, no. 4 (2008): 1201–35.

Thangaraj, Stanley. "Playing through Differences: Black-White Racial Logic and Interrogating South Asian American Identity." *Ethnic and Racial Studies* 35, no. 6 (2012): 988–1006.

Thelwell, Ekwueme Michael. "Foreword. H. Rap Brown/Jamil Al-Amin: A Profoundly American Story." In *Die Nigger Die! A Political Autobiography*, by H. Rap Brown, vii–xxxviii. Chicago: Lawrence Hill, 1969.

Theoharis, Athan G., ed. *The FBI: A Comprehensive Reference Guide*. Phoenix, AZ: Oryx, 1999.

Theoharis, Athan G. *The FBI and American Democracy: A Brief Critical History*. Lawrence: University Press of Kansas, 2004.

Thompson, Krissah. "Assata Shakur Was Convicted of Murder. Is She a Terrorist?" *Washington Post*, May 8, 2013.

Towns, Armond R. *On Black Media Philosophy*. Berkeley: University of California Press, 2022.

Umoja, Akinyele. "Black Liberation Army." In *Black Power Encyclopedia: From Black Is Beautiful to Urban Uprisings*, edited by Akinyele Umoja, Karin L. Stanford, and Jasmin A. Young, 112–17. New York: Bloomsbury, 2018.

Umoja, Akinyele O. "The Black Liberation Army and the Radical Legacy of the Black Panther Party." In *Black Power in the Belly of the Beast*, edited by Judson L. Jeffries, 224–51. Urbana: University of Illinois Press, 2006.

Umoja, Akinyele Omowale. "Repression Breeds Resistance: The Black Liberation Army and the Radical Legacy of the Black Panther Party." *New Political Science* 21, no. 2 (1999): 131–55.

Volpp, Leti. "The Citizen and the Terrorist." *UCLA Law Review* 49 (2002): 1575–88.

Waddell, Kaveh. "The FBI's Most-Wanted Cybercriminals." *Atlantic*, April 27, 2016.

Walker, Corey D. B. "The Infinite Rehearsals of the Critique of Religion: Theological Thinking after Humanism." *boundary 2* 35, no. 3 (2008): 189–212.

Walker, Tim. "Assata Shakur: Black Militant, Fugitive Cop Killer, Terrorist Threat... or Escaped Slave?" *Independent*, July 18, 2014.

Ware, Rudolph T, III. *The Walking Qur'an: Islamic Education, Embodied Knowledge, and History in West Africa*. Chapel Hill: University of North Carolina Press, 2014.

Washington, Nuh. *All Power to the People*. Montreal: Arm the Spirit/Solidarity, 2002.

Weheliye, Alexander G. *Habeas Viscus: Racializing Assemblages, Biopolitics, and Black Feminist Theories of the Human*. Durham, NC: Duke University Press, 2014.

The White House. "The List of Most Wanted Terrorists." US Department of State Archive, October 10, 2001. https://2001-2009.state.gov/s/ct/rls/fs/2001/5317.htm.

Williams, Evelyn A. *Inadmissible Evidence: The Story of the African-American Trial Lawyer Who Defended the Black Liberation Army*. Chicago: Lawrence Hill, 1993.

Wing, Adrien Katherine. "Civil Rights in the Post 911 World: Critical Race Praxis, Coalition Building, and the War on Terrorism." *Louisiana Law Review* 63, no. 3 (2003): 717–57.

Wynter, Sylvia. "On How We Mistook the Map for the Territory, and Re-imprisoned Ourselves in Our Unbearable Wrongness of Being, of Désêtre: Black Studies Toward the Human Project." In *Not Only the Master's Tools: African American Studies in Theory and Practice*, edited by Lewis R. Gordon and Jane Anna Gordon, 107–69. Boulder, CO: Paradigm, 2006.

Yazdiha, Hajar. *The Struggle for the People's King: How Politics Transforms the Memory of the Civil Rights Movement*. Princeton, NJ: Princeton University Press, 2023.

Young, Liam Cole. *List Cultures*. Amsterdam: Amsterdam University Press, 2017.

Young, Marilyn B. "Ground Zero: Enduring War." In *September 11 in History: A Watershed Moment?*, edited by Mary L. Dudziak, 11–34. Durham, NC: Duke University Press, 2003.

Index

Page locators in italics indicate figures and tables.

9/11: 3–6, 89, 105–6, 114. *See also* war on terror

Abdul-Rauf, Mahmoud, 62
abolition: contemporary movement, 137; slavery, 155n20
Abu Nidal Organization, 93
Abu Sayyaf Group, 101
Acoli, Sundiata, 53, 68
Act to Combat International Terrorism (1984), 83
administrology, 42
Africa, John, 60
Africans, 12–14, 55, 68, 72, *124*, 149n107, 152n181, 155n20
Ahmad, Eqbal, 21, 115, 132–38
Ahmed, Sara, 45
Aidi, Hisham D., 5
alerts, 97–98
Al-Amin, Jamil (H. Rap Brown), 77, 78–79, 85, 121, 152n172, 155n27
Al-Aqsa Flood, 131
Algeria, 132
Algiers, 37
Al Harakat al Islamiyyah, 99
Ali, Ishmail Muslim, 90, 123
Ali, Muhammad, 51–52
Ali, Noble Drew, 54, 155n24
aliases, 34–35, 98
Al-Liby, Anas, 92

"All Power to the People," 15
Al-Munawar, Muhammad Ahmed, 93–94, *94*
Al-Qaeda, 3, 92, 94, 95, 99
Al-Shabaab, 98, 99
Alsultany, Evelyn, 5
Al-Tamimi, Ahlam Ahmad, 92–93, *93*
America's Most Wanted (television program), 48
AMSA acronym (Arab, Muslim, South Asian), 21
anarchists, 37
anthropocentrism, 8, 25
anthropometry, 32–38, 43, 49–50, 84, 127, 148n70, 149n117 165n41. *See also bertillonage*
anticolonial movements, 47, 79, 112
antidiscrimination law, 109–11. *See also* redress
antiracism 17, 19, 135: Muslims, 117; Israeli defense, 131–32, 134–35; "official," 50, 71, 116; reclamation, 137–38
antiwar activists, 85, 90, 123
Appleby, Theodore, 58–61, 62
Arab, 13–14, 18, 21, 55, 88, 90, 92–94, 102, 104, 114–17, 140n10, 161n7, 165n45
archetypal Muslim terrorist, 4–6, 85, 87–101, 106. *See also* racelessness
Armstrong, Nancy, 35, 36
Arshad, Farhan ul, 89
Asad, Talal, 5
Assata (Shakur), 14, 20, 54, 60, 73–75, 79, 80

Assata Bulletin, 60, 62
"Assata Shakur, Excluding the Nightmare after the Dream: The 'Terrorist' Label and the Criminalization of Revolutionary Black Movements in the USA" (Bin Wahad), 107–8
Assata Shakur Defense Committee, 11, 80, 81
"Assata Taught Me" slogan, 125
Assi, Fawzi Mustapha, 162n13
astronomy, 7, 23–24, 27, 29–30
Attica, 58
Attica News, 11
average man (*l'homme moyen*), 7–11, 25, 29, 37, 47–50, 115, 128, 135, 140n18, 146n45; *bertillonage*, 32–42; binomial curve, 27–28, 30, 35; continued use, 7, 20, 23, 32, 49–50, 102; critiques, 25, 32, 143n15; deviations from, 27, 29, 30, 31, 36, 46, 78, 86, 102, 115, 135–36; different races/nations, 30–31, 108, 136, 146n58; FBI wanted posters, 8, 23, 36; fictional, 25, 28, 35–36; height and weight statistics, 28, 144n21, 145n36, 147–48n70; nature, 10, 26–27, 32, 50, 102; obliterative, 29, 32, 36, 49; policing, 7–9, 25; Quetelet's derivation, 27–32; racelessness, 86, 102; progressive replication, 135–37; the secular, 8–10, 25; Assata Shakur, 56; theology, 29, 32; universalism, 8, 30. *See also* Black Madonna figure; human; man; statistics
Aziz, Sahar, 5

Baraka, Amiri, 62
Barbary pirates, 104, 141n35, 163n35
The Battle of Algiers (film), 132
Bayoumi, Moustafa, 5
Bazian, Hatem, 5
Belafonte, Harry, 62
Belgium, 24
bell curve, 7, 21, 27–28, 35, 115, 136
Ben Rejeb, Lotfi, 142n35
Bergdoll, Grover C., 41
Berrey, Ellen, 105
Bertillon, Alphonse M., 7–8, 23, 134; average man, 7, 20, 35–36; biographical sketch, 32–33; cabinets, 7, 34–6; cards, 7–8, 34–36, 48; influence on FBI wanted posters, 8; photography, 34–35; race, 36–37, 127, 148–49n105. *See also* policing, *bertillonage*
Bertillon, Jacques, 32

Bertillon, Louis-Adolphe: 32–33, 147n69; polygenism theory, 147–48n70
bertillonage, 7–9, 32–42; adoption in United States, 32, 38–39; Bertillon cards, 7–8, 34–36; bodily measurements, 35, 38–39; cataloging processes, 35; colonial use, 37, 49; continued use, 32, 39, 49, 134; method of elimination, 34; photography, 34–36; standardization, 1–2, 7, 35–40; used by FBI, 8, 32, 34, 36–41, 84, 134. *See also* anthropometry; policing; scientific rationality
Beydoun, Khaled, 5, 115
Bhattacharya, Baidik, 9, 34, 36
bin Laden, Osama, 3, 11, 84, 161n6, 161n8
binomial curve, *see* bell curve
Bin Wahad, Dhoruba, 21, 107, 110, 114, 127–29
Bird, Joan, 52
Bishop, William N., 42
Black Islam, 14–16, 20, 21, 51, 77–82, 153n1; Black Muslim, 79, 112–13; FBI, 54–56; the Negro, 11–14, 55–56, 79; divinity, 14, 80, 82, 130. *See also* Islam; Muslims; Nation of Islam (NOI)
Black Liberation Army, 3, 12, 51–53, 64, 76, 126, 129, 153–54n9
Black liberation movement: criminalization, 11–12, 45, 52–53, 107–8, 127–29; legacy, 110, 127; *See also* Black Liberation Army; Black Panther Party; Black Power
Black Lives Matter movement, 11, 14, 125–26
Black Madonna figure, 21, 107–9, 115, 127–28, 164n5. *See also* average man (*l'homme moyen*)
The Black Muslims in America (Lincoln), 79, 112
Black Nationalism: The Rise of the Black Muslims in the U.S.A. (Essien-Udom), 79
blackness: racial blackness, 13–14, 17–18, 20, 54, 115, 119; innocence claim, 108, 116, 119; Islam, 12, 79–80, 137; political, 79, 129; proxy for race, 16, 96. *See also* racial blackness
Black Panther Party, 3; biographical approach, 74; Muslim members, 51, 53, 56, 75–77, 80, 155n23; prison escapes, 64, 75; repression, 52–53, 153n8; religion, 15; trials, 12, 57, 153n8. *See also* Black Liberation Army; Black liberation movement; Black Power

Black Panther publication, 53–54
Black Power, 15, 20; black political elite, 142n45; humanism, 15; Islam, 15, 68, 80
Black Power: The Politics of Liberation in America (Carmichael and Hamilton), 154–55n15
Black Solidarity Day, 64
Black studies, 8–9, 16, 21, 129–30, 137 167n78
Bonilla-Silva, Eduardo, 161–62n11
BOSS (Bureau of Special Services), New York, 153n8
Boyle, Robert, 153n5
Britons, 141–42n35
brown, 6, 162n14
Brown, H. Rap. *See* Al-Amin, Jamil (H. Rap Brown)
Browne, Simone, 72
Bukhari, Safiya, 20, 56–57, 75–80
bureaucracy, 35, 39, 42, 103, 150n135
Bush, George W., 2, 83, 111

Cainkar, Louise, 5
Camescasse, Jean-Louis, 37
Canada, 8, 37, 40, 90, 150–151n153, 167n69
capitalism, 5, 10, 13, 39, 47, 49, 70, 72, 77, 115–6, 137
Capital: Volume I (Marx), 136
Carmichael, Stokely (Kwame Ture), 154–55n15
Castro, Fidel, 120, 122
categories: Bertillon, 8, 34; cataloging processes, 35; relations, 111; incoherence of race, 3–4, 14, 16, 30, 87, 93, 136; photography, 26. *See also* archetypal Muslim terrorist; *bertillonage*; criminal identification; identification order; Negro category
Center for Constitutional Rights, 58
Césaire, Aimé, 44
Chan-Malik, Sylvia, 112
Chesimard, Joanne Deborah. *See* Shakur, Assata
CHESROB, 72
Choudhury, Cyra Akila, 143n50, 163n26, 165n45
Chow, Rey, 111
Christendom, 10–11, 86
Christian Identity Movement, 124
Christianity: 98; cultural destruction, 12; God, 10, 15; purity, 164n5; civilizational hierarchy, 141; Western, 60–61

citizenship category on wanted posters, 88–98, 91–94, *94, 95, 96*
City College of New York, 122
class struggle, 33, 37–38, 49
Cleaver, Eldridge, 73
Cleaver, Kathleen, 122
Clinton, Bill, 84, 120
Clinton Correctional Institution for Women, 63
Clinton prison (Dannemora, New York), 58
coalition building, 108, 117
COINTELPRO, 47, 128
Cold War, 73, 78, 120
Cole, Simon A., 8, 38
colonialism, 32, 37, 49, 77, 149n115, 163n27
colorblind logic, 161–62n11
colorless human, 30, 104
Comey, James, 50
common sense, racial, 6, 50, 86, 97
communists, 40–41, 64, 73, 85, 120–21, 152n172
complexion category on wanted posters: 1, 34, 38, 89, 91, 99, 101, 105; "Dark," 96, *96*, 99, *100*; "Light," 91, 93, 94, *94, 95*, 98, *99*; "Olive," 91, 92, *92*; "Tan," 99; "White," 88–90, *91*, 93, 98
Comte, Auguste, 24, 143n4, 143n15
Cone, James, 81
"conscientious scruples," 62–63
Coombs, Timothy Thomas, 124
counterinsurgency, 52, 113
counterterrorism, 113, 129, 161n5, 166n48
Crenshaw, Kimberlé, 110–11
crime rates, 46
criminal identification, 8, 23, 33–34, 42–43, 69, 117–18
criminalization, 5, 107–8, 127–29
criminology, 29, 36, 39, 46, 128, 167n69
critical race theory, 115
Cuba, 10–11, 20, 53, 67, 72–73, 107, 109, 119–22, 158n91
Curtis, Edward E., 5
cybercrime, 2, 48, 83, 89

Daily News, 63
Darwin, Charles, 143n15
Daulatzai, Sohail, 5
Davis, Angela, 5, 85, 121, 126, 152n172

INDEX 187

Davis, Lennard J., 28, 168n10
Davis, Ossie, 62
Dee, Ruby, 62
Debord, Guy, 44
decolonial thought, 17
decolonization, 50, 71
de-godded, 10
demography, 32
Dengrove, Ida Libby, 68, *68*, *69*, *70*
Department of Homeland Security, 2, 121
Department of State, 83, 160n2, 161n6
deportation, 110
Detective (IACP magazine), 41
deviation: astronomical metaphors, 27, 30; from Christ, 26, 27; comparative framework, 36; disappearance, 29, 31; unnatural, 26–27, 29, 102; from average man or standard, 7, 21, 29, 31, 36, 56, 78, 86, 102, 115, 128, 134–37; documentation, 46, 69, 72, 127; terrorism, 86, 102, 104, 110
Diouf, Sylviane, 13, 55
diversity, 50, 105, 109, 115, 118, 129, 157n79, 167n77
documentation: circulation 45–46; fixity of identity, 33; form, 1, 35; organization, 42
Domestic Terrorism list (DT), 2, 121; priority, 123–24; race, 90, *91*, 123–24; Assata Shakur, 53, 122–23
Donnelly, Kevin, 24
drone warfare, 3, 92, 94, 110, 128, 135
Durkheim, Émile, 28, 143n15
Dussel, Enrique, 10–11

Earth Liberation Front / Animal Liberation Front, 123
ecoterrorism, 3, 98, 123
Edwards, Erica R., 115, 167n77
El-Kurd, Mohammed, 135
embassy bombings in Kenya and Tanzania (1998), 84, 92, 95, 99
Esposito, John, 5
essentialism, 15, 113, 117; and anti-essentialism, 145n41
Essien-Udom, E. U., 79
Ethnographie moderne: Les races sauvages (Bertillon), 37
eugenics, 16, 28, 32, 39. *See also* Galton, Francis

Europe, 7–10, 70–71, 87, 136: Christendom, 10–11, 86; categories 49; colonialism, 37, 104; deviance, 36; Eurocentrism, 10; origins of race, 13, 19; origins of wanted notices, 43; pogroms, 135; recognition, 17; representation of others, 12, 13, 55, 61, 104, 141n35; secularization of, 29
exclusion and inclusion, 110–11, 114–15, 117, 157n79
extrajudicial killing 87, 110

facial angles and race, 31–32, 36
Fanon, Frantz, 17
Fard, Wallace, 54
fear/fearlessness, 20, 75–77, 80
Federal Bureau of Investigation (FBI), 1–2, 45–6, 54, 60, 69–71, 85; *bertillonage*, 8, 32, 34, 36–41, 84, 134; diversity, 50, 157n19; filing system, 39, 149n120; fingerprinting, 8, 39–40, 149n115; identification orders, 8, 42–48, 150n142; individual-focused logic, 3, 21, 127–128; *Law Enforcement Bulletin*, 150n148, 151n154; popular opinion, 47, 48; religion, 25; website, 45, 47–48, 87–88, 121–24, 139n3. *See also* Most Wanted program (FBI); Most Wanted Terrorist (MWT) list; wanted posters
femininity, 67–69
feminism, 79, 110, 125–26, 137, 164n12
Field, Henry, 165n41
Fields, Barbara J., 6, 16–17, 118, 165n45
Fields, Karen E., 16–17, 118, 165n45
fingerprinting, 8, 39–42, 149n115, 149n117
Finn, Jonathan, 105
First Amendment rights cases, 58–61, 156n37
Foerster, Werner, 53
Foreign Relations Authorization Act, 121
Fossella, Vito, 121
Fourier, 24
Fox, John F., Jr., 39
Franks, Robert, 120
Fritz, Jos, 43
Fuerzas Armadas de Liberación Nacional (FALN), 47, 121, 123
Fula, Yaasmyn, 128

Gadahn, Adam Yahiye, 93–95, *95*, 98
Gage, Beverly, 149n120, 150n135

Galton, Francis, 23, 30, 32, 39, 42, 44, 47, 143n15, 149n115
Garth, Leonard I., 60
Garvey, Marcus, 52, 54
Gaussian error curve, 27, *See also* bell curve
Gaza, 77, 131–32, 135
gendered orders, 68, 71
generational differences, 52, 107, 114–15, 126–27, 142n40
genocide, 64, 77, 131
geographies, 3, 6; peoplehood, 31; *Black as Muslim*, 79, 112; racelessness, 6, 101; the Negro, 61
Gilmore, Ruth Wilson, 5
Gilroy, Paul, 16
Ginzburg, Carlo, 25, 34, 49
God: Black Panther Party, 15; false divinity, 15; Islamic secular, 29, 145–46n43; Moorish Science Temple, 155n24; *mysterium tremendum*, 77; ownership, 20, 77, 80; private belief, 61, 155n23, 164n5; secular epistemology, 9–10, 15, 19, 26, 28–29, 32, 49, 56, 61, 77, 82, 135, 137–38; and *shirk*, 76; statistics, 26–27; theodicy, 26, 74, 80–82
Goldberg, David Theo, 17, 42, 103
Goldthorpe, John H., 24, 27, 145n36, 145n38
Gomez, Michael A., 13, 55, 155n19, 155n20
Gordon, Lewis, 26–27
Gotanda, Neil, 5
"The Government's Terrorist Is Our Community's Heroine" (Mos Def), 122
Grewal, Zareena, 5
Groebner, Valentin, 42–43
Guantánamo Bay prison, 21, 103
Guardian, 94
Guevara, Che, 77
Guillard, Achille, 32, 147n70
Gupta, Gautam, 89

Hacking, Ian, 8, 28, 30–31, 37, 143n4, 146n49
Haddad, Yvonne, 5
Haitian Revolution, 164n6
Haley, Alex, 12
Hall, Rachel, 41, 42, 128, 150n139
Hall, Stuart, 16
Hamilton, Charles V., 154–55n15
Hammami, Omar Shafik, 98, *99*
Hammer, Juliane, 5

"Hanafi Siege" or "Moslem Siege" (New York City), 63–64
Hands Off Assata committees, 122
Hankins, Frank, 9, 27, 145n36
Harrisburg Seven, 132
Helms-Burton Act (1996), 120
Henry, E. R., 39
hero, 8, 21, 25, 108, 122, 128, 135, 143, 144, 153. *See also* average man (*l'homme moyen*); noble man
Hezbollah, 109, 162
Hinds, Lennox, 58, 157–58n85, 158n94
hijab, 68, 157n78
Hoffman, Abbie, 57
Holden v. Board of Education of City of Elizabeth, 62–63
Hollinger, David A., 103
Home News (New Jersey newspaper), 58, 63
honor killings, 88
Hoover, J. Edgar, 8, 23, 34, 38–40, 42, 44, 144n19, 150n135, 150n142
human: as colorless, 30, 104; idealized, 15, 31; materiality, 8–9; race, 8, 19, 26–27, 116; the secular, 26, 127. *See also* average man (*l'homme moyen*)
humanity, 10, 30, 55, 112, 116, 132, 146: alternative notions, 113; the humanities, 3, 6, 109
Hume, David, 79
Hussain, Nasser, 21, 103
hyperlegality, 21, 103
hyphenated identities, 115

identification order, 8, 20, 42–48, 53, 150n142; Most Wanted posters, 48; Assata Shakur, 69, 85, *124*
identity, 12: based on race, 10, 18, 70, 115–17, 118, 143n50, 166n46; explanation, 108–13, 117, 145n41; fixed, 33, 110, 130; identification of the body, 36, 43, 150; Muslim, 56, 75, 77–78, 113–14; religious, 9, 12, 61, 130
imperialism, 5, 9, 32, 34, 49, 73, 110, 127, 132
Indian category, 14, 141–42n35
Indian nationality on wanted posters, 89–90, 162n14
individual criminal frame, 3, 21, 128
informant, 52, 67, 161n2
innocence, 21, 107–8, 116, 119, 128–29, 138

INDEX 189

International Anti-anarchist Conference of 1898, 37
International Association of Chiefs of Police (IACP), 23, 39–40, 120, 143n1
intersectionality, 10, 21, 164n12; analytical structure, 112–14, 164n12; immigrant rights movement, 114; innocence defense, 108; legal sphere, 110–11; man, 108, 113, 136;
invisible enemy, 104–5
Iranian Revolution, 55
Iranians, 114–16, 165n41
Iraq's Most Wanted playing cards, 41
Islam: and blackness, 12–16, 21, 51, 54–55, 59–60, 75, 67, 77–82, 137, 142n40, 153n1, 159n119; Black liberation movement, 72; Black studies, 21; courts, 53; epistemology, 56, 76–77; First Amendment rights cases, 58–61; obliteration, 12–16, 55–56, 59–61, 72, 80, 112–3; power and rivalry, 12–14, 15, 20–21, 56–7, 63–64, 68, 72, 75, 102–4, 130, 138; race and racelessness, 75, 85–86; revolution, 74–75, 81; secularization, 29, 119, 145n43, 165n24; terrorism, 85; ungendering, 20. *See also* Black Islam; Muslims
"'Islam and Revolution' Is Not a Contradiction" (Bukhari), 75–77
Islamic law (*Sharī'ah*), 29
"Islamic secular," 29, 145n43, 165n24
Islamophobia, 5, 113–14, 140n10
Islam: The Misunderstood Religion (Qutb), 75

Jaafar, Hilal Hasan Ali, 88–89, *89*, 90
Jackson, Sherman A., 5, 12, 29, 77, 79, 154n24
Jain, Shaileshkumar P., 89
James, Joy, 74, 153n5
Janjalani, Khadafi Abubakar, 99, *101*
Jewish question, 111
Jewish Holocaust, 44, 131
Johnson, Sylvester A., 12, 25, 54–55, 56
Jones, William R., 81
Joint Terrorism Task Force, 64
Joseph, Jamal, 52
Judy, R. A., 8–9, 13, 15–17, 25, 28, 30, 82, 104, 135, 167n78
jumu'ah, 57–58, 60

Kant, Immanuel, 8, 30, 104
"Kant and the Negro" (Judy), 30

Kashani, Maryam, 155n23
Khabeer, Su'ad Abdul, 153n1, 157n78, 159n118
King, Martin Luther, Jr., 127
King, Pete, 121
Kissinger, Henry, 132
knowledge production, 5, 8–10, 21, 23, 30, 61, 77, 128–29, 133
Kochiyama, Yuri, 62
Kumar, Deepa, 5
Kundnani, Arun, 5
Kunstler, William, 57, 59–61, 63–64, 158n94

Latour, Bruno, 144n17
Laplace, 24
Lazarsfeld, Paul, 24, 146n68
Leavenworth, Kansas, penitentiary, 40
legal sphere: 29, 61, 107–11, 115–17, 129, 140n9, 155n24, 158n94
l'homme moyen. *See* average man (*l'homme moyen*)
liberalism, 18–19, 61, 78–79, 104, 108, 113, 117–18, 129
Lincoln, C. Eric, 79, 112
Lloyd, David, 30
Lombroso, Cesare, 36, 143n15
Long, Charles, 26
Love, Erik, 5

Maghbouleh, Neda, 114, 116, 165n41
Mahmood, Flora, 89
Mahmood, Saba, 78
Maira, Sunaina, 5
Malcolm X, 51–52, 74, 127, 130; "Message to the Grassroots" speech, 79, 112
Mamdani, Mahmood, 111, 131–32
man, 8–10, 14–15, 25, 28–29, 30, 32, 56, 61, 77–78, 80, 82, 86, 102–3, 130, 132, 135, 137, 140n18; Man1 (*homo politicus*), 10; Man2 (*homo economicus*), 9–10, 14, 15, 28–29, 135; *See also* average man (*l'homme moyen*); noble man; hero
Marx, Karl, 24, 52, 72, 136, 168n10
masculinity, 15, 67, 69
mass culture, 128
Matar, Nabil, 141n35
materiality, 8–9, 17, 87, 133–35, 142n45, 144n28; Assata Shakur's religious freedom, 59–61, 63; body, 9, 34; definition, 60, 72,

134; demands, 58; pursuit by state, 45–46, 50, 120; religiosity, 60–61, 63; threat, 72, 104
May 19th Communist Organization, 64
McCrary, Charles, 61
measurement, 34–49, 115, 146n68: bodies, 7–8, 28, 31, 37–39, 127, 145n36, 147n70; crime rates, 46, 150n135; skulls, 36, 144n19, 147n70; minorities, 105; morals, 7, 24, 28, 31, 145n40, 147n69
Medovoi, Leerom, 104–5
Meer, Nasar, 5
Mehsud, Hakimullah, 92, *92*
MENA acronym (Middle Eastern and North African) 117, 140n10. *See also* AMSA, SWANA
Menendez, Robert, 121
"Message to the Grassroots" (Malcolm X), 79, 112
Middle Eastern, 18, 54, 88–89, 93, 104, 116–17, 140n10, 165
Middlesex County: 59; jail, 157–58n85
Mignolo, Walter, 103
millennial activists, 107–8, 114
Modood, Tariq, 5
Mohamed, Liban Haji, 98, 99, *100*
Mohammed, Fazul Abdullah, 96
Moorish Science Temple of America, 55, 60, 155n24
Moors, 26, 55–56, 104, 141n35
Morales, William, 121–22
Morning, Ann, 140n9
Mos Def, 122
Most Wanted program (FBI), 3–4, 43–45, 47–48, 84, 86, 88, 90–91, 97–99, 121–23: Additional Violent Crimes list, 89, 124; captures, 43, 45, 48; creation, 43–44; Cyber's Most Wanted list, 2, 83, 89; Domestic Terrorism list, 2, 53, 90, *91*, 121, 122–23; Endangered Child Alert Program, 48; Fugitives list, 2, 53, 89, 122, 151n153; Human Trafficking list, 2, 48; Parental Kidnapping list, 2, 83, 88–89, *89*, 90; Seeking Information—Crimes against Children list, 2, 48; Seeking Information—Terrorism, 2, 90, 93–95, 139n4; White Collar Crime list, 48, 89. *See also* Most Wanted Terrorist (MWT) list; Ten Most Wanted list; wanted posters

Most Wanted Terrorist (MWT) list: creation, 2–3, 19–20, 83, 84; Muslims, 88, 90–101; race categories, 4, 91, 98–99; racelessness, 3–6, 16, 20–21, 90–101, *91*
motherhood, 71, 75
MOVE, 60
Msalam, Fahid Mohammed Ally, 96, *96*
Mueller, Robert, 50
mug shots, 7, 34, 42, 67, 127, 165n41
Muhammad, Elijah, 51–52, 74, 79, 130, 156n39, 168n11
Muhammad, Khalil Gibran, 39
Muhammad, Warith Deen, 168n11
"The Muslim Cult of Islam" (FBI publication), 54
Muslims, 13, 86, 141n35; American nationalist symbols, 62–63; Muslim immigrant rights movement, 108, 114–16, 119, 130; Muslim Sabbath, 53–54, 57–61, 82. *See also* Black Islam; Islam; Nation of Islam (NOI)
Myers, Twymon, 121
mysterium tremendum et fascinans, 77

Naber, Nadine, 5
Napoleon, 33
National Bureau of Criminal Identification, 40
National Council of Black Lawyers (NCBL), 58, 71–72
nationalist symbols, 62–63
nationality category, 1–2, 89–92, 98, 101, 162
National Liberation Front (Algeria), 132
National Security Entry-Exit Registration System (NSEERS), 105
National Task Force for Cointelpro Litigation and Research, 128
Nation of Islam (NOI), 51, 79, 54–55, 58, 62–63, 68, 112, 168n11. *See also* Black Islam
nature, 19, 28–9, 54, 75, 86, 102, 104, 128, 135, 147n70: changeable by man, 10, 26–27, 32, 50; secularization, 9–10, 26, 103–4
Negro category, 11–16, 159n112; property, 70–71, 77; earlier images of Africans, 12–13; fabrication, 70, 80, 86, 112; scientific rationality, 61, 71; non-Muslim, 14, 55–56, 72, 75, 102; wanted posters, 69–70, 85
neoliberalism, 112, 118–19, 129, 166n46
Netanyahu, Benjamin, 132, 167n2

INDEX 191

neutrality, claims of, 9, 28–29, 32, 36–37, 43, 47–50, 61, 68, 85, 117, 130, 139n8
New Jersey police and state, 11, 20, 53, 58, 60–64, 67, 71–72, 119–22, 157n80, 158n94
Newsday, 73
Newton, Huey P., 15, 52, 73, 142n37
New World, 13, 55, 71, 159n107
New Yorker, 94
New York State Bureau of Prisons, 38
New York Times, 62, 67, 94, 98
noble man, 8–9, 14–15, 25, 28, 30, 77, 82, 128, 135, 140n18. *See also* average man (*l'homme moyen*); hero
nonterrorism lists, 4, 20, 88–91, 97, 162n14
normal: and Comte, 143n4; distribution, 28, 147n70; psyche, 86. *See also* bell curve
norms, 27, 29, 36: ideals versus, 28
North African as identity category, 21, 92, 102, 116–17, 140n10, 149n107, 152n181, 163n27

Obama era, 127
obliteration: average man, 29, 32, 36, 49; deviation, 29, 31; Islam, 14–16, 55–56, 61, 80, 112; materiality, 134; race, 12–14, 32, 55–56, 87; religion and Negro category, 2–14, 54–56, 59–60; social construction of race, 12; standardization, 36
Occupy Wall Street, 126
Odinga, Sekou, 52
Office of Management and Budget, 106, 117
Official Detective magazine, 66
Omi, Michael, 18–19, 117
oscillation, 29

Palestinians: genocide, 77, 131–32; God, 77, 137; racism, 131
Parental Kidnapping list, 2, 48, 83, 88–89, *89*, 90
Paris Commune, 33
Paris Prefecture of Police, 23, 32–35, 37, 149n107
passports, 33
Patel, Bhadreshkumar Chetanbhai, 162n14
Pearson, Karl, 32, 143n15
peasant uprisings, 43
photography: aliases, 34–35; categories, 35–36; mug shot, 7, 34, 42, 127, 165n41;

police archive, 34–35, 40; Shakur's refusal to be photographed, 159–60n123; wanted posters, 1–3, 42–43, 49, 64, 88, 92–93, 95, 110, 121, 124, *126*, 150n148, 151n156
Physique Sociale (Quetelet), 33
police: BLA target, 129, 153–54n9; breaking strikes, 40; DIY wanted posters, 50; Hoover's vision, 19, 39; infiltration, 153n8; lobbying, 11, 39, 72–73, 120–22; narrative of history, 23, 42; occupying force, 153–54n9; focus on Assata Shakur, 11, 20. *See also* Bertillon, Alphonse M.; Paris Prefecture of Police; policing
policing: average man, 7–9, 25; Muslims, 18; proletariat and colonies, 37–38, 49; scientific rationality, 33. *See also bertillonage*; Federal Bureau of Investigation (FBI)
political prisoners, 64, 75, 127, 159n104
polygenism, 147n70
popular culture, 48
popular support: 41, 44–45, 47, 126
populations: controlling and managing, 37, 49, 118; measuring, 145; properties, 24, 104; racial purity, 147n70; standard and substandard, 28
portait parlé ("spoken portrait"), 34
Porter, Theodore, 9, 24, 28–29, 146n68
preemption, 127, 167n69
premodern protorace, 26
prisons: conditions, 57–58, 64, 71, 75, 155n27; control units, 58; conversion to Islam, 75, 111; escape, 11, 46, 53, 64, 75, 119, 127, 129; prisoners' rights movement, 57–58, 61, 75; repression, 52; Shakur's correspondence, 11, 56, 64, 80, 125–26, 155n23, 164n5; Black nationalism and NOI, 39, 57, 155n27, 158n89; warfare, 154n9. *See also* Guantánamo Bay prison
probability, 7, 24, 25, 31, 145n36, 167n69
progressive era, 39–40
proletariat, 37–38, 49, 136. *See also* class struggle
propaganda, 41–42, 94
propensities, measurement, 7, 24, 27–28, 145n36
Pryor, Richard, 111
psyche, 34, 86
Puar, Jasbir, 5, 86, 103, 111

quantitative paradigm, 7, 24, 26, 31
Quetelet, Adolphe, 7, 9–10, 23–33, 29, 49, 78, 115, 135, 143–44n17; biographical sketch, 23–24; influence on Bertillon, 7, 20, 32–33, 35; Durkheim, 24, 28; Marx, 24, 28, 136; derivation of average man, 27–32; legacy, 23–24, 30, 136; height and weight statistics, 28, 144n21, 145n36; humanism, 24, 32; influence on FBI, 8, 84; political context, 23–24, 30, 38; *race-theirs*, 134; religious views, 26; secularization of statistics, 9–10; deviations from norm, 7, 29, 102. *See also* average man (*l'homme moyen*); Bertillon, Alphonse
Quijano, Anibal, 17
Qur'an, 74, 77
Qutb, Muhammad, 75
Qutb, Sayyid, 75

race: binary, 16, 30; Christianization, 12; countable minorities, 105; domesticated animals, 26–27; epistemological dimension, 9–10, 21; essentialism, 15, 113, 117, 145n41; ethno-racial pentagon, 103; European category, 17; incoherent analytical category, 3, 4, 14, 16, 30, 87, 93, 106, 118, 136; Islam, 77–78, 87; materiality, 8–9; obliteration, 12–14, 32, 55–56, 87; proxy, 16, 96; *raza*, 26–27; reclamation, 16, 135–38; *theirs and ours*, 21, 134–38; theocentric to biocentric, 8–10, 103–4; wanted posters, 4, 88–90, *89*, *91*. *See also* racelessness
racelessness, 3–6, 84–85, 90, 91, 93, 96, 98–99, 110, 139, 140n8, 161n8, 162n14; bin Laden, 84–85; colorblind ideology, 161–62n11; complexion, 91; extreme deviance from average man/norm, 86, 102, 110; extreme violence, 87, 110; hypodescent, 95–96; Islam, 85–86; looking Muslim, 4, 96–97, 162n14; Most Wanted Terrorist list posters, 3–6, 16, 20–21, 90–101, *91*; nonterrorism lists, 4, 20, 88–90; proxy, 85, 91–92, 96; white supremacy, 30, 104. *See also* archetypal Muslim terrorist; Most Wanted Terrorist (MWT) list; *race categories on wanted posters*
race-ours, 136–38
race-theirs, 134–35, 137
racial blackness: 17, 21, 55, 79, 108, 112–19,
129–30, 137, 162n11, 166n46, *See also* Negro category
racialism, 13
racialization. *See* racialization of Muslims
racialization of Muslims, 5–6, 18–19, 21, 86–87, 97, 115, 118
racial profiling, 115
racism, 13, 117–18, 130–38: intra-Muslim, 112; scientific, 44, 49, 72; Assata Shakur, 71, 107, 129; transformed into race, 16–17; war on terror, 103, 105, 113, 116; Western consensus, 71. *See also* materiality; Negro category
radicalism: Black, 52, 80; repression, 37, 41, 48, 117
radicalization theories, 113
Rai, Amit, 86, 103
Rana, Junaid, 5, 18, 97, 117
rationality: Enlightenment, 26; fear, 76; of race, 28, 138; scientific, 7, 8, 20, 33–34, 38, 42–43, 47, 54, 57, 61, 71, 84, 128–29; violence, 87, 103, 110, 129, 141
Ravachol, 37
raza, 26–27
Razack, Sherene, 5, 103
recidivism, 33, 39
reclamation, 16, 135–38, 154–55n15
recognition, 14, 17, 59–61, 63, 71, 77, 80, 114
redress, 87, 108, 110, 114, 116–18
Reed, Adolph, 115, 142n45
religion: Black religion, 79; discrimination, 4–5; epistemology, 9, 20, 28, 29, 49, 103–4; FBI, 25; First Amendment, 58–61, 156n37; inclusion, 117; religious freedom, 11, 58–63, 155n23; wanted posters, 10. *See also* secularization
Republic of New Afrika, 58, 64, 73, 75
revolution, 129, 167n77; Eqbal Ahmad, 133, 137; American, 104; anticolonial movements, 47, 79, 112; Black revolution, 52–54, 79, 85, 112, 121; innocence claim, 129; Iranian, 55; Islam, 51, 56, 74–77, 81, 113; policing, 23, 33, 36, 38; probabilistic, 7; Quetelet, 30; revolutionary violence, 129
Revolutionary Suicide (Newton), 15
rewards for information leading to capture, 1, 2, 46, 83–84, 90, 120–24, 160–61n2
Rewards for Justice program, 83, 160–61n2, 161n6

INDEX 193

right-wing, 118, 124
rivalry: Islam, 14, 21, 55–56, 72, 86, 102, 104; Muslim control of Mediterranean, 55, 141n35
Robinson, Cedric, 12–13
Roots (Haley), 12
Rosas, Gilberto, 18

Sadiki, Kamau, 74
Safi, Omid, 5
Sahiron, Raddulan, 98, 99, *100*
Said, Edward, 132
Said, Yaser Abdel, 88
Salafi Muslims (Philadelphia), 159n110
SaMarion, William, 58
SaMarion v. McGinnis, 58
San Diego, Daniel Andreas, 3, 4, 98
Sarton, George, 24
savages, 36–37, 141
Sayyid, Salman, 5, 105, 111, 113
Schrader, Stuart, 50
Schweber, Libby, 144n17
scientific racism, 49, 117–18; Jewish Holocaust, 44; no-god-but-man epistemology, 56. *See also* racism
scientific rationality, 42–43, 47, 84; Negro construct, 61, 71; policing, 7–8, 20, 33; theology, 56–57; ungendering, 71. *See also bertillonage*; rationality
Scotland Yard, 39
Seale, Bobby, 52, 57
Secretum Secretorum, 43
secularization, 20, 48, 60–61, 145–46n43, 156n55, 159n110; average man, 8–10, 25; Huey P. Newton, 15; Islam, 29, 119, 145–46n43; knowledge, 8–10, 25, 29, 49, 61, 77, 104, 156n55; left, 117, 165n43; nature, 9–10, 26; race categories, 26, 103, 145; statistical methods, 9, 25–27
Sekula, Allan, 23–24, 35, 42
Selod, Saher, 5, 115
Shakur, Afeni, 52, 126, 128
Shakur, Assata, 3–4, 11–12, 52, 53, 56, 62–63, 67–68, *68*, *69*, 69–72, 74, 77, 80–82, 85, 107, 119–125, *124*, 154n12, 158n94; Black Lives Matter, 11, 14; Black Madonna, 21, 107–8, 127; correspondence and writings, 14, 20, 54, 56, 60, 64, 73–75, 79–81, 120,

125–26, 155n23; courtroom drawings of, *68*, 68–69, *69*; Cuba, 11, 53, 72–73, 107; extradition attempts, 10, 11, 73, 119–20; Domestic Terrorism list, 53, 122–23; escape from prison, 11, 64, 75; Islam, 4, 11–12, 14–15, 20, 51, 53–54, 57–61, 63, 74–75, 79–82, 138; incarceration, 53, 56, 58–59, 63, 71, 157–58n85; Most Wanted Terrorist list, 10, 21, 45, 53, 73, 82, 106, 107, 119; "Muslim or men's clothing," 11, 64–67, *65*, *66*; symbol, 74, 125–30, 153n5; trials, 53, 56, 58–64, 159–60n123; ungendering, 20, 56, 71–72, 158n85; wanted posters, 11, 20, 64–67, *65*, *66*, *68*, *69*, 69–70, *70*, 85
Shakur, Lumumba, 52
Shakur, Mutulu, 126, 128
Shakur, Salahdeen, 51–52
Shakur, Zayd, 53, 153n9
Shelby, Tommie, 17
Shukrijumah, Adnan, 92
Silah, George, 90
Silah, John, 90
Silva, Kumarini, 5
"sincere believer," 61
Sing Sing Prison (New York), 38
Sinnar, Shirin, 90
slavery, 13, 74, 86, 122; piracy, 141, 163n35; Bertillon's writings, 37; enslaved African Muslims, 13, 72, 155n20; property, 70, 77; Negro compared to Indian, 37; obliteration of Islam, 12, 15, 56, 61, 72; rebellion, 55, 154; slave narratives in Arabic, 167n78; ungendering, 71; wanted notices, 43
social construction of race, 12
social physics, 25, 29, 33, 143n4, 143n15
social sciences, 6–7, 9, 16, 21, 23–24, 31, 36, 39, 49, 73, 77, 86, 104, 111, 134, 143n15
sociological science, 24, 104
sociology of race, 6, 87, 118, 161n11
somapolitics, 34
Soviet Union, 84, 120
Spanish in the New World, 55
spectacle, 44, 48, 116, 128
Spillers, Hortense, 20, 71–72
Spivak, Gayatri, 117
Stampnitzky, Lisa, 126–27
standardization, 1–2, 7, 28, 31, 34–40
state: countable minorities, 105; administra-

tive practices, 42; identification orders, 42; religious protections, 59–60; statistics, 25

statistics, 7, 23; bell curve, 7, 21, 27–28, 35, 115, 136; birth and death rates, 25, 28; Black dysfunctionality, 39; census taking, 25; deviance, 26; secularization, 9, 25–27; and theological explanations, 9, 27. *See also* average man (*l'homme moyen*); Quetelet, Adolphe; probability

St. Louis World's Fair of 1904, 40

Student Nonviolent Coordinating Committee (SNCC), 85, 152n172

Sunni-Ali, Bilal, 52

surveillance, 6, 46, 50, 52, 67, 72, 105–6, 110

Süssmilch, 27

SWANA acronym (Southwest Asian and North African), 21. *See also* AMSA; MENA

Swedan, Ahmed Salim, 96

Syed, Shafiuddin, 89

tabloid journalism, 41

Tabor, Michael "Cetewayo," 52

Tehranian, John, 116

Ten Most Wanted list, 2, 45–48, 84–85, 88, 121–22, 151n156, 152n171, 161n6, 166n55

terrorism: Eqbal Ahmad, 133–35; American television programs, 104–5; counterterrorism, 113, 129, 166n48; Cuba designation, 73; environmental, 3, 98, 123; international versus domestic, 90; official definitions, 125, 133, 134–35; raceless, 4–6, 16, 20–21; terrorism studies, 86. *See also* 9/11; archetypal Muslim terrorist; Domestic Terrorism list (DT); Most Wanted Terrorist (MWT) list; war on terror

"Terrorism: Theirs and Ours" (Ahmad), 21, 132–38

theodicy, 26, 74, 80–82

theological naturalism, 26

theological thinking, 113, 164n24

Third Circuit Court of Appeals, 60–61

Third World, 73, 78, 137

Thomas, Paul, 30

Toynbee, Arnold J., 79

typology, 111–13, 129

Uddin, Noor Aziz, 89

Umoja, Akinyele O., 154n9, 158n94

UNESCO declarations on race, 44

ungendering, 20, 56, 71–72, 158n85

UNIA movement, 52

unions: 40–41, labor movement, 137

United Nations, 64, 131

United States: antidiscrimination law, 110–11; Barbary pirates, 104, 141m35, 163n35; *bertillonage*, 38–39; ethnic cleansing, 131–32

United States Bureau of Investigation, 42, 150n142. *See also* Federal Bureau of Investigation (FBI)

university politics, 11, 114–15, 118, 167n77

US Marshals Service, 151n153, 160n123

victimhood, 135, 138

Violent Crimes—Murders list, 88

visibility: 4, 97, 116–17

Volpp, Leti, 5

Walker, Corey D. B., 113, 164n24

Wallerstein, Immanuel, 135

wanted posters, 20–21, 44, 150–51n153; announcement and attention, 45–46, 69, 127; atomizing, 3, 21, 128; average man, 23; circulation, 121–22; digitization, 45, 47–50; DIY, 50, 161n7; form, 3, 6–8, 38, 43, 48–49, 102, 127–28; identification order, 42; location, 44–45; public as target audience, 8; rates of apprehension, 46; rewards, 1, 2, 83–84, 122; route forms, 150n148; scientific genealogy, 48–49; scientific paradigm, 21, 102; Assata Shakur, 11, 20, 64–67, *65*, *66*, *68*, *69*, 69–70, *70*, 85. *See also* categories listed on wanted posters; Most Wanted program (FBI); Most Wanted Terrorist (MWT) list

war on terror, 4–5, 18, 86–87, 93, 113, 132–33, 108; climate impacts, 3; Guantánamo Bay, 21, 103; invasion of Afghanistan and Iraq, 203; unmarked enemy, 104–5; rival, 13–14, 21, 64, 86, 102–4; Most Wanted Terrorist list, 2–3; preemption, 127; racelessness, 87. *See also* 9/11

Washington, Albert "Nuh," 75, 80–81, 155n23

Washington Daily News, 44

Weitzman, Steven, 25

White, Avon, 67

White category, 85, 88–90, *89*, *91*, 93, 98, 123

INDEX 195

white supremacy, 8, 25, 30. *See also* average man (*l'homme moyen*); hero; noble man
Whitman, Christine Todd, 120
"Why Has the FBI Placed a Million-Dollar Bounty on Assata Shakur?" (Cleaver), 122
Williams, Evelyn, 57, 67–68, 154n9, 158n94, 159–60n123

Williams, Mabel, 73
Williams, Raymond, 30
Williams, Robert F., 73
Winant, Howard, 18–19, 117

Wing, Adrien, 115
Woodruff, Barbara, 125, 126–27
World Trade Center attack (1993), 84, 160–61n2
World War I, 128
World War II, 41, 44
Wynter, Sylvia, 9–10, 15–16, 28, 38, 55, 61, 78, 82, 116, 134–35, 159n112

Yardville State Prison, 63
Yazdiha, Hajar, 114-15
Yousef, Ramzi, 160–61n2

Zionism, 131, 135